THE TRUTH

THE TRUTH

Robert Firestone, PH.D.

A N D

Joyce Catlett, M.A.

MACMILLAN PUBLISHING CO., INC.

NEW YORK

COLLIER MACMILLAN PUBLISHERS

LONDON

Macmillan Publishing Co., Inc.
866 Third Avenue, New York, N.Y. 10022
Collier Macmillan Canada, Ltd.

Library of Congress Cataloging in Publication Data

Firestone, Robert.
    The truth.

    1. Psychotherapy. 2. Truth. 3. Defense
mechanisms (Psychology)   I. Catlett, Joyce,
joint author. II. Title.
RC480.5.F47   616.852   80-26383
ISBN 0-02-538380-9

10   9   8   7   6   5   4   3   2   1

Printed in the United States of America

*To our patients and friends who contributed
the truth of their personal experiences as
well as their intellectual analyses.*

Contents

Acknowledgments

THE AUTHORS would like to express their appreciation to Jeremiah Kaplan, who had faith in the value of this book in spite of the challenge it presents to psychological defenses. We would like to thank Cecilia Hunt, whose editing helped make this book more readable by a wide audience.

We are also grateful to Barry Langberg and Tamsen Firestone, who contributed their ideas to the organization and rewriting of the manuscript; to our agent, Frank Tobe; and to the many typists and proofreaders who worked with our word-processing consultants to complete the final draft: Linda Clark, Eileen Parkes, Jan Brown, Susan Short, Anne Baker, Sara Bartlett, Patty Lubin, Sonya Rousso, Robyn Parr, Marcia Mirman, Catherine Cagan, Scott Cranmer, Richard Catlett, and Tom Chester. And, finally, our thanks to Linda Benvin for all her help during the production of this book.

Introduction

I HAVE SPENT THE PAST TWENTY-FIVE YEARS working with my patients and friends trying to overcome one of the most puzzling and
frustrating aspects of human nature, the stubborn and unconscious
resistance to a better, more emotionally rich life. Though we know
that people's psychological defenses, which protected them from pain
when they were children, later play destructive limiting roles in their
adult lives, keeping them insulated, mechanical, and cut off from
their feeling of love and compassion, it has often been difficult to
understand why those defenses are so hard to give up when they are
no longer needed. Over the years I have come to understand that
not only are these defenses deeply rooted, but they are also inter-
twined with those of the larger society.

Out of my work I have developed a broad concept of a cure for
neurosis that will help those who are brave enough to accept the
truths about their early lives, their present relationships, the society
at large, and the reality of their finite existence.

There are two guiding principles in this book. The first is that
there is no simple, quick cure for individual unhappiness or for society's ills. The second is that nonetheless people really can change.
They can change their lives enormously. This second principle challenges the deep-seated myth that people and things are basically unchangeable, in spite of many social and technical advances. Most
people believe, on a deep level, that "People are what they are" and
that "You can't change human nature." On the contrary, there is no
psychological problem or emotional malady that is impervious to
change, providing a person has both motivation and understanding.

My experience observing and interacting with people in experi-
mental social milieus has impressed me with an unhappy truth about

most people: the perversity with which they refuse to accept nice treatment and a positive environment; it is perhaps the greatest limiting factor in psychotherapy and in people's lives in general. Unbelievable as it may sound, most people cannot tolerate the kind of life they really desire. Most of us reject or manipulate our environments to keep from feeling an emotional experience that contradicts our early conception of reality. This is a major reason for our resistance to change.

Learning to live with the truth is the only way to get what we want and enjoy it. As compelling as fantasies or illusions can be, they cannot satisfy our deep need for a sense of reality. Nothing but the truth can truly fulfill that need. For each of us our defense system is our illness; it "protects" us from the truth. It is a painkiller and an anxiety reducer, just like a drug. Withdrawal from the addiction to defenses and illusions is the cure, but it is not an easy cure. The truth can be like a bad-tasting medicine, but it can effect real and dynamic change in us. In learning what originally caused us pain and distress, what we originally had to protect ourselves from, we can stop blaming the outside world for our misery and begin to do things to challenge and dismantle our defense system. This self-examination will make us anxious, but as we adjust to the anxiety, we can begin to change our lives.

My optimism about writing this book sprang from my feeling that people, by understanding the nature of their defenses and the myths of their culture, may well decide to challenge them both. They might choose to go against the habitual patterns that deaden them. By understanding how pain and neurosis are passed down from generation to generation, they might decide to break that chain. They could choose to live by an implicit code of morality that minimizes psychological suffering, a morality that doesn't fracture their feelings and experiences or those of others, a morality that enhances their well-being and personal development. If this book can be a step toward creating a society that is sensitive to the emotional and psychological fulfillment of all its members, I would feel more than deeply gratified.

Robert W. Firestone

THE TRUTH

The Truth
About the Individual
and Society

1

Your Defenses—How They Kill You

OUR SOCIETY ACTUALLY EXISTS as a kind of negative afterimage. We all live in a crazy, backward world, often unaware of the lies and double messages we are given. If we could be free for a moment to catch a glimpse of our true situation, if we could view our society as a visitor from another planet, we would be stunned at the nightmare in which we live. The things we are expected to believe about ourselves and about society are frequently completely the opposite of the way things really are. Unhappily, the individual and all the members of our society are often unconsciously working together to maintain a largely defensive and dishonest way of living.

As a clinical psychologist I have devoted my life to studying and understanding human psychological suffering and to helping alleviate that suffering through psychotherapy. This has been the compelling interest in my life. For the past twenty-five years, I have been working with individual patients and discussing the problems with colleagues and friends. Initially, I practiced intensive individual psychotherapy with schizophrenic patients and then extended my interest and practice to include more "normal" neurotic people. Also, at different times friends and acquaintances who were not patients have volunteered to participate in my search.

I have found that there are truths and ideas that can be of considerable assistance to anyone who wants to understand the source of his pain and who hopes to find an honest way out of his suffering. Truths may be painful, they may destroy illusions you have about

[3]

yourself and your life. But facing the truth is the only way to live
your life fully.

One crucially important truth to face is that destructive processes
in your way of living may be deadening you as a thinking, feeling
person. Usually you don't know what you are missing because you
have never allowed yourself to taste the difference. We often unconsciously turn our backs on our real feelings and real desires and
this self-denial is the core of a self-destructive process that deadens
us emotionally and cuts us off from our deepest personal experiences.
What is ironic is that the self-destructive process originated in the
defenses that protected us and helped us to avoid painful feelings as
children. What began as ways of freeing ourselves in situations we
couldn't change or run away from became our imprisoning agents.

I want to make it clear that having emotional problems does not
mean you are sick. Whatever is now bothering you emotionally exists because at various points in your early life you tried desperately
to avoid emotional pain that you were not capable of dealing with.
There are many ways of cutting off pain. You may have protected
yourself against the pain by blocking it off, soothing it away, imagining it wasn't there, vowing never to let it happen to you again, or
even literally falling asleep to escape. Over a period of time, like
everyone else, you built a defense system, using all these methods
and many others. These defenses that you built long ago are now
what cause most of your misery. You are like a knight in a suit
of armor who cannot move freely. You are trapped in your iron
fortress.

A woman whom I have known for several years is locked into a defense system that she built long ago. Gretchen is a forty-three-year-
old woman whose defenses have kept her distant from many people
in her life, especially men. Gretchen's father had been an amateur
auto mechanic and when she was seven years old she had been
pressed into the role of a mechanic's apprentice. In a cold garage she
sat for hours at a time, handing her father a wrench, spark plugs,
engine parts, etc. If she was slow, her father became angry and called
her names. If she cried, he only became angrier. If she wouldn't stop
crying within ten seconds, he spanked her. She usually stopped and
then was told to go to the house and wash the tears and dirt smudges

from her face. When she came back, her father passed inspection on her clean face. Then she was ordered to sit down again and continue assisting.

This scene was repeated many times throughout Gretchen's childhood. Gretchen grew up thinking that all men were mean and critical like her father. For her first two years in high school she avoided boys, but then she met Joe. Joe was looking for a girl who wanted to please, someone who would idolize him. Joe was the football star, but his ego needed constant feeding. Gretchen went steady with him for a year and then was dumped when Joe fell in love with Gretchen's best friend and eloped on the evening of the senior prom. This painful rejection confirmed her view of men and she secretly vowed never to fall in love again. But Gretchen didn't spend her life in spinsterhood. She married and had two children. But once again she had chosen a man who was like her father, a man who was critical and demanding.

Gretchen's self-protective vow didn't help her. It imprisons her to this day—and it imprisons her husband and children. She cannot feel much affection toward them. In cutting off her loving feelings toward men, she cut off most of her natural affection in general.

Gretchen had other options. She could have given up her assumption, her prejudice that all men are mean. She could have taken a chance, developed a relationship with an uncritical man, and challenged her self-protective attitudes. But she didn't. Instead, she chose to marry a man who would criticize her. She clung to her defensive attitudes. Her choice was neurotic.

Gretchen developed into a deeply cynical woman and her point of view about men was unshakable. Unconsciously, she anticipated anger and criticism from any man, and she went out of her way to provoke it. In the office where she worked, she hovered around her boss, waiting for dictation. Her behavior was servile, but her facial expression was hard and set in deep, sullen lines. She often acted incompetently and made clerical mistakes. She provoked her boss into the same kind of rage that her father had expressed toward her years before. Her view of men was again verified.

In her marriage Gretchen played the victim, but she did not see it. In her view her husband was mean and critical. True, she had chosen a man who was somewhat critical, but in trying to make her marriage correspond to her early family life, Gretchen had to work hard to make him be as mean to her as her father had been.

One of Gretchen's constant provocations involved the mail. Her husband, Mitch, liked to have his mail put together on a table in the hall so that he could easily find it in the evening. Gretchen almost never placed the mail where Mitch wanted it. It would get mixed up with the children's schoolpapers or sometimes even thrown away. Mitch actually pleaded with Gretchen to keep his mail together in one place. He really didn't care where; she could even leave it in the mailbox. He just wanted to be able to find it when he got home from work. Gretchen withheld this simple courtesy for years. It might have seemed like innocent forgetfulness, and Gretchen would never admit that it was anything other than absentmindedness, but it wasn't.

One summer morning before setting off on their vacation, Gretchen and Mitch had a very direct confrontation. Again, if Gretchen's actions had in reality been unintentional, Mitch would never have reacted as he did. This is Mitch's account of the events of the day:

On the first day of my vacation, I was looking forward to traveling with the kids and Gretchen across the country to visit our folks. I had been busy packing the camping equipment and loading the station wagon. When I finished, I sat in the front seat for about twenty minutes waiting. Gretchen had said she would be right out. Finally my patience ran out. I went back into the house. Gretchen was on the phone to one of our neighbors. I couldn't believe it. I was furious. The kids were sitting around waiting for her, too.

I whispered loudly to Gretchen, "Who are you talking to?" Gretchen shot me a look that could have killed. A look of contempt that I'd seen hundreds of times before, but it had never registered with me that much. That look had always made me stop cold in my tracks and feel like apologizing for bothering her. But not this time. I just became more furious. I felt enraged. I was glad that my daughter was there in the room because I felt like smashing Gretchen right in the face. By now she was smiling that fake smile of hers and hating me with her eyes.

I swear, I shook with the feeling. I remember gripping the edge of the bar until my knuckles turned white. She finally hung up and walked really fast toward the bedroom. I caught up with her and (this is what I'm ashamed of) I grabbed her by the arm hard. I said something like, "Just one minute! I've been waiting for you and the kids for the past half hour. Don't you ever keep me waiting again, do you hear?"

I squeezed her arm harder. She looked like she was going to cry. She told me to let go of her arm. She said that she didn't know what I was talking about, that she'd been hurrying as fast as she could. She was whining and crying and saying that I never noticed that she needed help getting the kids ready and that she's with the kids all summer and they drive her crazy and that I should be more firm with them. She went on and on. I yelled at her to shut up. I was shocked at the sound of my voice. I had hardly ever shouted at her like that. Then she really cried and sobbed. I remember her saying, "You're scaring me. You're scaring the kids. What's come over you. Please stop yelling at me."

She looked like a pitiful little girl. Suddenly I wasn't angry anymore. I felt sorry for her and scared by what I had done. I looked around to see if the kids had heard. They weren't there. For that I was grateful. I would have been humiliated for them to witness that scene. I went out to the station wagon. The kids were there, waiting. They stared at me. I felt terrible. I don't think I've ever felt as bad as I did at that moment. In a few minutes we were driving down the highway. The sun was shining and everything looked as if it would be a great vacation. But I felt nothing of that. I was depressed and worried. Strangely, I started thinking about money, about having no savings, that the station wagon was over four years old, that I was a lousy provider.

Gretchen had been able to provoke the kind of response she wanted, first by keeping Mitch waiting and then by acting the helpless, innocent child. She had been successful in her manipulations, but both she and Mitch were miserable as a result. The outcome is a common one. We often sacrifice a good time and nice feelings with the one closest to us just to keep our defense system intact. This is just what Gretchen did on the morning of what could have been a pleasant vacation.

Some men feel that all women are out to trap them and take away their freedom. This feeling might have been accurate during a particular man's childhood; his mother may have refused to allow him the independence he needed as he grew older. But if today he picks a woman to marry who is extremely possessive of him, he, like

Gretchen, is making a neurotic choice. His defense system is the trap, not the woman he marries. As an adult, he has far more control over the situations in which he puts himself.

One of the great dangers of defenses is that they are indiscriminate. You begin by not trusting one person, usually for a very good reason, and you can end up trusting no one. Once you are burned, the scar tissue that originally protected you from further damage now only causes disfigurement. The defense that once saved you now causes you more pain.

I see neurosis as a process of reliving rather than living—choosing bondage instead of freedom, the past instead of the present. Neurosis is a childlike clinging to our defenses, our fantasies, and our connections to our parents long after this behavior has ceased to be appropriate.

Defenses are not easy to shed. It is even difficult to break them down when there is a change in environment while a person is still young. Eric was a young boy who didn't want to take another chance on people.

Eric was seven years old when his mother became too ill to take care of him. His father was unemployed and spent much of his time drinking at home and physically abusing his son. A close friend of Eric's mother took him into her home to look after him until Eric's mother recovered. The friend had known and loved Eric since he was an infant and it had caused her a great deal of pain to see him neglected by his mother and mistreated by his father. Eric liked his mother's friend and had always responded warmly to her. Over the next several months, the friend and her husband tried to repair the damage that had been done to the child. These were two people who, with their genuine affection and intelligence, should have been able to help this battered child. But Eric rejected their warmth and love. He became sullen, unruly, provoking, and mean. And in anger he tried to destroy several of his new toys.

It was tragic. Eric couldn't tolerate the positive atmosphere of his new home because his defenses were already too well developed. He tried to provoke the same kind of treatment he was familiar with at home. Eric was sure he couldn't afford to take another chance and perhaps be hurt more, even though he was in a situation where the odds were totally against his being mistreated.

We are—all of us—not too different from Eric, though our early lives may not have been as traumatic as his. The cynicism, the lack of trust, the things you keep secret because you're ashamed, the whole process of being inward and secretive to "protect" yourself hurts you far more than any external event in your life today. Refusing to take any more chances because you want to protect yourself is more than a no-win solution; it can be profoundly self-destructive.

Defenses take different forms. There are the ones that soothe us, put us to sleep physically and emotionally, kill our pain, help us build a false image of ourselves and a false sense of security, and keep us emotionally dead: Smoking, excessive drinking, overeating, compulsive sex, long hours of television viewing, all of these may be the defenses we use to keep anxiety and pain at low levels. They are what we call ego-syntonic. All defenses are addictions, and these particular ones are harder to break because they make us feel better temporarily.

The first step toward learning to live with the truth lies in knowing what your problems are. Your problems are your defenses and your system of defenses is a neurosis. Ironically, your system of pain-killers is what is causing you so much pain.

One of the first steps toward giving up your defenses is to realize that you're not too different from anyone else—we are all well defended. All of us suffered varying degrees of emotional pain as children, but we're not sick or deeply disturbed. When we were children, in our attempts to ease anxiety and pain, we formed imaginary connections with our parents. Our parents probably felt that we belonged to them and we drew some satisfaction and security from that illusion. Naturally we felt less alone and vulnerable if we thought we were permanently connected to someone, even if it was only a fantasy, and even if the relationship was largely negative. Because it made us feel secure, as we grew older we probably attempted to re-create this relationship with our parents in other people or institutions, or even within ourselves, in our heads, if all else failed.

Deep down, we still feel, as so many parents have said, that "The family will always be there" and "No matter what happens, we can count on our families." What we fail to see is that this conscious or unconscious image of a close family structure is often an attempt to avoid the real pain of facing the feelings of rejection and aloneness that we experienced as children. We avoid painful truths from the past and pay the cost by giving up real experiences and personal dignity in the present.

Many parents gave up the real affection they had for their children and substituted role-determined feelings and behavior that society says are appropriate. Birthdays, anniversaries, weddings, and funerals are occasions that offer clear-cut examples of the results. We're supposed to feel something at these events, but what we allow ourselves to feel is very often not real. In fact, we may kill off any spontaneous feeling in order to be able to show the "right" (socially accepted) emotion. This defense of showing an "act of love" instead of real affection is not a minor form of dishonesty. It damages us and those people closest to us. Knowing the difference between real feelings and role-determined feelings is a very important step toward change, toward feeling whole:

A father cried at his daughter's graduation. But at a restaurant later the same day, he made a sarcastic joke when his daughter reached across the table to say that she had felt happy when she spotted him in the audience.

In the first situation, most of the father's feelings were sentimental (he was remembering his own graduation), proud (he hoped that people would notice that his daughter was the one getting the award for outstanding scholarship), and dramatic (this was the big moment, a huge step forward in his beautiful daughter's life; also, others were teary-eyed, so it must have been an intensely moving moment). His responses had tended to be more role determined than real.

He *had* experienced a catch in his breath and a lump in his throat when he first noticed his daughter entering the auditorium. She was leaving for summer school at a distant college and he had thought simply, "God, I'm going to miss her." This was a real feeling, but it was too painful for him. So he withdrew into his familiar internal world, which had very little to do with his real feelings. Later at dinner, when his daughter spoke to him affectionately, he cruelly cut her short because he could not tolerate the reawakening of the earlier real feeling. In addition, he added one more twist. When he saw her face fall after his "joke," he said, "C'mon, I'm just kidding—can't you take a joke?"

This father had unintentionally hurt his own daughter because of his defensive nature. The genuine feeling he had had cracked his defense system for a moment and he couldn't tolerate it. The daughter, in turn, was largely unaware that her face had registered her hurt. She was more conscious of being ashamed that her father's remark could "get to her" and almost unconsciously tensed her face and body. On some level she vowed to be more on guard from then on.

As a child, small and vulnerable, you did not have the power to leave or to take active measures to cope with stress and pain. You defended yourself against pain and anxiety as best you could under the circumstances. However, these defenses that worked when you were a child tend to persist beyond childhood and they become neurotic and self-defeating when you generalize them and extend them to other persons and situations.

Defenses that are appropriate to the child who is at the mercy of his environment and who is in truth a passive victim of life are not appropriate to a striving, active adult who can control his world to a large extent. Unfortunately, the fear of change often causes us to persist with the defense long after the original situation that stimulated it has passed. Our childhood defenses and false hypotheses about life later restrict and hurt us and damage the people we are close to.

These defenses extend everywhere. As a group we pool our individual defenses and this makes up our social order or society. And, closing the circle, the social order in turn confirms and supports the individual's defense system and negative world view, making it difficult for him to change, to live nondefensively.

Defenses limit and kill off our everyday experiences. They numb us as feeling persons and rob us of our dignity. A passive victim has no dignity, he only feels hurt pride. This is a tragic way to live, but there is a way out. By giving up some of your prized ways of looking at yourself and at the world, you will be able to feel like a real person again with dignity and trust and respect for yourself. As you begin to experience more of yourself and your strength, you will begin to see the possibility of an adventuresome life instead of a boring, senseless, repetitive existence. You will have more control of your fate in your personal relationships and in every aspect of your life. You will develop the mood of an adventurer. An analogy to this kind of life is drawn by Don Juan in *Journey to Ixtlan* by Carlos Castaneda when he describes the mood of a warrior:

One needs the mood of a warrior for every single act . . . otherwise, one becomes distorted and ugly. There is no power in a life that lacks this mood. Look at yourself. Everything offends and upsets you. You whine and complain and feel that everyone is making you dance to their tune. You are a leaf at the mercy of the wind. There is no power in your life. What an ugly feeling that must be!

A warrior, on the other hand, is a hunter. He calculates everything. That's control. But once his calculations are over, he acts. He lets go. That's abandon. A warrior is not a leaf at the mercy of the wind. No one can push him; no one can make him do things against himself or against his better judgment. A warrior is tuned to survival, and he survives in the best of all possible fashions.

A warrior cares very much about how he lives; he is in control of his life. I feel that all of us can care very much about how we live and how we express our lives. We all have choices, and one of the best choices we can make is to try to live fully alive, nondefensively.

2

The Mixed Messages of Society

ONE OF THE MOST SHATTERING BLOWS an individual can sustain is to have his sense of reality distorted or denied. A correct perception of reality is central to a person's well-being. To mislead him or confuse his perceptions of the world around him is extremely destructive, yet this action is carried out thousands of times a day in families everywhere.

It has been shown by numerous researchers studying the origins of severe mental illness or psychosis that it is not simply rejection that severely harms children. It is denying and hiding rejection with double messages that has the most damaging effect. Having this sense of reality fractured by parents whose words they trust and believe literally drives children crazy. Rejection and emotional deprivation are serious enough issues in young children's lives, but if their parents also pretend that they are *not* rejecting them—if they tell them one thing and do another—they may cause more harm than most children's egos are capable of handling.

On a larger scale, our society is so permeated with these same kinds of double messages that one can predict a corresponding effect on a social level. If our sense of reality is being subtly twisted and distorted, if our perceptions are constantly being confused, then we must expect drastic consequences. Mixed messages—where we are told one "fact" yet see something else happening—are prevalent in our society and do have a devastating effect on all of us. It is important to our emotional well-being that we be aware of the contradictions that every day impinge on our sense of reality.

For example, in our society we profess strong support for close, enduring relationships between men and women, yet the reality is that men and women very often are not friends, are not loving toward each other. In fact, despite the "sexual revolution" and male and female liberation, they are still enemies in the battle of the sexes. Their learned, stereotyped attitudes about each other are as discriminatory and deep rooted as racial prejudices.

People place a high value on a happy marriage, yet for most couples the marriage ceremony signals the end of romance. Most relationships deteriorate, either rapidly or slowly, and this fact is simply hidden away in the bedrooms of the unhappy couples.

Parents are supposed to love their children and raise them to be happy, fulfilled adults, yet most parents are not emotionally free enough to love their children, and most children end up resenting their parents, even after they themselves have become adults. Most books on child rearing do an untold amount of damage because they promote coverups; they teach parents to act the "proper" responses rather than express their genuine feelings. Years of dishonest behavior causes serious damage because it confuses a child's sense of reality. No parent is successful at pretending to love his child. On some level the child knows when he is being lied to, being given two contradictory messages. Unfortunately, the child often has to sacrifice his own sense of reality and try to fit in with the lie.

Freedom and a democratic form of government are highly valued by all of us, yet most people do not choose to live free, spontaneous lives, the kind of lives that reflect their own points of view. Free from the obvious external authorities, people still prefer to set up others as authorities, who rule their lives in more subtle ways. Internally, most people are not free either; they are prisoners of their own defense systems.

These are just a few of the thousands of contradictions we face in our everyday lives. However, most people are so emotionally dead, so cut off from their real existence and from their real feelings that they rush through life not noticing the insanity around them. They are immune, insensitive to the suffering and miseries of their own lives. They can watch situation comedies on television and laugh at the sarcasm, the meanness, and the mutual nastiness in the dialogue of the characters. They are amused and entertained by these portrayals of their own marriages and families. However, the humor avoids the destructiveness in the relationships on the screen and in our own homes. The humor condones the hostility as normal.

The lies and dishonesty of society begin with the individual. We have all grown up in families that have their own contradictions that mirror society at large. Despite the fact that each family or group has its own unique life-style, there are many general attitudes, behaviors, roles, and routines in society that most of us accept uncritically. Many of these socially approved patterns of behavior and points of view reflect the individual defense patterns of each person. Thus, *society represents a pooling of individual defense systems.* The combined defenses of all of us who live in our society tend to support the particular defensive life-style of each person.

Generally, a couple start out with genuine love, sensitivity, and respect toward one another. But precisely those characteristics that are highly valued by the other person are those qualities that become unconsciously withheld. Because love and openness were withheld within our original family, we tend to resent another person who genuinely acknowledges us and loves us because it contradicts our earlier experience. Thus, as adults, when routines set in, the beloved begins to resent the lover, and each member of the couple begins to reinstitute his defenses. Each progressively blocks out the other, and individually they are often the most destructive when the other person is being the most outgoing and warm. Finally, both members of the couple are defeated and have lost the feeling of compassion for each other.

Withholding and withdrawal can start very early in a relationship. There was a young man on his honeymoon who told his bride that he loved the way she looked, especially her hair. He said that he liked the way it fell softly to her shoulders, and that he felt proud to walk down the street with her looking so beautiful. The next day his wife went to the hairdresser where she had her hair cut and was given a permanent wave. When she returned to their hotel room her husband was shocked. He felt as if a mean trick had been played on him, and it was true: his new wife had already begun withholding something he admired.

Many of us are aware of how many times we have started off with the best intentions toward loved ones, somehow gotten sidetracked, and then just could not reconnect with those feelings. Many of us can remember how good we felt at the beginning of our relationship with our mate, and we wish we could recapture those feelings.

Many of my patients have complained to me about their husbands or wives. When I reminded them that they had chosen their spouses, they would universally say, "Well, _____ wasn't like that when we first met." To a large degree these husbands and wives were telling the truth. Their mates had increasingly backed off from the loving way they were at first.

For some people this backing away starts even before closeness has a chance to develop. Many people find it too difficult to tolerate even more than one date with someone; they feel doomed to go from one person to another, making little contact. Many people cannot bear feelings of both friendship and sexual attraction for the same person, although this combination of feelings makes for the happiest kind of relationship.

People Try to Maintain the Fantasy That They Really Love Each Other Long After the Romance and Tender Feelings Are Gone. The man and woman who are still together yet have retreated from closeness and genuine affection for one another are in a truly unhappy position; this basic dissatisfaction is at the core of their emotional life. These individuals have formed a strong dependence on one another and at the same time will not accept the true reality of their lack of feeling for each other. This loveless dependency increases the destruction between them.

The same man who has described an awful and hopeless situation with his wife, when asked, "Why don't you leave her?" invariably answers, "Because I really love her." It requires a great deal of imagination to see love between these warring couples. By this time they may be habitually treating each other with insensitivity and disrespect, yet they do not want to see that long ago they ceased to be friends and are now substituting a pretense of love and loyalty. This deception may go on for a long time as the members of the couple attempt to cover up the fact that they have lost the real feelings of love they once had.

Ronald and Sharon, for example, had a fantasy of being in love. They both felt that they had one of the nicest relationships among their circle of friends. Almost immediately, however, Sharon took it for granted that Ronald was hard to please and critical of the way she looked and spoke. She had forgotten that he had once been attracted to her looks, the way she dressed, and her soft voice. Ronald didn't seem to mind very much that Sharon was too tired at night to make love and that she didn't seem very happy to see him when he came home from work each night. They had been married for only three years, but the romance was completely gone.

Sharon thought she had discovered other ways to please Ronald. She was a perfect hostess and an immaculate housekeeper, and she took pride in keeping the checkbook balanced. But Sharon had only substituted serving Ronald for being affectionate and sexual with him. Both Ronald and Sharon were deceiving themselves about their relationship. They were no longer in love with each other but were caught up in role playing.

The Denial of Truth Within the Couple Is the Fundamental Dishonesty Within the Family and the Society.   The need to protect these untruths leads to hostility toward anyone who might see and expose the truth; an outsider's point of view must be suppressed to protect the illusions. We often feel angry toward the people who might reveal our own destructiveness. All of us feel ashamed and even paranoid when we are rejected or are destructive and rejecting to others. We would feel humiliated if we were overheard fighting with our mates.

By the time a child is born, very often the couple has hardened into a dishonest style and has long since retreated from basic feelings of love for one another. It is likely that love will be progressively withheld from the child as well. When these feelings are withheld, there is a great deal of shame and covering up. The myth of family love and closeness must be upheld. The family will cling to one another desperately and dishonestly, attempting to prove the lie of its closeness. It is terrified of exposure and distrustful of outsiders, though family members often treat each other with less respect than they would a stranger on the street.

Form (the roles and routines of family life) is substituted for substance (the real feelings) when friendship is gone. This substitution can occur because parents feel that their children belong to them and because the parents are so defended that they cannot allow real acknowledgment, positive or negative, of their feeling. The contradictions of family life and the coverup of this basic dishonesty are present in society at large. All of us are drastically influenced by the contradictions we see around us, by the discrepancy between what everyone says he wants and what he really thinks or how he really acts.

Cynical Attitudes Abound in Our Society, Yet Personal Happiness Is the Stated Goal.   We all say we want happiness and act as if we are seeking it. Yet if happiness were achieved, it would interrupt one of our most prevalent defenses: the thousands of cynical thoughts we entertain about the world, about ourselves, and about members of the opposite sex.

"All women are bitches."

"Men only want sex."

"Women are just after security and want to tie you down."

"You can't fight city hall."

"Men are always trying to keep women down."

"There are no honest politicians."

"A woman's place is in the home."

"Men aren't supposed to cry."

"The rich and powerful must be corrupt."

These attitudes, supposedly based on extensive previous experience, serve as self-fulfilling prophesies and contribute to a general feeling of helplessness. It is hard to imagine that people really believe they could find happiness in the harsh world described by the above thoughts. They are deceiving themselves about seeking happiness, just as many couples pretend to still be in love.

Personal Freedom Is a Cherished Value in Our Society, Yet It Terrifies Most People.   Everyone says that he wants the freedom to live his life to his fullest potential. Yet most people run from freedom as they would from the plague. They prefer to feel victimized by the political system rather than live freely in a democratic government. They use these attitudes to support their feelings of powerlessness. Their search for personal freedom is doomed because of their fear and cynicism.

What people do with their freedom often proves that they are really terrified of it. A prominent professor had achieved a certain amount of prestige in his field and felt that his career was successful. Having reached this happy situation, he found himself more open to the reality of his miserable relationship with his wife of twenty years, who was severely mentally disturbed. He felt restricted by this insanely controlling, domineering woman, and now, with a spirit of determination, he decided to obtain his freedom. He divorced his wife and slowly began to make some new friends. For a few months he enjoyed the exhilaration of his freedom. Soon, however, this usually sober man could be found in the cocktail lounge of the university faculty club, drinking heavily. Within two years of his divorce he was fired from his position and admitted to the alcoholic ward of a local hospital.

In this extreme example a man essentially destroyed himself after gaining the freedom he had so longed for. Even though he had become externally free, he was still a prisoner of his defenses. It would have been very difficult for this man of intelligence to admit that he was terrified of freedom. Even today he is probably unaware that he ran away from the life he had said he wanted all during the confining years with his wife. His desire for freedom and his actions after gaining his freedom constitute a strong mixed message.

Mixed messages and cynical attitudes are capable of having an insidious effect on you because they interlock with your defense system. There is also a strong social pull to go along with these contradictions, to imitate other people. You can help yourself resist this social pressure by becoming aware of these mixed signals. Becoming more observant of the discrepancy between people's words and their actions can clear up the confusion you feel when receiving this kind of mixed communication. Also, if you learn to trust your own perceptions, you will dilute some of the effect of these conflicting messages.

A young couple I know had been dating for several months. They usually met three or four times a week for dinner and then spent the night together. One evening after they had felt very close to each other, Paul expressed some deep feelings. He told Alice that he was starting to care for her a lot, more than he had for any other woman. He said that she had the qualities that he had always fantasized about in the woman he hoped he would someday meet. He said he wanted to spend more time with her, and perhaps they could live together someday.

Alice was happy to hear all this, but her good feelings didn't last. In the weeks that followed, Paul stopped calling for dates as often as he used to. After a few weeks Alice realized that they had only spent one evening together during the previous ten days. When she asked Paul if he was pulling away, he became angry and offended, denying the true message of his behavior. She felt terrible and confused. Until then she had believed her lover's words and hadn't noticed that his actions had been the opposite for a long time. She would have been better off if she had paid more attention to his actions.

You can practice a similar kind of scrutiny on yourself. Question habitual patterns of behavior that contradict your supposed goals. How many times have you said you wanted love in your life and then pushed others away? How many times have you pretended that others were denying you what you wanted when in reality you were probably denying yourself?

In relationships it is vital to be honest with yourself and others about those times when you are not feeling loving. More than anything else, try to be honest with your children. Deceiving them with white lies in the name of protection confuses them and tends to distort their sense of reality. Children read your actions anyway, and it is your behavior that they imitate, not your words. It is far better to tell a child that you can't feel much for him at the moment than to try to avoid the pain of that honest statement. One of the most destructive things you can do is confuse and deceive a child about your feelings toward him.

If you attempt to live a life of integrity, where you make your behavior correspond to your stated goals, you will gain in confidence and good feeling. And you won't be contributing to the damaging effect on others that mixed messages create.

3

Why Your Parents Didn't Love You in Spite of Good Intentions

To the extent that our parents are cut off or emotionally deadened to their own feelings, they will deprive us of love and sensitivity. Contrary to their best wishes and dreams for us, their personal system of defenses will deeply restrict their ability to provide us with the emotional support necessary for our development and growth. The degree of damage they do will be in proportion to their reliance on a system of defenses in their own lives and that naturally varies from one person to the next. If our parents are very withholding, they will deny affection to each other and deprive you as well. Conversely, to the degree that they are emotionally free and experience life and feeling for themselves, they will pass on their love and joy.

If they are self-denying, self-pitying, and self-victims of life, they cannot offer much to you. Holding back their natural feeling of tenderness toward you hurts everyone involved. In depriving themselves, in not giving themselves value, parents do an injustice to themselves, and this carries over to their children.

Audrey was lucky. She was a pretty, vivacious teenager who was raised in a family of four children where it was clear that the parents enjoyed being with their children. Their spacious house was always filled with friends—the children's friends and the parents' friends. There seemed to be very little friction between the members of this large family. There appeared to be almost no generation gap: the teenagers preferred bringing their friends home to staying out late at night. There were very few rules for the young people and there seemed little need for any. Audrey's sisters and brothers weren't stay-at-homes either. Each one led an independent life outside of the home, excelling in athletics and creative projects. Audrey, at sixteen, was already employed as an architect's assistant and was learning drafting.

It was obvious that here was a family in which there was a great deal of love for, interest in, and spontaneous enjoyment of life. The parents had taught their children by example that this could be an exciting world to live in. Without being pollyannas they experienced the highs and lows of life, not trying to erase any significant event from their own lives or the lives of their children. As a result, Audrey was maturing into an exceptional young woman, respected and well liked by her high school classmates.

Next door to Audrey lived a boy named Craig. An only son with a sister three years older than he, Craig had a fantasy of being adopted by the family next door. He had every reason to nourish this secret wish. Craig's parents provided every material thing that Craig and his sister needed or wanted, except any real interest in them. In contrast to the atmosphere next door, Craig's parents simply did not like people, especially their neighbors. They often complained about the noisy kids next door even though the houses were well separated from each other by very wide lawns.

The father, a salesman who traveled extensively, was rarely home, and when he was at home, he spent his time trying to "whip Craig back into shape." This father had a deep fear that if his son were left under the influence of his mother he would become a "sissy." So the father's time at home was devoted to discipline and teaching the boy the value of "hard work." Craig and his father were impossible to be around when they were working together on a project, such as home auto repairs or yard work. Vicious words of disrespect flew between the two. The father sarcastically criticized Craig, while Craig was sullen and resentful.

Craig's parents were just as miserable as Craig, yet they seemed unable to remedy the situation. Needless to say, Craig was a very different person from Audrey. If Craig's fantasy of being adopted by Audrey's family had come true, however, it is very doubtful that Craig could have acclimated himself to the growth-enhancing atmosphere of the home next door. Long before he had reached high school his defensive patterns were well established, and a withholding, resentful style was deeply ingrained in Craig's nature.

Audrey's parents and Craig's parents stand in sharp contrast with each other, especially in the dimensions of the ability to give. The two home environments had very different effects in the formation of these two young people's personalities.

I would define parental love as behavior that enhances the well-being and development of children. "Love" would be all that is nurturing and supportive of the unique personality and development of the child. It would be a gross distortion to define "loving" as any responses that are detrimental to psychological growth or that cause painful wounds to the psyche.

A friend of mine remembers an experience she once had when she was about five years old. Nancy was awakened by her mother very early one morning and was told that she was going to visit her grandparents. Her father said they would be staying there a few days and would have a nice time vacationing at the grandparents' large home in the country. Nancy was excited and she hurried as her mother helped her dress. Instead of going to the home of her grandparents, however, her mother and father drove Nancy to the hospital for a scheduled tonsillectomy. The next thing Nancy knew, her parents had disappeared, leaving her in a strange room with people she didn't know. Nancy remembers the feeling of deep betrayal and panic as the anesthesiologist placed the mask over her face, quieting her cries and screams for her mother.

By not preparing Nancy for her tonsillectomy, by tricking her, her parents unknowingly and unnecessarily scarred her. They withheld the truth—an explanation of what she was about to experience—and they lied instead. They avoided a discussion that would have made them feel pain and anxiety. They were not protecting their small, vulnerable daughter as they claimed, they were shielding themselves from pain.

Whenever Nancy heard the sound of a siren, she was told by her mother that it was an ambulance on its way to deliver a new baby to a happy mother. Up until Nancy left for college her mother prepared a bag lunch every day of Nancy's school life and made all the phone calls for her appointments. The first time Nancy had to make her own doctor's appointments at the university she had an anxiety attack. Even in her twenties, partly because of her petite five-foot height and her little-girl appearance, Nancy gave the impression of a fourteen-year-old. This overprotection had prevented her growth in ways perhaps unknown to anyone.

Nancy "grew up" to be a young woman who was functional in some areas but anxiety ridden and extremely defensive in many other areas. She paid a high price for her parents' overprotectiveness and defensiveness—parental defenses that limited her growth. Without meaning to, she will probably pass on these same defensive attitudes to her children, perpetuating the damage into the next generation.

Nancy's parents were incapable of sharing their lives with their children. Their separate, isolated, secretive style of living together as a family amounted to little more than perfunctory greetings and superficial conversation. They unconsciously sacrificed their children for their own defense system, because they were insensitive to the needs of their children.

In my observation of families, I have noted countless examples of well-meaning parents carrying on behavior that is destructive to their children while claiming to love and have the best interests of their children at heart. These parents are telling the truth, albeit defensively, when they tell their child that they did the best they could. As in the case of Nancy's parents, they have often been too psychologically damaged themselves to provide the necessary ingredients for a healthy climate for their children. No matter how well meaning they were, they were unequipped to raise children. And even being well meaning is not necessarily an expression of an underlying love for their children.

Many parents feel a strong sense of affection toward their newborn infant, but as the baby grows older, they begin to withhold it. Some parents cannot even tolerate their young baby's budding recognition of them. They cannot stand the trust, the loving looks and smiles their infant begins to express during the first year of its life. These looks stir up the parents' feelings about themselves as lovable. This simple appreciation of them is too much for some parents. It brings back the pain and anxiety that they had suffered at the hands of their parents, which they had successfully suppressed for years with psychic painkillers and the deadening behaviors defined in their relationships.

When a parent holds back love from his child, he feels unconscious guilt because at some level he knows that he has stopped feeling his original strong feelings of affection. He feels guilty, too, because it is unthinkable, even immoral that he may not have the so-called normal feelings of love toward his child. The fact that parents are *supposed* to love their children creates a sense of pressure and obligation in most parents. It would be better for all concerned if parents could realize that it is humanly impossible to love their children all the time. Then parents might feel less guilty about not feeling love and affection and might be open to more honest communication and less pretense with their children.

There is a way out of this continuing destruction of our children and ourselves. Part of the solution lies in exploding the myth of unconditional love. There is no such thing as unconditional love or security, and the pursuit of it in our parents, mates, friends, or children is futile. Attempting to establish that kind of safety leads to frustration and misery in our close relationships. It is the primary source of marital discord and suffering. There is, however, the possibility of real safety and adult security in ourselves and in our honesty.

We no longer need what we needed as children. The extent to which we realize this fact and become free and independent of childhood expectations determines to a large degree what type of parents we will be to our children.

Facing the truth about you and your parents frees you. The only way you will be able to avoid the destructive pattern of reliving your past with people in the present is to face the truth about what happened to you in your family.

There are specific incidents in your early life that tend to stand out in your memory. Some may be pleasant to recall, others very unpleasant. In recalling these events, try to remember what you felt at the time. Put yourself in the shoes of the little kid you were and experience the sadness or the pain that you must have felt at the time. When Nancy remembered the incident of the tonsillectomy, she felt again the deep distrust and fear she had experienced that day in the hospital. She said with sadness, "If they had only told me what was happening, I would have had someone to talk to." Then she went on to picture her large house, where each person seemed to be alone in his own separate world with no words passing between them. She again felt the loneliness of those years. As a result of reexperiencing this lonely feeling she came to understand why she found it very difficult to talk to people whom she didn't know well. With this insight came more courage to talk with others and trust people more. However, if Nancy had overdramatized this memory and simply felt sorry for herself, she probably would not have used the insight to help her change.

Understand important determining influences on you in your development, but don't get stuck blaming others. As an adult you are capable of overcoming the effect of early negative experiences. A cynical hatred toward your parents often gets unconsciously transferred to the very people with whom you want to be close now. Hatred of your parents damages you just as much as an idealization of them will. It is essential not to get stuck brooding over the past and feeling victimized by the fact that your parents didn't love you as much as you needed or wanted. It's natural that you will feel anger about having been hurt, but nursing the anger won't help you.

Many children don't love their parents either. In the space of one or two years in his early life an individual may be damaged so much that if he spent his entire adult existence working out his neurosis he would never succeed in reclaiming all of himself. By the age of two or three, many children are no longer the innocent, pure beings we like to think they are. They have become sullen, corrupt, and conniving. They have learned to exploit their parents with powerless, babyish, pouting behaviors to get the things they want. It is the truth that many children don't love their parents either, and they behave in ways that make this truth all too evident.

Craig, the boy who fantasized about being adopted by the family next door, was a miserable person by the time he entered kindergarten. He wouldn't sit still in class and constantly interrupted the teacher with loud talking. In a parent-teacher conference Craig's mother told his teacher that Craig acted in ways that often made him unbearable to be around. He seemed to crave punishment while at the same time begging verbally for tangible signs of his parents' love and approval. He had no interest in his parents except in what he could get from them. He had extended these negative feelings toward other parental figures too, e.g., his teacher.

Craig, at the young age of five, was well on his way to becoming an exploitive, destructive adult. He was no longer an innocent person. He had essentially become very much like his parents.

Some children grow up to become adults who are bitter and who hold grudges against their parents. They may attempt to be unhappy and unsuccessful in order to "blackmail" their parents through guilt. Almost any parent feels guilty to some degree about how he raised his children and can be vulnerable to the accusations, spoken and unspoken, of a child who grows up to be a corrupt, miserable individual.

For example, the daughter with a broken marriage can blame her divorce on her mother's failure at marriage. The son who can't keep a responsible job can always lay blame at his father's doorstep, saying that his father was too critical and suppressive, thus discouraging his son's initiative.

Parents really do long for their children to succeed, first of all because they wish them well anyway, but secondly and more importantly, because it lets them, the parents, off the hook. They can breathe easier knowing that whatever they did wrong, at least their child is now a happy, responsible adult. If the idea of letting your parents off the hook is an intolerable idea to you, remember that revenge doesn't satisfy your real needs.

Emotional Hunger Is Not Love

What most parents mistake for love of their children is their own driving hunger and need for the child. Their unfulfilled hunger for love and care from their own parents causes them to focus these desires on their children. Many parents mistake their strong possessive attachment to their offspring for genuine feelings of love. In one therapy group a mother cried out, "What is this burning feeling inside of me if it isn't love for my daughter?" Moments before uttering these words, this mother had spoken to her daughter, Sylvia, who was also a member of the group, very condescendingly and disrespectfully. She had intrusively criticized Sylvia's choice of friends and her appearance. She obviously had little respect for Sylvia as a separate individual, yet she was claiming to love her deeply.

A few months later, at Sylvia's wedding, her mother again displayed her insensitivity by constantly touching her daughter's clothes and body in an exaggerated display of physically intrusive behavior. At one point in the evening, when Sylvia gently removed her mother's hand from its clutching grip on her blouse, the mother asked, "What's the matter? Do you mind? After all, I'm your mother." What this mother was experiencing, to an obviously abnormal degree, was emotional hunger, an intense feeling that she had always tried to satisfy by keeping her daughter close to her, both physically and emotionally. The marriage of her daughter threatened this "closeness," and the mother was clinging even more desperately than usual.

A young child who is caressed by a hungry, needy parent will not feel loved and secure, but instead may become unresponsive to physical touch later in life. To the child, the hungry touch at times may feel physically soothing: it cuts off pain and lulls the child to sleep.

David was an appealing, tow-headed five-year-old when I first met him. His long eyelashes were set at half-mast, however, in a half-asleep, glazed look. Each morning it was a battle to get David awake enough to get him ready to go to nursery school. He was grouchy, whiny and complaining, and almost totally immobile.

This behavior only occurred around his mother. In his therapy sessions David was active and full of spunk. Following each session, David invariably ran to his mother, climbed into her lap, and within minutes had assumed the position of a sleepy, cross infant. His mother initiated each contact by pulling his head close to her breast, stroking his blond hair, and cooing to him in a soft voice. Even when she was trying to be firm with him, her tone of voice had a dull, droning quality that was capable of putting the most wide-awake adult to sleep. In fact, one evening at a small gathering, some friends became very drowsy as they listened to David's mother explain to him why he had to go to bed.

This mother's soothing behaviors were an acting out of the emotional hunger she felt toward her young son. By acting on these strong feelings of need within herself, she was able to relieve some of the intensity of her hunger, but at the expense of David's independent aliveness.

The so-called loving touch of an immature parent may be experienced by a child as possessing, sucking tentacles that drain the child rather than nurture him. However, in some cases, and in David's case, the child will seek out this type of affection, even as an adult, whenever he wants to kill his emotional pain. Others will tend to have feelings of being trapped or suffocated when they feel close to someone later in life. Still other individuals may experience genuine affection as physical or psychological pain.

The hunger and dependent needs of some parents may also be expressed in the parents' proprietary interest in the child's health, friends, thoughts, career, and in general, every aspect of the child's life. In a sense, this kind of parent feeds off the accomplishments of his child, takes credit for his talents, and pushes his child to perform for friends. Children raised by emotionally hungry or immature parents suffer much pain and embarrassment from this exploitation in their early years. Many will soon lose interest in the areas in which they originally showed talent or curiosity.

When parents are needy themselves, the extensive needs of the child for love and security are threatening to the parents' defenses. The child's needs are therefore discouraged in many ways and he is made to feel that he is wrong for wanting. The child feels that he is dirty or bad or unlovable and eventually adopts this identity as part of his self-concept. The child is discouraged from crying when he is in pain because the crying indicates to the parent that he is somehow inadequate. Neither the parent nor the child wants to know that the parent is inadequate in his ability to love and to provide security.

One of the major reasons that parents are unlikely to love their children much of the time is that they themselves grew up with a negative self-image. If they do not love themselves, have a negative view of their bodies, and are ashamed of their own bodily products, they cannot pass on love and tenderness to this unique, remarkable creation of theirs. People who do not really like themselves are incapable of genuinely loving others. In fact, they are more likely to dump their negative feelings on others and act out their hurt. Nowhere is there an easier place to dump our negative perceptions of

ourselves than on our children. In one family I know, the son was
the scapegoat for his father's feelings of inadequacies:

Bruce continuously doubted his own masculinity. In the course of
therapy, it became clear that Bruce's father had pronounced latent
homosexual tendencies. Unwilling and therefore unable to see these
impulses in himself, he dumped these perceptions on Bruce by developing fears that his son would become effeminate. Although
Bruce did not develop homosexual traits, his father's fears led Bruce
to doubt his maleness. He became afraid of being "too close" to a
woman, because she might be able to sense his lack of confidence.

If you are now a parent or plan to be one in the future, I want to
emphasize that this chapter is not a diatribe against parents. Parents
are people who were once the children of whom I speak. I place no
blame on parents, but neither do I have unlimited compassion for
those who continue these damaging behaviors once they become
aware of what they have been doing. Certain destructive behaviors
are easily brought under control, others take more time. Giving up
your own negative self-image and self-hatred would be an important
step in interrupting the misery and suffering that may have been
perpetuated one generation after another in your own family.

Idealizing your parents damages you. By idealizing your parents
you must retain a negative image of yourself. You will be clinging to
the image of the "good," strong parent while seeing yourself as the
undeserving, unworthy child. The truth is that every child is born
innocent and lovable and does not need to earn love and affection
through change or hard work.

When parents withhold their love from their child, he distorts
himself, trying, hoping, and hungrily longing for that love. He has
no choice but to think that there is something wrong with him if he
is not loved. He cannot afford to believe for one minute that his parents are unloving or weak or inadequate or even cruel. He needs
them for survival.

Nancy's perpetuation of her own self-protective defenses beyond
her childhood years was a defense against the terror of discovering
that her parents were inadequate, fearful people. In her present
life Nancy is frightened of being independent of them because of
their overconcern for her.

While she was attending college fifty miles from her home, she felt guilty knowing that her parents would be worrying about her every day. In hopes of allaying this guilt and in an attempt to get some recognition from them, Nancy phoned home each evening "so they won't worry about me." She invariably hung up the phone with an empty feeling, not realizing that she was feeding her parents and that they were giving her nothing.

As in Nancy, the hope of finding love and approval by working hard, by changing oneself, by taking care of one's parents, this hope is eternal in most of us. We bend ourselves out of shape in the desperate attempt to find this kind of love not only in our parents but in parental substitutes in our lives today.

When you are able to feel what happened to you as a child and feel it in a deep way, you will have no desire to pass on this hurt to another person, either your children, your friends, or your parents. You will want the damage to stop with you.

Have some compassion for your parents and understand that they too were hurt and misunderstood when they were young. By compassion I do not mean making excuses, for there are no rational excuses for the senseless destruction of children. Neither do I mean to underestimate the serious limitations under which we all operate because of our upbringings. I am only suggesting that the same compassion that you have felt for yourself when remembering your innocent years be extended to parents who were once in that vulnerable position themselves.

One scene stands out in my mind: a wedding. The two persons getting married had worked for years to overcome some of the ways in which they had been crippled emotionally by their parents. Behind the bride and groom stood their parents, with tears in their eyes, radiant and happy. No one condemned them. There was a deep sense that they were all in this together and that there was no one to point a finger at.

Many of the guests were aware of the destructive process these young people had worked through. Knowing the truth had not changed them into cynics about life. On the contrary, this young couple and everyone who was present were embracing life courageously, with full knowledge of the risks involved. The truth had not discouraged these people or made them pessimistic about the future. The truth had set them free.

4

Social Pressure

"CANDID CAMERA" ONCE PROVIDED a humorous example of social pressure for the benefit of millions of people in the television audience. A department store elevator opened its doors to a person pushing the "up" button only to reveal five or six people standing with their backs to the open door. Time after time each shopper, unaware that he was being filmed, stepped into the elevator and stood like the others, facing the rear. It was a hilarious show that probably left most viewers with a small question mark in their minds about what they would do in the same situation.

What Is Social Presure?

Social pressure is a strong pull from important people in your life and from society in general to *do what other people do, not what they say.* This pull exists on two levels. On one level, you are affected by the general cynicism of people in society, which undermines our faith in other people and relationships in general. On another level, there is the pull exerted by people who are close to you and who want less for themselves than you want for yourself. For example, can you imagine sharing the joy of a beautiful new sports car you have just acquired with a friend who is stuck driving a beat-up old car? Can you picture your feeling good about having a good-looking woman or man in your life when you are with a friend who "can't find a date"? There are thousands of examples of this phenomenon, where it seems natural to hold back your feelings and hide your successes to "protect" a friend. You instinctively hold back so as not to hurt another's feelings.

This process may seem innocuous on the surface, but it can become part of a serious self-denial or holding back. We may even become a little paranoid about showing our joy, vitality, and childlike enthusiasm about life. On a deeper level we may unconsciously deprive ourselves of much that we value in life in order to stay in step with others who are choosing negative, empty lives.

Nowhere is this spell so powerful as with your parent of the same sex. I have often felt that the role model of the parent of the same sex is the single most limiting psychological factor in a person's life. When you strongly identify with someone as you are growing up, he has a tremendous impact on your development and a powerful tie is formed. When you surpass this person, you become anxious and guilty because you begin to lose the connection with the model that has given you so much security in the past. You really feel out on a limb. Many times you scurry back to safety by giving up your accomplishments and satisfactions. Much of this process is unconscious, but you may have had glimmers of this phenomenon in your own personal experience.

We model our defenses after our parents and other family members, especially older siblings. Much like the young antelope that stiffens in fear when his mother senses the presence of a predator, we unconsciously imitate parental reactions to the stress and anxiety they feel in their personal lives and become anxious ourselves at the same stimuli.

In other words, our style of defense becomes very similar to that of our role model within the family. We tend to become afraid any time we act differently from this person, because we have depended on him for our sense of identity. To some degree we have even internalized the role model's fears and mistake them for our own. To put it overdramatically, it is as though we were "possessed" by this person. That's why horror movies like *The Exorcist* are so terrifying. All of us have incorporated our parents, with all their limitations, as a basic part of our identity. We have often incorporated any hatred they had toward us, and we grow up hating ourselves to a considerable degree.

If our parents were unable to feel or display much physical affection for the opposite sex, we will grow up feeling anxious about showing warmth and affection. If a parent was a chronic failure vocationally, we will be apprehensive about achieving success in our jobs. True, many of us succeed in spite of having parents with handicaps, but rarely without some toll in our psychological functioning. Generally, there is extra guilt and anxiety in those areas where the parents were limited.

We are truly fortunate if our parents as models are successful, functioning adults. To this extent we may imitate them without detrimental effects. We do not need to feel guilty when our parents are strong. This increases the range and possibilities for our own lives.

The parent who is limited, on the other hand, will have the reverse effect of narrowing our range of vitality. I have half-jokingly warned men of my acquaintance to carefully look over the mothers of the women whom they love and would marry. Of course, the same applies to women in relation to sizing up their future mates. Unfortunately, the best way to predict the performance of our loved ones may be to observe their parents of the same sex.

Destructive Social Pressure in Action

Our own defenses tend to make us internally self-denying in the same style as our families. Other people who behave in similar styles can be the source of an external social pressure on us.

Carol and Andy were driving from Los Angeles to San Francisco to attend the wedding of their closest friends. On the way they began to talk about getting married themselves sometime in the near future. They talked of having a baby, who the baby would look like, and what name they would choose for it. The drive along the mountainous coast was beautiful, and they both felt happy to be together. Carol felt especially close and very affectionate with Andy. She felt free of worries, was relaxed, and was enjoying the first day of their four-day weekend.

Soon they reached the restaurant and spotted the cars of the other members of the wedding party. They went in and sat down in a booth with Carol's sister Barbara and Ted, her boyfriend. After a few minutes Carol noticed that she was getting sleepy and bored with the conversation. She looked at Andy closely, and he didn't seem to look as attractive to her as he had in the car. She looked across the table at Ted and Barbara and wondered if they had been arguing. They were sitting far apart and not talking or looking at each other. Carol felt embarrassed to be sitting so close to Andy.

As they left the restaurant, Andy asked her, "What's the matter with you? Why did you pull away from my touch just now as I was helping you on with your coat?" At first, Carol was surprised. She hadn't noticed the incident he mentioned. Then she thought of Ted and Barbara, and she knew they had affected her mood.

Carol was responding to a specific social pressure from Barbara, who was seriously cut off from her feelings toward Ted. Barbara was denying herself close contact with Ted, and so Carol felt a pull to erase the difference between her sister and herself. On a societal level Carol was reacting to a general taboo against men and women being very affectionate to each other in public.

A few months earlier Carol and Andy had been guests at a large medical convention dinner. They had been sitting close together and holding hands when one of the doctors they had just met said, "Oh, look at those two, aren't they cute—just like newlyweds." They both cringed with embarrassment at this attention. Carol again recalled that embarrassment in the restaurant with Ted and Barbara. She wouldn't tolerate the anxiety of being different from her sister, so she sacrificed the close moments she could have had with Andy.

Since we learned our defensive style from our parents, we will become aware of a pull to step back into line as soon as we feel very different from them in the area of their particular defenses. In turn, we too become part of the social pressure because we affect others negatively whenever we live defensively and deny ourselves the things we want in life. In this sense it is immoral to deny oneself. In giving up our goal-directed behavior, in being "selfless," we give up all that we have to offer others—which is just being ourselves. By being self-denying we all damage others.

The Unconscious Aspect of Social Pressure

One young woman, who at twenty-five had never gone out with a man but had been involved with another woman in a homosexual relationship for two years, began to feel more interested in meeting men. Through her therapy she became freer and more assertive in other areas of her life and for the first time expressed an interest in overcoming her shyness in relation to men. Soon after expressing this desire she met a man whom she liked very much and started dating him. Over a period of a few months this woman lost many of her sexual fears and was enjoying her newfound freedom. She felt gratified and happy that she had finally discovered herself as a woman in this relationship. She gave up the relationship with her girl friend after several month of conflicting feelings.

The man began to grow fond of her and talked with her about the possibility of their making some kind of a commitment to each other because of the seriousness of their relationship. On the evening of this talk, the woman had a terrifying nightmare that left her shaking and crying. She had dreamed that she was walking through a bombed-out city alone and frightened. Suddenly she saw her mother, dressed in a faded yellow bathrobe, beckoning her to come back. Her mother looked so weak and pathetic that the woman could not bear to leave her there among the ruins. Superimposed upon her mother's face was the face of the girl friend whom she hadn't seen for months. She returned to her mother's side and picked her up and began carrying her through the empty city. She awoke still feeling the weight of this phantom of her nightmare around her shoulders.

Within two days she had her answer to the young man's question about a more serious commitment. She told him that she needed time to think it over, that they had been seeing each other too frequently, and that the rest of her social life had been suffering because of all the time she was spending with him. She had a few more dates with him and then broke off the relationship completely. Soon after the breakup she returned to her former homosexual relationship.

The young woman's nightmare of her mother corresponded very closely to the real picture the mother had presented while the daughter was growing up at home. This woman rarely left the house except to shop, attend church, or go to a movie. She had divorced her husband shortly after the birth of their daughter and never sought the company of men. She bought nice clothes for the daughter, but very little for herself. And she *did* walk around the house during the day in a faded yellow housecoat, dusting and "straightening up." For this young woman, the call of the self-denying mother had been too compelling to resist. Thus, in the following days she *unconsciously* destroyed the relationship that had brought her much happiness. Her anxiety about being so different from her mother expressed itself in the nightmare of which she remembered only bits and pieces.

Everyone has heard the saying, "All the world loves a lover." Yet when the lovers decide to get married, another set of clichés appears and is recited to the happy couple in the spirit of fun and good humor. Overheard at many bachelor dinners: "This is your last fling, buddy. Now you're really going to have to settle down. There goes your freedom. No more bowling or baseball games with the fellas." Or at the bridal shower: "You're going to have to keep him in tow, please him, and cater to him, keep him thinking that he's the boss." Or the advice given to both of them: "Now you two are going to have to be serious. Marriage is a big responsibility."

Harriet's marriage to Tim was nearly ruined by social pressure before the wedding even took place. As Harriet was planning their large wedding, and as the guest list mounted, she began to have misgivings. As her friends phoned to reply to her invitation, they offered her advice about how to maintain the togetherness that characterized a good marriage in their minds. "You're still going to paralegal school? Even after the wedding? I would think that you would be too busy for all of that. Will you quit school when you get pregnant?" A close friend wanted to know if she were going to quit her job as a legal secretary now that she was "setting up housekeeping." The best man asked her about a group of friends that she often socialized with: "Won't you miss seeing these people after you're married?" No thought of leaving her close circle of friends had even entered Harriet's mind until the best man asked this question.

Harriet didn't quite know what was affecting her as the important day approached, but it might well have been the pressure toward couple "togetherness" at the imagined expense of her independence that was making her feel less excited about her wedding.

Remarks and questions such as the ones Harriet received along with the well-wishes of her friends form the substance of the social pressure that protects the dependent ties of marriage but kills the friendship aspect. Harriet's and Tim's relationship will continue to be under pressure to form this kind of tie once the ceremony is over.

The pressure can eventually transform the initial love and friendship into the role-designated feelings and behaviors that are so common in many marriages. Society's cynical expectations and predictions that romance will fade once the "honeymoon is over" may soon come to be this couple's own expectations. They may become content with what they have, especially if there are few obvious conflicts between the two people. One couple, married twenty-five years, expressed self-satisfaction with their relationship by declaring: "We may not love each other that much, but we're faithful."

This couple had succumbed to the pressure to accept the fading of romance and the loss of true love and excitement as inevitable. They seemed resigned to this state of affairs, never realizing that this loss was unnecessary and could be prevented. They were losing the best moments and years of their lives, years in which they could have continued to enjoy the love they had known at the start.

In neighborhoods everywhere the housewives' coffee klatches exert a strong social pressure to denigrate, put down, and criticize men. These informal "women's clubs" are used as forums for open discussion of the stereotyped attitudes toward the opposite sex that these women have learned from their mothers.

Their complaints about their husbands support the kind of social pressure that professes, "Men are mean, and there's nothing a woman can do about it." These same women more than likely greet their husbands at night with a far different story. They probably cater to them, praise them, and treat them with special deference.

At a political level many individuals support conformity to the prevailing social order, or to an organization or to a cult, only because they are seeking guidance and security in the form of authoritarian leadership. They would tend to elect someone who is an advocate of rigid law-and-order measures and who fears individual freedom. They feel safe serving blindly and submitting uncritically to authority. This type of person would be supportive of the very social pressure that keeps him locked into his own defense system.

People will often perform acts in large groups that they wouldn't consider committing alone. The transcripts of the Nuremberg trials are a case in point. They reveal that the orders to execute millions of human beings were passed down from the highest authorities. Lesser officers and soldiers murdered these people in blind obedience. They dealt with their guilt by disclaiming responsibility, saying, "I was just obeying orders." Collectively, many people will commit heinous crimes that they could not even bear to think of as individuals.

The crowd standing below, watching a suicidal person teetering on the ledge high above, has been known to shout, "Jump! Jump!" Probably not one of these people would shout this encouragement to die if he were alone on the sidewalk below.

It is group pressure and conformity that makes many of us uglier, more cynical, and far more destructive to each other than we would ordinarily be. The "herd instinct" may be nothing more than this intense social pressure to imitate each other's actions. Each of us may have some repressed area that could be drastically affected by the right combination of social pressure and our inner defenses.

Usually, the effects of unconscious social pressure are much more subtle and hard to pinpoint. Henry and Alice, for example, are a happy, loving couple. There is a special quality about the way they are with each other. They are not exclusive, and they enjoy close friendships with other people. One afternoon they asked Michael, a college roommate of Henry's, to drop by for a visit. The three people spent the afternoon swimming in the pool and then went to a fine restaurant for dinner. Michael seemed quiet and somewhat awkward. He was obviously more comfortable talking with Henry. He attempted to talk with Alice about conventional topics, but he really wasn't very interested in her part of the conversation. As the evening wore on, Henry and Alice felt very self-conscious and were quieter than they had been at the beginning of Michael's visit.

What Henry and Alice didn't realize was that just being around this isolated, cynical young man had affected them in a very negative way. The time spent together had been ruined by Michael's unspoken, almost unconscious thoughts. He had a deep-seated suspicion of women and was living his life according to his inner thoughts, which reflected his father's attitudes toward women and marriage. Years before, Michael had unconsciously determined that marriage was not for him. On a conscious level he doubted that he would ever find a woman who would love him.

Michael, Henry, and Alice didn't speak about these subjects during the afternoon, but Michael's silent thoughts had spoiled the mood of that day. The process that had so affected Henry and Alice was the same one that originally caused Michael to form his own cynical attitudes toward women. He had picked up his father's silent disdain toward his mother and the general unhappiness of the marriage. It was the undercurrent of hostility in Michael's home that had done the damage to Michael, just as it had affected the loving mood of Henry's and Alice's afternoon.

Cynical Attitudes Act as a Strong Social Pressure to Interrupt Our Pursuit of Happiness. Many people are like Michael in that they have given up on themselves. Their cynicism is so deep, their ways of viewing themselves so absolute that they become hopeless about ever changing themselves. They perceive others categorically and exclude them from the possibility of being friends. They may think thoughts like: "You can't change human nature" or "It's foolish to become attached to anyone because you'll get hurt."

Our society is permeated with cynical attitudes about sex, age, friendship, happiness, and genuine affection between men and women, as is demonstrated in the following incident.

Cindy and Mark were parked in Mark's car in a lot at the college campus. They were talking about their relationship and what it meant to both of them. They were sitting close together when they heard a rap on the window. A campus security guard shone his flashlight in and asked, "What are you two doing in there?"

"We were talking," answered Mark.

"Are you sure that's all you were doing? It sure looks suspicious."

"No really, officer, we were just talking." Cindy leaned toward the window so that the officer could see that she was respectable looking.

"Look here, how old are you two?"

"I'm eighteen and she's thirty-two," Mark replied.

"Lady, what are you doing, robbing the cradle? Look, kid, you'd better get home and don't let me catch you parking here again."

"But this is where my class is held, in that building over there. I have a right to park here for that class, don't I?"

"Listen here, don't give me any of that or I'll turn you in. If you want to mess around with older women, do it somewhere else."

The hostility and sarcasm displayed by this man is not that unusual in our society. There was absolutely no rational thought behind his cynical destructiveness. It is interesting to note that this man was most degrading to this couple in relation to their ages. Cynicism and hostility separate people from each other based on artificial boundaries, such as age, race, occupation, social class, and sex. It is that kind of separation that also subtly supports the erroneous view that parents are necessarily wiser and children "too young to understand." Children submit to the societal pressure to perceive their parents as wise, good, strong, and almost perfect.

Initially, children see the human weaknesses in their parents and may feel compassion for them; however, the taboo against real exposure of a parent's weaknesses, faults, or negative traits is very strong in our society.

Everyone tells the child, "Your folks are the greatest. Look at all they've done for you." No one tells him how awful they may be under the guise of protecting him. As a result, he may deny the weak points in his parents' makeup and instead feel fearful and inadequate himself. By lying and building up his parents, he must weaken his own self-image.

The young child learns to evaluate himself as his parents did. If the child is not accepted and loved for himself, he will tend to feel unworthy and unlovable. He needs to feel that the parents are good and strong, that if he is rejected it is *not* because the parents are inadequate or unloving but because he is bad. The child needs to preserve the strong, good image of the parents at his own expense. To feel secure and go along with society's rules, the child uses the idealized image of the parents to obscure their *real* weaknesses. In the same manner he uses the bad, weak image of himself to blot out the real inadequacy of his parents.

When Richard was a young boy, he often went to the beach with his father. His father happened to be a man who was terrified of the sea, who had never been on a boat during his life, and who had never learned to swim. He carefully hid his fear from his son, but through the father's tense actions his anxiety was communicated to the boy without a word being spoken. Richard grew up frightened of the ocean even though he had a natural curiosity about it. For many years he stayed away from the sea; then he and some friends decided to buy a sailboat.

As he became acquainted with the small boat within the confines of the marina and as he ventured further out to sea on day cruises, Richard began to question his long-standing fear of the ocean. He recalled sensing his father's fear and agitation during the trips to the beach so long ago. Richard realized that his father had been afraid of the water, but that as a boy he, Richard, had been fascinated by the ocean and the beach. He now knew that he had protected the image of his father as a brave, strong man by thinking of himself as the one who was afraid. Richard soon discovered that sailing and feeling at home on the ocean were natural to his style of life. His strong reluctance to see his father in realistic terms had come from the social taboo against a less-than-idealistic view of a father and from his own internal guilt—an unconscious social pressure.

Coping with Social Pressure

Becoming more aware of any double messages you may be picking up can lessen the effect of social pressure in your life. It is good to remember that it is *behavior* that affects you and that you tend to imitate. It is not the words of people that cause this kind of pressure. The people in the elevator didn't have to say one word to have an obvious effect.

It is also important to realize some facts about the nature of anxiety, guilt, and fear. These emotions will be aroused when you are closest to success in your struggle against social pressure. At the point when you are separating your own point of view from the attitudes of your parents, you will experience anxiety. If you can learn to tolerate it and to sweat through these changes, you will hold on to the territory you have gained, and the anxiety will eventually dissipate. The added weight of social pressure will increase the intensity of the anxiety brought on by being different. But if you make sure you are around people who are strong themselves and who don't deny themselves their honest strivings, then you will get implicit support, a kind of positive social pressure.

Understanding how negative social pressure works is vital to your ability to control its effect on you. It is valuable for your own development not to be deceived by people who are self-denying martyrs and victims of life. You are not required to hide your accomplishments and successes just because someone else wants very little. Being courageous in going against the self-denying tendencies, both in yourself and others, plays a constructive part in your growth and development. It is important to take a chance on standing out from the group, not in a defiant style, but just for yourself.

Patterns of Defense

5

Reliving vs. Living—Destructive Repetition

T RYING TO WARD OFF AND SOOTHE painful experiences in our early childhood, we unintentionally become prisoners, locked into a defensive style of living. We often, in spite of our wishes, re-create the kind of life we had hoped to escape or outgrow. By continuing to ease our pain with the methods we learned as children, we give up the luxury of completely experiencing life. In this sense, we are not free individuals. Instead, we live defensively.

There are six dimensions of defensive or neurotic living. These dimensions are not isolated; they overlap and merge with each other. Each individual's unique life-style may make use of any or all of these aspects of defensive living.

The major aspects or dimensions of neurotic living are:

Reliving
Withholding
Playing the victim
Using psychic painkillers
Relying on fantasy
Bonds (destructive ties)

A major dimension of defensive living is the destructive repetitious process of reliving rather than living: It is the attempt to re-create a parent in other persons or institutions. Most people have experienced some degree of pain while growing up because their needs for love and nurturing experiences were not fully met. For those who suffered a great deal of emotional deprivation and rejection in their childhood, the need to repeat the patterns of their early lives may become compulsive.

When a child experiences much emotional deprivation, he will feel the anxiety and pain within his entire being. Small and vulnerable, he is helpless in the face of the truth that his parents feel or express little love for him, and so he represses this awareness and looks for ways to ease his fears and suffering. Knowing that he is totally dependent on his parents for his physical survival, he is forced to block out his feelings of being unloved by them. His primitive thought process put in words would be, "If they don't love me, they might abandon me and I'll die. That's an intolerable idea, I must and will believe they love me."

As he grows older the child will attempt to exclude any experience that conflicts with the deep belief about the certainty of his parents' love. The guaranteed way to accomplish this is to make sure his life mirrors his original childhood experience, that it excludes the possibility of different, more positive experiences.

In an animal experiment young pigs were fed a minimum subsistence diet, food that barely kept them alive for an extended period of time. Later, when as a part of the experiment, more nutritious food was made available to them, they preferred to eat the substandard food that they were used to.

A child, too, becomes habituated to a negative environment and negative behavior patterns, losing any conscious desire to escape or change. Re-creating a similar environment and repeating the same patterns in his adult life serve to reduce and perhaps even completely block the awareness of his initial pain, fear, and anxiety about abandonment.

There is another phenomenon reported from animal studies that is analogous to the human's propensity to repeat hurtful patterns of childhood. In an experiment dogs were strapped into a harness that made them unable to move and were then given electric shocks. Later the dogs were placed into a two-compartment box where they were supposed to learn to escape the shock by simply jumping across a low barrier from the shock section to the nonshock section. The dogs that had been restrained so that they couldn't escape stayed in the shock section until they were dragged away, even though they were now free to jump across the barrier. Other dogs, who had not been harnessed (helpless) when first shocked, quickly learned to jump to freedom.

It is true also for a child who is unable to do anything to change his situation that he will often cut off his awareness of pain and remain passive, accepting the same hurtful situation as it "happens" to him again and again throughout his lifetime. When one studies the patterns in human interactions, it is amazing to see how often adults choose a partner or mate whose behavior resembles one of their parents. A daughter who was pampered and praised for her childish performances will probably marry a man who treats her like a princess. Many times a son will marry a woman with the same characteristics as his mother. Frank was a man who found such a woman, someone with whom he could repeat the unhappiness of his childhood.

Frank grew up hating his mother. Of the three children in his family, he had been singled out from his two sisters by his mother to "keep" for herself. Frank was a sickly child, suffering from a chronic sinus condition, and as a result, over a period of years he had to make many visits with his mother to an out-of-town doctor.

Frank remembers those visits well. "I sat for hours in waiting rooms. Mother was always checking to see if I was feeling all right or if my clothes were getting wrinkled. I was humiliated but mostly I was ashamed in front of my father when we returned from these trips. My mother would describe the latest report about my health and my father would silently look at me with disgust. He thought that I was a mama's boy and there was nothing I could do to change his opinion of me because I was so weak and sickly looking."

Before he had developed his illness, Frank had been a rough-and-tumble kind of kid, always exploring his environment. He especially remembers a very early routine, which he related to me:

I can see myself as a small kid, about two or three years old. I am walking and running around the house having lots of fun just looking at things, exploring dark corners in the cellar, discovering old pieces of machinery laying around the garage, even taking an old alarm clock apart. Suddenly my mother is standing over me, frowning. She grabs me up and throws me into a crib (which I slept in until I was five) and tells me that I have to learn to stay out of things. She was putting me to bed for my "nap." I stayed in that crib for hours every day. I remember studying the design on the mattress cover. It was the only thing I had to look at. Once in a while my mother would let me out of the crib, but only to bring me out into the living room to show off before her friends. She would ask me to repeat the "cute" sayings that I said once in a while, or she insisted that I recite a line of poetry which she had taught me. It was at these times I loathed her the most.

When Frank was in college he was attracted to and finally married a girl who had a strong need, because of her own insecurity, to control his activity. She sulked when Frank went to baseball games with his friends and when, on occasion, he stopped by his old college roommate's house for a quick drink after work. Soon Frank found himself cutting out all of these extra activities. Instead, he spent more and more time at home, working on house repairs and gardening.

In discussing his marriage with me, Frank began to wonder about his wife's concern about his health, which had improved since his childhood and gave him no concern.

You know, Marcia takes an incredible interest in vitamins and eating nutritious foods. She insists that I eat correctly, whatever that means, and that I eat the kind of health food meals that she likes. I swear, she's almost as fanatical as my mother was.

This conversation took place between Frank and me three years after he had married Marcia. When he mentioned in passing that his wife resembled his mother in this one characteristic, he didn't connect it with anything else in the overall pattern of repetition in his life. Frank was irritated by Marcia's interference in his eating, but he put up with it good-naturedly for many more years. According to Frank, Marcia had one outstanding talent: an ability to entertain his business associates in their home.

Marcia is a wonder at throwing these parties. She's the perfect, gracious hostess. She's great as a conversationalist, too. We always end up talking about something interesting, usually something about my work at the lab. [Frank was a nuclear physicist.] I think that she has a knack for guiding the conversation where she wants it to go. I think, too, that she likes to hear me talk because that's the way the evenings end up, with me and a couple of other men discussing the latest findings in the field. I love those evenings.

By the time Frank and Marcia had been married ten years, the sparkle was wearing thin on the dinner party conversation and Marcia was tightening her grip on Frank's freedom. She made all the decisions about who they would have over, where they would go on vacations, which hotel they would stay at, which private school their children should attend. Frank's resentment grew and he even began to view in a different light those evenings he had so loved.

I realize now that Marcia is a manipulator. I know she guided these afterdinner talks in my direction, but it was very similar to my mother's attention to my cute childish sayings. I finally came to know that everyone else was bored with those evenings except me.

Today Frank feels stifled by Marcia's domineering style of relating to him and to his friends, yet he feels powerless, just as he did when he was a child, to remove himself from a situation that has been degenerating for years. He is afraid to risk a fresh start with someone else and he has not been able to stop Marcia's slow erosion of his life. He has felt too comfortable for too long either to effectively call a halt to her controlling techniques or to seek a new life without her. He is locked into a prison of his own making. Frank has successfully repeated his past, to the detriment of himself and of Marcia. His defeat is unreal, however, because as an adult he does have the power to change things or to remove himself from the situation.

How many times have you seen the initial excitement and attraction at the beginning of a relationship fade and the love go? How many times has the sexuality of a new relationship evaporated just as one partner begins to develop strong feelings of affection? How many times has a businessperson achieved success only to lose his enthusiasm and drive when he is recognized for his accomplishments? How many friends do you have who complain about the same problem year after year?

You may have noticed that some sorts of things happen to you over and over again. There may be patterns in your own life that seem to repeat themselves and appear to be beyond your control. One woman I knew was involved with a series of passive men who seemed incapable of supporting themselves in the career of their choice. Her first relationship was with an artist who refused to work in the field of commercial art (where he could possibly have made a living) because he didn't want to "prostitute his creativity." This woman supported his career with her own income for a period of two years. Following this, she was involved with a Ph.D. candidate, working to support him while he wrote his dissertation. When I questioned her about her choices of men, she said, "But these are the only men who have attracted me. I guess I like feeling needed by them, but I think I resent them too."

Gradually, this woman came to recognize the truth: She just wasn't attracted to a man she couldn't take care of. Her puzzlement over her selection was a first step in recognizing that she had a pattern of being involved in relationships that did nothing to enhance her self-respect. In a sense she felt that "no independent man who could make it on his own would choose me." She had to feel indispensable to feel any security at all. Her relationships each ended in the same failure: These men came both to need her and to resent her deeply.

There is a tremendous amount of waste incurred when people act out their past family relationships in their jobs. Many executives do, indeed, rise to the level of their incompetency and languish there year after year. Having received "tenure," they often rest on their laurels, rarely achieving any more outstanding successes in their fields.

The acting out of repetitive patterns takes place at all levels and in all fields with workers unconsciously holding back their talents, enthusiasm, and capabilities from their employers. Lawrence, for example, usually performed well on the job and was time and again promoted to a position next in line to the boss. This was always the point at which he "went into action." Lawrence had certain ideas about the way things should be run in the companies where he worked, and he didn't hesitate to tell his bosses about his ideas. At board meetings and executive dinners, he tried to sell his ideas in a persuasive manner. But he had the knack of indirectly insulting the higher-ups' intelligence, the very people whom he was trying to win over to his point of view. He always antagonized his bosses.

Lawrence was bent on being fired or otherwise punished by persons in the position of leadership. He was consistently undermining his chances to do the kind of work he was fully capable of. His resentment of authority was a long-standing pattern. When very young he had stubbornly refused to comply with his mother's rules about bedtimes, household chores, and many other routines of his home. His mother usually gave up easily and threatened him with punishment "when your father gets home." Indeed, when his father returned home in the evening, Lawrence was usually punished either physically or verbally with a stern lecture. In his harassment of his immediate superiors, he was attempting to repeat the punishments of his childhood.

Some of Lawrence's methods of aggravation point out the lengths to which he would go to bring this kind of punishment down on his head. Not only did he brag about the value of his ideas, but if they were voted down, he acted indignant and self-righteous. He had the attitude of somehow having equal status with the boss or the board of directors. In other words, he acted like a big shot, as if he were more important and more intelligent than anyone else in the company. In one place of employment, he sometimes smoked a cigar while working in the same room with his boss, knowing all the while that the man hated the odor of stale cigar smoke. In another office he insisted on trying to rework the entire inventory systems even though he knew the previous manager had just completed a new, efficient system.

Often, we seek out environments that are so similar to the atmosphere of the homes we grew up in that we don't have to act to "feel right at home." We place ourselves in authoritarian institutions where the rules and routines are followed to the letter with no questions asked. Lawrence had chosen this kind of environment when he joined the marines at the age of eighteen. He fit in well with the regimentation at boot camp and enthusiastically took part in the drills and rigid upkeep of barracks. It was almost as if he were at home, but living under the immediate rule of a father figure instead of his mother.

In Vietnam he distinguished himself by his adherence to orders and by his coolness under fire. He told me that he felt somehow guided and looked after by his officers, almost as if he were invulnerable to danger because he was protected by strong leaders. These leaders were strict disciplinarians like Lawrence's father and so he felt secure and comforted with familiarity and regularity in the midst of the chaos of war. For Lawrence his years in the marines were a repetition of his years at home with his father. The regulations were restrictive and punitive enough to begin with. It was not necessary for him to aggravate and provoke punishment as it was later in the more democratic environment of a civilian job.

We may also attempt to provoke punishment if we meet someone who is loving or if we experience something positive. Encountering a significantly warm, positive experience in our present-day life, we may be driven to wipe it out, deny it, or change it because it is too great a contrast to the painful events of our childhood. We cannot bear the truth: Our parents may have withheld their love from us, may not have been very good to us. So we arrange our lives in a way that avoids the possibility of receiving real warmth and consistent love, and we never have to feel the pain of knowing what we didn't get or how we were hurt.

Anyone who tries to block out the realization of the pain and emotional deprivation that he experienced as a child resorts to a variety of mechanisms in his desperate attempt to keep things eternally the same. There are three principal ways in which we maintain and perpetuate our neurotic equilibrium. Our defenses are sustained basically through *selection, distortion,* and *provocation.*

1. Selection: We choose those individuals with the same or similar traits as significant individuals in our early lives.

2. Distortion: We distort our perceptions of people and events in a direction that corresponds closely to the people and events of our childhood. We tend to focus a kind of selective attention on any new person in our lives, always on the lookout to prove that he is like the people in our past. We often project onto him, see in him these very qualities we resented in our parents and siblings; this, of course, guarantees the eventual decline of trust and openness in our new relationships. We may actually misperceive and misinterpret events so that they can't contradict what we want to go on believing. Carried far enough, this process can become seriously maladaptive.

3. Provocation: We behave in such a way as to provoke the kinds of responses that we received in our families. We often do this with loved ones.

Lisa used all three of these defensive styles in trying to push away a love she had discovered only a few months previously. Lisa met Dick shortly after she began working in the accounting office adjoining his. She was immediately attracted to him and had eagerly pursued him, which was uncharacteristic of her. When Dick asked her to go out the first time, she was ecstatic. For several months things went smoothly and Dick was really beginning to care for Lisa. He was thinking of asking her to marry him. It was at this point that Lisa began to change, almost imperceptibly at first. Gradually, she became more distant and less enthusiastic about the relationship.

Lisa had grown up while her father had been involved in a rigid discipline of studying for a medical degree. His years of study had spanned most of her childhood. During this time he had insisted upon strict rules of silence in their home when he was there and on several occasions had become extremely angry with Lisa when she broke the rules.

In choosing Dick, who was pursuing a career as a certified public accountant and was often preoccupied with studies, Lisa was trying to reproduce the circumstances of her childhood. But Dick was not a stickler for rules and rarely became annoyed with Lisa when she wanted his attention. So Lisa's new circumstances were not as negative as those with her father and she had to resort to other defenses in her attempt to relive her past. This is the way she talked about an evening she spent with Dick:

"One night I was ten minutes late meeting Dick and his associates at a restaurant for dinner. As I approached the table, I looked at Dick's face, trying to determine whether he was angry. I saw that he was frowning and felt that he must be angry with me for being late. As I sat down next to Dick, I whispered to him, 'Are you mad at me for being late?' I could tell he was really angry by then. He ignored me for the rest of the dinner and when we were driving home, he told me that he had been very embarrassed by me at dinner. I can't understand him. I had been very quiet so that Dick could discuss business." Lisa's voice took on a complaining tone as she told me about the evening.

The truth was that Dick had been embarrassed by Lisa's nervous behavior. Making a silent resolution never to invite Lisa to this kind of business dinner, he had attempted to continue the conversation, but his mood had been ruined by the anger he felt toward her. Her childish question and frightened look had been completely inappropriate to the circumstances. These responses had irritated Dick, not her lateness. Dick had not even noticed that she was a little late.

This ordinary and seemingly innocuous event was just the beginning of a serious pattern of insecurity for Lisa. She began to demand constant reassurance from Dick that he loved her and approved of her actions, even her ideas. Her exaggerated need for comfort, guidance, and security further aggravated Dick. At first he attempted to give her reassurance and to "love her out of it," but when this failed he felt increasingly angry and resentful. In the process of "proving" his love and affection, he became less free to pursue his own goals. This contributed to his anger and to a sense of guilt and failure as well.

Some people constantly ask, "Do you love me?" or say, "Please say you love me" or "You don't say you love me as much as you used to." Their pathetic demands for reassurance provoke the very rejection that they fear so much.

Lisa was involved in the systematic destruction of the relationship that she had valued so highly at the beginning. She was so well defended as a child against feeling the real rejection from her father that she couldn't tolerate real love in her adult life, especially love that might be consistent and enduring.

Lisa's manipulations in her attempts to be rejected were to a large degree unconscious. She really believed that Dick was angry when he wasn't, that he was ignoring her whenever he was preoccupied with studies or work, and that he wasn't attracted to her as much as he claimed. She lacked any awareness that these were her distortions; instead, she thought that it was Dick who was changing and pulling away from her. She couldn't bear the anxiety of not knowing if she would be rejected. She had to provoke the rejection before it might happen. She protected herself from the possibility of being hurt by pushing Dick away first. Like many of us, Lisa was involved in reliving her earlier family life rather than living her own life in the present.

Coping with Life Instead of Reliving

All of us have the tendency to look outside ourselves first for the cause of our problems. We blame a person we are close to and insist that it is he who is mistreating us, losing interest and rejecting us. It may be difficult at first to do the reverse and look to ourselves for the cause of our sufferings. However, this is the first step toward stopping these destructive, repetitive patterns.

IDENTIFY THE PATTERNS

Obviously, it is important to identify behavior patterns that prevent good experiences with other people. If we look closely, we can become aware of how our attempts to reduce risk and vulnerability produce instead the very rejection we wish to avoid. Resisting our tendency to run away from our real life into the unreality of reliving past experiences is worth the effort.

In reality each person is responsible for most of the negative events that he feels just "happen" to him. Learning to recognize your own specific patterns or distortions in your relationship with others is one way to resist repeating these destructive patterns. Be open to other people's ideas. Compare your own perceptions with the perceptions of others; it's a way of searching for the truth and testing reality.

It is not just important for your own sake to be aware of the times when you want to provoke anger or rejection from a person you are close to. It also hurts the other person when you try to get a negative response from him. When people feel loving toward you it makes them feel good, and when you distort these feelings, they naturally feel bad and are often confused. If we do finally manage to provoke them and make them angry with us, they also begin to turn some of their anger inward and dislike themselves.

BREAK THE PATTERNS

When you take a genuine chance on being close to someone else, you may be breaking deeply entrenched old patterns of behavior. Taking risks and being vulnerable, while exposing you to hurt and rejection, also exposes you to a lot of positive experiences. Becoming sensitive to other people's points of view and to constructive criticism without killing yourself with guilt gives you a chance to be aware of your mistakes and modify your patterns of behavior in the future. If you are open and honest with yourself about *your* contribution to the unhappy times in your relationships, you can put an end to this destructive way of relating.

If you find that your patterns of reliving are too difficult to isolate and change through a pattern of self-analysis and you are still unable to help yourself, you may need to seek the services of a qualified professional. Look for a psychologist or psychiatrist who is expert in identifying and working through destructive repetitious behavior.

Facing and accepting the anxiety of change that comes while breaking these habitual patterns will give you a sense of being in control of your own life. This anxiety can be tolerated and it diminishes as you live more and more in the present.

As an adult you don't have to continue repeating your childhood with the new people in your life, hoping that they will somehow fill your unmet needs from the past. No one can satisfy your longing for what you never received as a child from your parents, not even your parents now. To involve other people in this hopeless search is to lose what you have today trying to gain what you had so little of in the past.

Learning to really experience and live fully aware in your present life will open up new dimensions for you. You will no longer be limiting your life.

6

Withholding—How It Hurts You

A Basic Hostility Toward Self and Others

HOLDING BACK OUR NATURAL RESPONSES in favor of protecting our defense system and the fantasy of self-sufficiency may mean, among other things, holding back our natural love and affection, our sexual responses, our special gifts, and our natural abilities.

When a child suffers from emotional deprivation or rejection, he turns inward toward fantasy to gratify his needs and he then feels pseudoindependent. In a sense he incorporates the image of his rejecting parents, who are "all-powerful," into himself and feels a false sense of self-sufficiency. A child will come to depend on fantasy to the degree that he is frustrated and pained in the real world. Later, he will unconsciously reject real giving from others who love him to hold on to the safety of the fantasy world over which he has complete control. He will resist emotional transactions with others, refusing to take love from outside or give love to others.

Most people who use this defense are almost completely unconscious of having and depending on a fantasy world. It's not like having imaginary friends or hallucinations. The fantasies, for the most part, exist deep in the unconscious and we only become aware of them by examining our behavior and noting the ways in which we act against our own best interests.

The more we use fantasy as a defense against pain, the more we will resist giving. In holding back we deprive ourselves of our greatest joy and happiness—the natural expression of our love and compassion for others. The high price we pay for our illusions and false security is in guilt and suspicion. For when we choose inner gratification over love of others and self, we become suspicious, even paranoid, that other people will discover what we are doing. This is why we cover up our withholding as much as we can. If it is exposed we become very angry and fearful.

In extremely disturbed individuals the fantasy of self-sufficiency can become all-encompassing, with the person withholding almost all his natural responses. Paradoxically, the more he imagines that he is independent and needs no one, the more dependent he really is on others for care. In mental hospitals maximum care is needed by those patients who delude themselves that they are the greatest, the strongest, and need nothing from anyone. One schizophrenic man was so withholding that he refused to urinate in a toilet. He had been incontinent for over a year and a half and was terrified to part with that product of his body. In his delusions his urine was "milk from my penis" and was thus a vital part of his self-nourishing fantasy.

An experiment was attempted with this man in which the therapists gave him large amounts of water while he was seated on the toilet, trying to force a break in his withholding and pseudoindependence. This man was so acutely withholding, however, that the water he drank was expelled through the pores in his skin as drenching perspiration and he still retained his urine.

This psychotic man is an extreme example of withholding carried to its ultimate conclusion. After a period of time, the experiment, together with the therapist's interpretations, interfered with the patient's fantasy. It was after repeated reassurances by the therapists that they would fill him up with real love and care that he was willing to take the risk, both of giving up his urine and of receiving care from the therapists. He no longer suffers acutely from his fear of being drained.

Much less extreme forms of withholding can cause damage to the individual and to the people around him. People withhold many of their responses in practically any situation of everyday life. For example, the career of housewife provides endless opportunities for withholding love and care. A woman can choose, consciously or unconsciously, simply to not give, all the while feeling overwhelmed by her "job." Her work may literally never be done. These words were often spoken by Sonya, a housewife who had once been a highly efficient nurse professionally, but who now held back her capabilities and her efficiency from her family.

Sonya was one of the most withholding people I have known over the years. She and Don and their three teenagers lived in a nice four-bedroom home. The most incredible fact about Sonya was that she worked hard all day and accomplished nothing. The house was an unbelievable shambles. Unironed clothes lay in piles around the living room while the ironing board stood in a corner of the dining room. There was not an inch of bare counterspace in the kitchen which was not covered by dirty dishes or food. On the dining-room table stood empty or half-filled pop bottles and cartons of milk together with the kids' schoolpapers. The door to one of the bedrooms was always locked. It contained boxes of clothes and books which Sonya said she was going to sort through "when she had time" and give away to Goodwill. This room had been crammed with boxes since the family had moved to the neighborhood four years before.

Sonya didn't want a neat, livable home. She didn't want to give this to her family; in fact, she strenuously withheld this from them while acting overworked. She constantly begged Don to help her, which he did from the moment he walked in the front door each evening. She whined and nagged the children to clean their rooms, but they were already imitating her patterns of not giving, so their rooms stayed messy. One boy, Albert, who was somewhat less withholding than the rest of the family members, regularly cleaned the room he shared with his brother, but it quickly resumed its usual messy state when his brother got to it.

A large woman who was constantly dieting, Sonya was also a heavy smoker. While she ironed, Sonya smoked and watched the soap operas on television. As a child Sonya had been rejected by her father, who was far more interested in her brothers than in her. In addition, her mother was babyish and inadequate, so that early in life Sonya had formed her own methods of giving herself love, beginning with the overindulgence of food. She could not tolerate any intrusion into her self-sufficient system of taking care of herself, of giving herself the love and nourishment she had missed. Keeping a clean house felt far beyond her capacity to give. It overtaxed her self-nourishing defense system. She literally felt afraid of being depleted emotionally by caring for others in the house.

It was inevitable that Don and Sonya's children grew up to become withholding. The two sons worked long hours at their jobs, sometimes putting in many hours of overtime each week, yet they were not successful. One of the sons was eventually fired because of inefficiency. The other son, Albert, is just now slowly improving his work habits. Through counseling sessions he is beginning to break into this defense of withholding. He finds it difficult because the patterns of behavior are so deeply ingrained by now, but he has optimism in further changing himself.

The tragedy of the withholding defense is that because of it children are damaged unknowingly; adults waste hundreds of hours resisting accomplishment while thinking that they are working hard, and relationships are ruined by one or both persons withholding the love they once expressed. Withholding is one of the most serious and brutally damaging patterns.

The child's only recourse when faced with parents who withhold from him is to pull inward and to learn systematically to withhold his own basic love feelings. Later, when these patterns have become automatic and habitual, the child unconsciously retreats and withholds when a person is loving or nice to him. He may even feel like lashing back angrily at those persons who value him for what he is.

This is the pattern that George learned from his family while he was growing up. One incident that happened when he was twelve is characteristic of the ongoing withholding in his family.

One summer, George, his two sisters, and his father had enjoyed a two-week vacation in the Canadian woods. The fishing had been highly successful and George's father was happy and relaxed. On the way back to civilization, however, the mood had changed. George's father seemed irritable and worried about minor details that hadn't bothered him while they were camping. Then, at an Indian trading post where they had stopped to buy souvenirs, George asked his father if he could purchase a hunting knife. His father exploded in anger, grabbed George by the collar of his jacket, and shook him in full view of several people. "You little ingrate, aren't you ever satisfied with what I give you? You've had enough for one vacation." George was shocked and humiliated by his father's display of temper.

Years later, all that he remembered of that trip was this one negative incident.

George's father had reached the limit of his tolerance for feeling close with George and his sisters. It had been easier to feel close and relaxed away from the routines and destructive interactions with his wife at home. George learned the lesson that good feelings are only temporary. When he became an adult he found it very difficult to maintain a loving relationship beyond a certain period of time.

Withholding is a holding back of truthful, open, positive responses to others, especially from those you care deeply for. For example, you may feel happy and excited to see the one you love when you come home from work each evening. If, however, you don't express this excitement, for whatever reason, you are hurting yourself and your loved one. You may tell yourself, "Why are you so excited? You've only been gone since this morning. Don't act like a child, be cool." You have effectively talked yourself into denying your natural response in order to protect your defenses.

Withholding Physical Affection and Sex

An infant needs a certain amount of tactile stimulation by a caring person if he is to survive. Some studies have shown that institutionalized infants will "give up" and literally die unless they are picked up and handled by nurses or attendants. Many of our parents have said as a rationalization, "Of course I loved you. I just had a hard time showing it. But I knew that you could tell that I loved you anyway." Thus, we in turn now withhold our affection because it is painful and sad to express it, and we defensively say, as our parents said, "It isn't that important." But it is. The only way the child can know that he is loved is if this love is demonstrated to him. A person can "feel" intense love within himself and never express it outwardly. This unexpressed love never reaches the "loved" one and does him no good at all.

A seemingly insignificant incident in Laurie's life highlights the process of withholding as it often occurs between married couples. Laurie and Greg had been married almost a year when one morning Laurie had an impulse to telephone Greg from the office where she worked. She was feeling especially good toward her new husband and wanted to ask him to join her for lunch. It would be a nice surprise and a continuation of the romantic evening they had spent the previous night. Thinking of asking him to lunch made Laurie feel happy and excited.

An hour later, when she found the time to call Greg, she opened the conversation by asking his opinion of a practical matter that had arisen concerning their joint tax return. It completely slipped her mind to ask Greg about having lunch. It wasn't until a few hours had passed that she remembered her earlier impulse. She realized that at some point between the time when she initially thought of the idea until the time of the phone call, she had become embarrassed by her romantic thought. At the sound of Greg's voice on the phone, she had immediately thought of a more practical matter. Laurie had withheld an opportunity for contact that she and Greg would have enjoyed.

Once you begin to hold back your physical responses, whether affectionate or sexual, you are turning your back on something basic in your nature. This withholding affects every area of your life. Not only do you damage the people close to you, especially your children, but you become cut off from yourself and your own feelings. You begin to lose your sense about what you really feel. Essentially, you sell yourself out; you have gone against something that is natural to you.

All of us have noticed our loved ones looking good sometimes and at other times looking faded. We have all seen a strikingly radiant woman whose glow draws all men's eyes. A woman of equal beauty, in terms of physical features, who is not alive or energetic might easily go unnoticed. When we hold back the flow of our natural feelings and retreat from our natural wants into a protective mode, this shows up on our physical features. But what is more important, it takes a heavy toll on our overall psychological functioning and may limit all aspects of our spontaneity.

A woman may begin to withhold her sexuality when she becomes pregnant. She may have grown up with a model of a "neuter" mother who may have taken good care of her children but who seemed to have no sexual life, or if indeed she had one, it was well hidden. A woman can feel embarrassed combining sex with pregnancy or maternity. She may be thinking to herself, "It's one or the other. Now that I'm about to become a mother, I should concentrate on that. It's more important."

Physical affection and sexuality are closely related and withholding one affects the other drastically and also affects other areas of your life. You cannot withhold physical responses without that having a drastic effect on your entire life.

Mary was a freshman in college and had been dating Tony for over a year when she decided that she should end their friendship because of the guilt she felt about being sexual. She stopped seeing him suddenly and threw herself into her schoolwork. Her grades fell off sharply, and she became tense and irritable. Her friends couldn't understand what had happened to the happy girl they had known at the beginning of the semester. They did not know enough about the situation to realize that they should urge her to make up with Tony and start having fun again. Originally, Mary had only wanted to end the sexual part of the relationship, but in doing so she had found that she didn't even feel friendly or affectionate with him anymore. In holding back her sexual response, she had blocked her other feelings as well and seriously damaged her psychological health for a period of time.

Men, too, are affected when they withhold sexual responses or when they are withheld from by women in their lives. They often lose their vitality. They may seem to become old before their time. If they are withheld from sexually, they may have to resort to fantasy to become aroused. In this way they lose personal contact with the woman during sex and also lose contact with their own feelings. Having an impeded or nonexistent sex life, they may throw themselves into their work with a vengeance and may develop physical ailments from the stress. It is a serious matter for men and women to withhold these important expressions of love or to be denied them.

Withholding General Competence and Work

Children begin withholding their ability to perform even before they reach school age. Our society values incentive, initiative, and hard work. Our families stress these values to the children. There *is* real value in the work ethic; we often derive our best feelings of self-worth when we work hard to accomplish what we have set out to do. However, some parents want their children to succeed not so much for the sake of the children's happiness but so the parents can feel good about themselves.

A father who has had limited success in business may push his son harder in that area. A mother who wanted a career but who gave it up for marriage may want her daughter to have a career and may pressure her in this direction. This kind of pressure makes it difficult for the child to separate what he wants from what the parent wants for him.

The child may begin to withhold the natural activities that he likes to do because he senses the demand in his parents for that performance. In addition, if his parent has withheld from himself the possibility of success and is failure oriented, the child will imitate the parent's self-denial, often in the same area where the parent failed. He will feel a strong sense of contradiction and conflict. On the one hand, he feels pressure to achieve, but he will also tend to fail in order to protect his parent.

Jeff was one of those people who felt forced to protect his image of his parent. Jeff's father was a German immigrant who came to America in the 1920s. His father had difficulty learning the language and never rose above the position of assistant foreman in a factory that employed only eight or ten workers. His father complained about his lack of advancement and blamed it on the language barrier, yet he refused to attend the English for foreign students classes at the local high school.

Jeff's mother and sister worked in laundries to supplement the family income. Jeff was sent to college on these women's savings. On the basis of his college reputation, he was hired by a wealthy furniture manufacturer and placed in the sales department. Soon Jeff was surpassing his fellow salesmen in commissions. His customers liked him because he was personable and charming, and they felt that they could trust him.

Jeff's boss, who also was about to become his father-in-law—Jeff had met and fallen in love with the boss's daughter—decided that he would make Jeff his new sales manager. The promotion was a wedding gift to Jeff and to his daughter. Several months after the wedding, Jeff began coming home late from the weekly sales meetings which he had instituted. It was soon discovered that Jeff was drinking heavily at these meetings and on the job. His sales performance fell off drastically and within a year there was talk of firing him from his position in the firm.

Jeff had not been a withholding person until after he had achieved what he wanted. Then his sales record had gradually turned into "something he was doing for them," for his wife and his father-in-law. They had become the demanding parental figures in his mind, and he became resentful toward both of them. He had taken the work that he loved to do, had twisted it in his mind into something that was expected and demanded of him by others, and from then on had held back his natural talents. He protected an idealized image of his father by becoming a failure after he had achieved success. He was unable to bear the guilt of surpassing his own father who had been a failure.

This is not an unusual story. How many times have you heard, "He couldn't stand success" concerning someone who had seemingly gone sour after unusual success of one kind or another? Withholding your competence and your talents because they were tied up with your parent's self-image is one way of remaining a dependent child. It is a destructive attempt to remain connected to your parents and to provoke a punishing parental response from your loved ones.

Refusing to Be Adult—a Serious Form of Withholding

Lynn worked as a registered nurse in the pediatrics ward of a local hospital. Over the years she had worked her way up through various positions to a point where she was ready to take on the role of floor supervisor. Lynn really wanted the position. She talked to her immediate superiors about the possibility of being promoted and on the basis of her good record and some innovative procedures she had initiated, she was given it. At last she had what she had wanted for a long time.

Around this time Lynn's boyfriend and some of his college fraternity brothers had purchased a sailboat together. Lynn was really excited about this because she loved sailing. She asked if she could be a part of the project of refurbishing the boat for a cruise to the South Pacific, and she was given the responsibility of stocking the galley, varnishing the interior wood, and cleaning the cushions for the bunks.

On the first day that she took over her jobs on this vessel, she worked hard, really enjoying the physical work and the salt air. As the captain left late in the afternoon, he mentioned to her that the cushions should be brought back into the boat before she left. She said that she would remember to do that and thanked him for giving her an opportunity to take the trip. Early the next day the captain arrived at the boat only to find that the cushions had been left out and that it had rained during the night.

This incident was the first in a series of mistakes Lynn made. Two weeks later she was found sleeping on the night shift at the hospital. The next month there was a death in the pediatric section. A premature baby had died during the night and it was determined that one of the contributing factors had been the injection of an incorrect intravenous solution. The mistake was traced to Lynn, who was fired the next day.

This very dramatic example of normal, everyday withholding highlights the destructive retreat from love and success. Usually this process occurs as a progressive, barely noticeable decline which may not be detected until a long time after it starts—when things reach the breaking point.

Behind this particular tragedy lay a stubborn refusal on Lynn's part to be adult. She had done well as long as there was someone above her in the nursing ranks so that she didn't have to assume final responsibility. Sharing the boat work on an equal basis with the men had been another opportunity to be adult on a level different from the typical doctor-nurse relationship she was familiar with. Lynn had refused this opportunity also, although with far less drastic results.

The refusal to be an adult in one's life is a stubborn hanging on to the unconscious fantasy of being a child forever. There are several reasons why a person would elect to remain a child. First, it may be an attempt to avoid facing one's own eventual death. As one woman recently said, "When I was a child, I knew that the next logical step was to be an adult. When I turned twenty-one I thought, 'Now the next logical step is old age and death.' I absolutely didn't want that next step, so I rejected the step of being an adult. I thought of myself as much younger than I was to avoid knowing that I was really an adult."

A second reason may be that we are still using our failures to be successful as a final way of holding on to our parents. If we were to grow up to handle our own lives in a capable manner and be happy doing it, we would be letting our parents off the hook.

The game of withholding our affection and our abilities from our parents is a destructive ploy we learned, perversely enough, by example from our own parents. Becoming more adult in the true sense of the word is vitally important to all of us. It means that we will no longer be withholding as our parents were. This fact distinguishes us from them. Herein lies the third reason for remaining a child. The terror of having an identity different from our parents leaves us feeling alone in the world. But, that is reality. We are all separate and alone anyway.

The Internal Voice That Controls
the Withholding Response

Withholding affection, abilities, and adult behavior is a process that is controlled by a seemingly protective voice. This voice is not necessarily conscious. It is not heard as one would hear a hallucination, or an audible sound. It exists more as a feeling, a general attitude toward the self and toward others. It is responsible for a self-critical attitude and a critical attitude toward others. The voice encourages us to be secretive and inward. It warns us against trusting other people; it is an expression of our cynicism. This voice represents the incorporated parental defense system, both spoken and unspoken. It contains those thoughts and attitudes of our parents that were the most rejecting of ourselves and of people outside the family. The voice is angry at us and at other people. It always acts to separate us from others. It may start out by praising or soothing us, but it changes soon to criticism and self-destructive attacks.

Your inner voice may be similar to Marsha's. Marsha had been studying all week for an exam, but one sunny afternoon she said to herself, "I've really done great studying this week. I deserve a break. I'm going to take the afternoon off. I can cut one class. I owe it to myself to take it a little easy." Marsha told her friends that she was cutting class and then went to the beach. Later, she felt very guilty, and her inner voice said, "Now I've really ruined it. I'm so stupid to miss class this week."

Then, turning her attacks on others, she thought, "My friends knew that this was an important class and that I shouldn't have missed it. Why didn't they tell me about it?"

Marsha first soothed herself with praise and then tore into herself savagely for cutting her class. Then, as often happens, she directed her aggression at others. Misdirected anger is often focused on those people who love and befriend you the most. The voice can be misleading and may at first appear constructive. However, it is basically harmful because it is part of the self-destructive process and is the major regulator of all your repetitious behaviors.

The voice represents the rejecting attitudes of your parents that you incorporated into yourself when very young. It consists of their negative point of view, which may have been spoken or unspoken, but which you have taken in through the processes of incorporation and imitation.

The voice affects your moods and your feelings toward others. It can make the difference between a good day and a miserable one. If you can become aware of the times when and why you are experiencing a transition from being fairly happy to being depressed or cynical, you can begin to control these moods, because you will know where most of your misery is coming from.

Elaborating on your criticisms or attacks on yourself can help increase your awareness of the process. Saying the attacks in the second person "you" instead of the first person "I," almost as if a parental figure were talking to you, is a good way to verbalize these thoughts. If you are angry at someone or at yourself and are really in a bad mood, the words will probably surface more readily than if you are only mildly upset. For example, your voice may have a lot to say about the person with whom you are involved emotionally. Marsha hurt herself by often doubting the nice feelings her boyfriend, Hank, expressed to her. Said in the second person, her voice went like this: "Do you really believe him when he says that he loves you? Remember, men are interested in one thing, sex."

The voice of a young man awkwardly approaching a young woman for the first date might go something like this: "Why would she want to go out with you? You're not as good-looking as the other men she's dated. You're too quiet and shy and you aren't any fun. She's probably going to turn you down and then you'll be humiliated." The young man may also have sensed the self-critical inner voice of the woman he wanted to date, and she may have sensed this, which only increases their awkwardness.

In both of these cases, the negative thoughts are directed against the self; in addition, suspicion, distrust, and predictions of rejection are felt about the other person. If you can verbalize these attacks instead of just being crushed by them, you will have a better understanding of your specific kind of self-destructive attacks and cynical thoughts about others. Gradually, you will see that these negative attitudes toward yourself and toward others are not your real point of view.

Answering these criticisms and accusations with realistic evaluations of yourself and acting in your own best interests will weaken the control this voice has had on your behavior.

A realistic answer to Marsha's voice about her boyfriend might go something like this: "I believe him. He's an honest person. He tells the truth and I know from his actions that he enjoys my company, that he likes being with me. He feels really attracted to me and I like that a lot. And as for sex, he likes it with me. I really like it, too. I feel attracted to him, too." The young man could answer his self-critical thoughts like this: "She might like to go out with me. I'll never know if I don't ask her. I don't have to entertain her; I'd just like to get to know her. I may not be that good-looking, but most women have said yes when I have asked them out."

A realistic appraisal that is nondefensive is the most effective method for weakening the power of these negative thoughts. Standing up to this internal parental voice puts you in touch with your real, positive feelings toward your loved ones, yourself, and the important events in your life.

When you answer the voice, admit both your negative and your positive traits. It is never acceptable to allow your voice to tear you down even if the facts are true. If a man is overweight, there is no useful reason for him to stand in front of his mirror berating himself: "You're so fat, you're disgusting. How can you stand yourself? No wonder you're so unpopular. Look at yourself, you're a repulsive creature." Or if someone has a lower than average IQ, there is no value in degrading himself in his own eyes by calling himself stupid and unlovable. Admit your faults and weaknesses, but have compassion for yourself. It never helps to be mean and sarcastic about your human weaknesses.

In your realistic answers to the voice, say what you want and what actions you plan to take. The voice is often self-denying, but you don't have to be if you are acting from your own point of view. Separate yourself from this negative force in your life and it will be an emotional separation from the rejecting part of your parent. You will gain more control over your life.

Being aware that it is your incorporated parental voice that is harassing you when you want to feel loving and yet are not feeling responsive will help you maintain a consistently close relationship with the people you love. This self-knowledge is essential in sexually close times. Try to figure out what the attacks might be, but continue to be affectionate and loving if you can. In other words, go against the destructive voice with positive actions. Being sensitive to the other person will help you to put his feelings above your own desire to withdraw emotionally. You can probably recall how you felt when someone took away his affection from you after you had grown to love him. Withholding is a cruel response; it really does hurt—both you and the people close to you.

Being honest with yourself and others can often turn negative situations into positive ones. For example, one evening Marsha and Hank were making love; after a few minutes both of them realized that something was wrong. Marsha didn't feel very affectionate, and Hank couldn't seem to become aroused by Marsha's lying close to him. Instead of proceeding with their love making and trying to pretend that they were feeling something when they weren't, they stopped and talked about how they felt. Marsha told Hank that she would just like to lie close to him and be affectionate with him, even though she felt a lot like holding herself back. When Marsha said these words, Hank felt relieved of having to perform and he relaxed. They talked for a few minutes while continuing to be close and affectionate. Within a few minutes they began to make love and this time they both felt deeply toward each other during the experience.

They had broken their pattern of withholding by admitting honestly that they weren't feeling very much toward each other at first. By talking honestly and continuing to be physically affectionate to each other and by being respectful toward each other, their sexual feelings soon returned.

It is important to remember that if you see people from your own point of view and not from the voice's, you will usually feel a natural affection and attraction toward people you love. Go with that feeling and not with the tendency to withhold. It is gratifying to know that you can be a real friend to people who are close to you. Once you have broken your withholding habits or if you are honest about the times when you feel like pulling away, you have become a friend. You can be trusted to be consistent in your actions and honest about your feelings. This is a valuable gift to be able to give.

It is natural to assume that the people who care for you will rarely or never wish to hurt you intentionally, just as you don't want to hurt them. Keeping this fact in mind, you can learn to be objective in situations where there is conflict between you and your loved one. You can become more aware of the times when your loved one may be withholding from you because he is cut off from his own point of view. If he is "listening" to his self-critical voice more than wanting to be with you, you will feel hurt to some degree by his withdrawal. If you confront him with your accusations, you may only succeed in pushing him further inside himself and further away from you. It would be better to tell him that you miss his affection and that you hope he will feel more like himself sometime soon. This is the time to be compassionate, not critical or condescending, for after all, there will be times when you may become withholding too.

In all your relationships and friendships, learning to be realistic and objective about other people's withholding habits will make you more sensitive to yourself as well as others. A lifelong pattern of withholding cannot be broken in a day. It is a challenging struggle for all of us, but the reward of warmer and more gratifying relationships makes it very much worth the effort.

7

Playing the Victim

IN HER SESSION ONE DAY, a woman complained to me that her husband never came home on time for dinner. Dinner was ready at 6:30, but he often came in as late as 8:30 without calling to let her know that he would be late. She asked me, "Is that right?" I tried to explain to her that the key question wasn't whether it was right or not, although one would tend to agree with her in principle. What she said may have been correct, but in any case, it was irrelevant. I wanted her to see how she was viewing the situation: as a passive victim.

Many people think they are entitled to good treatment. The truth is that they are neither entitled nor not entitled to it. The important issues are what is going on and how you feel about it. This woman would have been better off actively facing the facts of the situation and feeling her emotional reactions rather than distancing herself by judging it and feeling victimized.

If you are being robbed, you don't sit around thinking, "This shouldn't be happening to me. It isn't right." Instead, you react. You may call the police or try to run away. Constructive action is the opposite of victimized brooding.

Even in an extreme situation, such as a concentration camp, feeling victimized is not adaptive. Feeling your anger, planning an escape, attempting to survive, any and all of these courses of action are preferable to indulging powerless, victimized feelings. Your attitude is a vital factor in determining whether you will survive or perish, succeed or fail in life. The woman whose husband was late for dinner had every right to feel angry and to consider constructive action if she wished, but to simply try to justify feeling victimized was maladaptive and ultimately meaningless.

Maintaining a Child-Victim Role Leads to Chronic Passivity. The victimized feelings of a child may very well be appropriate to the situation in which he finds himself. He is without power, helpless, and at the mercy of his parents. Often, events do happen to him that are far beyond his control and understanding. The adult who is still playing the child-victim role is like a deer who sees a lion approaching and instead of fleeing the danger becomes paralyzed. The person just keeps noticing over and over that the situation is dangerous and doesn't make the appropriate adaptive responses. There is no mature, coping behavior, but rather complaining and being overwhelmed by the external situation. The person often focuses exclusively on the issue of the fairness or unfairness of the events.

Feelings do not require any justification. They are automatic responses to favorable and unfavorable events, and no one can be judged wrong for what he feels. In fact, it is better to experience feelings than to deny them or cut them off. Actions based on feelings are a different matter. "Acting out" cannot be viewed separately from its consequences. It is perfectly all right to feel murderous rage, but to make sarcastic remarks or strike a blow is destructive acting out and in most cases morally wrong.

In the case of the woman mentioned above, the tip-off that she really preferred the child-victim role was that she never made any substantial attempt to change her circumstances. Like so many of us, she preferred to complain endlessly about her unfortunate circumstances while passively registering her dissatisfaction.

The victim deals in judgments and "shoulds" in his interactions with others. He operates on the basic assumption that the world should be fair: "I should have been loved by my parents." "My children should call me or write to me." "After all that I've done for her, the least she could do . . ." These preoccupations with rights and shoulds are irrelevant to the real problems we are all faced with; they lead to inward brooding, righteous indignation, and vengeful feelings.

The person who assumes a self-righteous stance is playing a sophisticated version of the child-victim or martyr role. This kind of person is hoarding a tremendous amount of anger because the world isn't the way he likes it or things aren't going his way. He hides his feelings of childish, helpless rage by issuing judgments and evaluations of others, by insisting on authoritarian methods of punishment for those who make mistakes, and by disclaiming any personal responsibility for events not going right.

The Paranoid Process

Paranoid thinking is a disorder of focus and perspective whereby the subjective world of the individual (feelings, reactions) is experienced as happening to him rather than originating in or being caused by him. Genuine anger that would be felt in reaction to the frustration of not getting what he wants is distorted into a feeling of having been hurt or wounded. The difference between these two reactions may seem subtle and hard to grasp at first, but it is very important. The primary cause of this process of distortion is the inability to accept aggressive or competitive feelings in oneself.

The person denies his own angry, aggressive feelings and projects them onto (sees them as coming from) the external world and other people. This leads to a kind of chronic passivity in relation to events and to the expectation of harm from the outside. With this expectation and an abnormally high sensitivity to aggression in others, there is a tendency to distort and even to invent malice in other people. The person expects from others the anger and competitiveness (in a magnified version) that he denies in himself.

When I was working my way through school as an assistant at an animal hospital, I met Oliver, who had severe emotional problems at that time. He had started to develop a paranoid fantasy that a particular doctor had it in for him. He became increasingly nervous, angry, and sullen around this doctor. He started to make mistakes, such as sterilizing two left-handed gloves and giving wrong information to the patients who called him on the phone. Finally, it got to the point where he was in danger of losing his job. I told him about it and advised him that he'd better be careful or he was going to be fired. He was very angry at me for telling him this and was even more careless and sullen on the job and more provoking in the kinds of mistakes he was making. Finally, he was fired. What he predicted had come true. He made it come true, and all the time he felt like the victim of the doctor. He even blamed me for giving him the message that he might be fired.

Anyone trying to help a paranoid person by giving him a realistic picture of the situation will also be included in his paranoid thinking. If it is pointed out that it is his actions and not some outside cause that is bringing on the disaster, he will become even more angry.

Paranoia often occurs in a relationship. One person's focus may shift from feeling his own love and affection toward the other person to worrying about what the other person feels about him. When they were first married, Ben knew exactly how he felt about Lucille. He felt happy whenever they were together and loved her very much. He didn't wonder much about what she felt toward him at any given moment. He simply enjoyed the flow of his own positive feelings toward her.

After they had been married several months, however, Ben began to wonder about Lucille's love for him. She had just started a job as secretary to three young executives and Ben imagined that these men would attract Lucille's attention. He began to ask questions each evening when Lucille arrived home from work: "Who did you eat lunch with today?" "Do you remember our wedding day? Do you still love me as much as you did then?" "How long do you want to keep working before we start thinking about having a baby?" "Why can't you make arrangements to get home just a little bit earlier?"

The questions confused and irritated Lucille, who loved Ben just as much as she always had. Ben had lost much of his loving feelings because he had withheld his feelings of happiness soon after the wedding. Neglected by his mother as a child, he began to be unhappy in anticipation of being ignored now by Lucille. As soon as he had begun withholding his own feelings, he focused a paranoid attention on Lucille's feelings instead. He really believed that she didn't love him anymore, while ignoring the truth that it was he who had cut off his own feelings of love and happiness.

After many months of being cross-examined by Ben, Lucille realized she didn't like him very much anymore, was angry at him, and indeed began to find the men at the office more attractive than Ben. His nagging suspiciousness had killed the love she had felt for him when they were first married. Ben's paranoid suspicions actually came true. In the last months of the marriage, Lucille made one last effort to renew their love, because she really didn't want to lose Ben. At her suggestion they went away for a second honeymoon, and Lucille tried to recapture the romance of the first days after the wedding. She was tender and loving with Ben because she still genuinely felt that way on some deep level. Ben only found more fault with her and kept on complaining that she didn't love him.

Lucille finally left the marriage. She left because she was beginning to hate herself for the times she had given Ben the benefit of the doubt that he was right and she was wrong. She left to preserve her peace of mind. Lucille lost Ben to his inward, defensive process, his paranoid thinking.

The disordered focus of paranoia is frequently evident in the business world. It is true that some business practices are unfair, that some people in business are crooked, and that you can get "taken" in a bad business deal. However, fixing attention on the negative aspects of a business deal and not carefully checking out all the details of the transaction obviously is a paranoid process and is not conducive to successful business.

Randall was a dealer for an automobile manufacturer in a small town. After World War II he was able to purchase a trainload of new cars, which were then in short supply, through a deal that was slightly questionable but not illegal. Randall made a huge profit on the sale of these cars and as a result, a larger company in a neighboring town offered to buy his company and retain Randall's name and his services as a manager. The arrangement would have yielded Randall a large amount of money quickly, with a guarantee of continuing profits. Randall refused to consider the offer despite the pleading of his associates and his wife. He insisted that he had heard a rumor that one of the partners in this large company had had a shady reputation in the distant past. He said that he was suspicious of this man who now had a great deal of wealth and power. When asked about the sources of his information, Randall admitted that it was gossip, but he wouldn't check into the credit references of the company to see if the owner might indeed be suspect. His paranoid thinking and refusal to take any constructive action placed Randall in the category of a small-town car dealer for the rest of his life. No further opportunities came his way, and he can be found in his old age complaining about the lack of business in a small town.

Although his own business deal had been a little shady, Randall had disowned any feeling of personal dishonesty. Instead, he projected it onto the outside world, fearing that others might cheat him. For Randall, feeling like the victim went hand-in-hand with his paranoid suspicions of other businessmen. If Randall had taken the appropriate action of checking out the details of the other company, and if the deal had been consummated successfully, he would have lost his opportunity to remain the victim and complain about his fate. He obviously didn't want success at the expense of his defense system, and that's why he didn't seize the chance for profit when he could.

The process of punishing, accusing, and feeling unfairly treated is debilitating, leads to rage and more punishing feelings, and forms a circular downward spiral. It is vital to your development to stop playing the role of victim because it precludes further emotional growth and causes untold damage to people around you and to yourself.

Realistically speaking, a person has no inherent right to have his needs met. One does, on the other hand, have a natural right to want and to need, and to feel upset when one's wants and needs are frustrated. For example, imagine that you're sitting in your car at a stoplight and the light turns green. An old, crippled man is still in the crosswalk, slowly hobbling toward the opposite curb. You're in a hurry and hate him for delaying you. You have a right to feel angry and to hate him because he is frustrating you in getting to your destination, even though this anger cannot be "justified." You don't need to try to rationalize away your anger by saying, "He's a poor, unfortunate human being, I shouldn't hate him." Nor do you have the right to act out your anger and proceed through the intersection and run him over.

If you can be sensitive to the damage and pain you are inflicting on the person you love when you pretend to be a victim in the relationship, you can become aware of the specific ways this process is working and hurting both of you. Blackmailing another person with guilt by being a victim or allowing yourself to be manipulated by someone who is playing the victim role always damages both of you.

Anna, as a child, had been treated like a baby in her large family of eight children. She was the youngest and even her nickname was "Baby." She was given anything she wanted if she begged long enough for it. When she married Edgar she expected the same kind of treatment. When she didn't get it, Anna began playing the jealousy game to get the attention she wanted. She was enraged by Edgar's refusal to grant her every wish. She projected her anger onto him, seeing him as an ogre, while insisting and acting as if she were sweet and long-suffering. Edgar happened to be a man who was calm in general but who could be provoked into violent anger if there was a suspicion of a rival.

One night Anna "confessed" to Edgar that she had been going out with a close friend of his because she "knew" that he must have been cheating on her. This was too much for Edgar and he lunged at her, grabbed her by the neck, and was trying to choke her when he suddenly came to his senses. He let go of her and sank onto the couch sobbing in horror at what he had almost done. Anna sustained bruises on her neck and body and had to have her older sister take her to the hospital. Anna was listed as another case of the battered wife syndrome, but Anna's sister was one of the few people who knew the truth behind the story Anna had told the officials. She knew how Anna had provoked Edgar beyond his endurance and about the irreparable harm Anna had done to the relationship and to both persons involved. This is an extreme example of the kind of damage that can be sustained when one person is playing the victim in a close relationship.

Don't Play the Victim—It Hurts You More Than It Hurts Them

The destructive urge to play the victim role can be controlled. You can control it in yourself by acknowledging that the world does in fact contain many inequities. There are innumerable social injustices which are discriminatory and unfair to individuals or to groups of people. Even though there are active remedial solutions in a democratic society, many of us prefer to feel victimized in a personal way. This isn't useful, and it's inappropriate.

You don't inherently deserve to receive anything in the way of good treatment from another person, so it is not meaningful to speak of someone being unfair to you in that sense. The world doesn't owe you anything either, not a living, not happiness, not pleasant surroundings, nothing. To think that you deserve to be given something better than you now have is to feel like a victim. This attitude encourages a futile, hopeless, passive stance, and what is worse, it solicits sympathy from others.

Sympathy kills. Take the story of Anna above. The sympathy she received from the hospital officials and from her relatives only served to strengthen her belief that she was indeed a victim. She felt better for a short time, but the more people sympathized, the worse she felt. She became more and more convinced that Edgar was the villain, that she was innocent, and that bad things were always happening to her. She was encouraged to continue her paranoid, victimized posture and felt even more justified of her innocence, which was thoroughly provoking to Edgar.

Responding with sympathy to other peoples' complaints and their sad tales about life can be very unhealthy to them. Soliciting sympathy for yourself is not productive either. There is a way to share someone's sorrow and pain and a way to listen without offering this destructive sympathy and advice. Friends can be sensitive and compassionate toward you without being protective or sentimental. Your choice of friends can be crucial at the time when you are giving up a victimized role.

In general, you can't have a great effect on the conditions of society, but you can change yourself. It is far more hopeful and useful to view life from this perspective than to get stuck blaming failures on outside circumstances. The most important aspect of changing yourself will be how you take action to change situations you are unhappy with.

One action that you could take would be to drop certain words from your vocabulary, words like "fair," "unfair," "should," "right," and "wrong" that support a passive orientation to life when applied to the personal actions of others in relation to you. Many people in authority—parents, teachers, doctors, nurses—are among the worst misusers of these words. The word "should," for instance, often carries a double message. The mother says to her child, "You should go to bed now. You should get your rest." She might mean anything from "You look tired now, so go to bed. You'll probably feel more rested in the morning" to "Get out of my sight, you're bothering me." Both messages can be covered by the word "should." When used in adult relations, it implies that one person is wiser and more qualified to know what's best for the other person. "Should" assumes that the other person is incapable of mature judgment in some area; it is a condescending message.

You can really become an active agent in determining the direction of your life. If you feel stuck in a bad relationship, if you feel restricted in getting ahead in your career, if the same sorts of unfortunate events seem to keep happening to you, look closely and see if a passive attitude on your part has had more to do with these events than you previously thought. Avoid complaining about your problems to others in a style that "dumps" the problem on them. By changing your speaking habits, you will discover a different kind of conversation, one that includes taking full responsibility for your feelings and actions yet leaves you and the other person free to explore alternatives.

When you play the victim role, your orientation toward the external world is paranoid. You are involved in a process in which the focus of your attention is extremely distorted. Your real feelings of anger and frustration are short-circuited and projected onto the world around you. You vigilantly watch to see if someone is disapproving of you, is angry with or critical of you, or is indifferent or ignoring you.

There are hundreds of other ways you may keep this paranoid process going in your everyday life. Sometimes you may imagine that your friends are discussing you in your absence or that they don't really tell you what they think to your face. In your marriage or your closest relationship, you can find many situations in which you imagine your mate is being mean and inconsiderate to you. If you spot each of these thoughts when they come up and can identify them as paranoid, you will be able to shift your focus away from these thoughts back to what you really feel toward the other person.

One of the most effective ways to give up your paranoid orientation and your feelings of victimization is to let go of angry, mean
thoughts you may have toward the people closest to you. For example, if you have been blaming your loved one for making you
feel bad, tell him about your thoughts without making him feel as
if he really might be guilty.

Jerome felt that Sharon's decision to go back to college was a mean
act in relation to him and had been harboring angry, self-pitying
feelings for weeks. Finally, he decided to tell her, because he could
see that she was feeling guilty about her decision and was about to
change her mind.

This is the way he told her about what he had been thinking: "I
don't want to make you feel guilty any longer about your decision.
I've been feeling neglected and I even started feeling sorry for myself about the fact that you wouldn't be here as much if you were
attending college. I realized that I had been sulking like a little kid,
and I don't want to play that kind of game with you any more. The
truth is that I will miss you at times when you're at school, but I
don't want to act in any way that will make you feel guilty for doing
something you've wanted to do for a long time." This approach removes the burden of guilt and blame from the other person and
frees both partners.

If you decide to give up any stubbornness you may have about
being "right" in your relationship, you will find these suggestions
easy to follow. Being right has no functional value in a personal relationship and only serves to perpetuate the feeling of a misunderstood victim.

Honestly admitting your suspicious thoughts about others and even
just stopping your train of thought can reduce the feeling of having
to "make points" and the need to be right, to be the innocent one.
The tendency to indulge these thoughts and feelings will gradually
diminish and result in an improvement in the quality of your relationship or at least in your feelings about yourself. It is hard to assess
the damage that playing the victim has done to a relationship until
you stop playing. Then it becomes obvious. You will be gratified
by the changes that will occur once you stop accusing others of causing your unhappiness.

Relating to another person in terms of a sense of obligation is another way to set yourself up for paranoid thoughts. Again, this is where the use of the word "should" often comes into play. "If you loved me, you wouldn't want to go running off with your friends all the time, leaving me here with the housework. You should spend more time with me." Or to a grown child: "After all I did for you, the least you could do is call me once in a while. You know I get lonely. You should consider my feelings and call."

In your relationships you have every right to ask for what you want, and the other person has every right to refuse. Moreover, the other person has every right to ask and you have every right to refuse. If you tie your frustrations at not getting what you want or ask for to feeling that someone or something was obliged to satisfy you, then paranoid feelings are inevitable. If, however, you take full responsibility for your own feelings, if you shift the focus of your life back to a clear knowledge of what you want and what you feel and away from an overconcern with what others feel toward you, then the world will be in a more realistic perspective for you. You will know that you are in charge of your life. The self-limiting, victimized perspective will no longer control your life.

8

Painkillers

A NEUROTIC LIFE-STYLE is characterized by a progressive cutting off of real feelings to avoid experiencing pain and anxiety. In the course of attempting to minimize suffering in our early lives, we end up not only blocking out pain but limiting our emotions of joy and exhilaration as well. The methods we use to dull our pain may become addictive because, like drugs, they temporarily make us feel better. But as we do with drugs that temporarily reduce our anxiety, we become increasingly debilitated by the effects of cutting off from our feelings.

Anxiety rises whenever our suppressed feelings threaten to break through to consciousness. This can complete the destructive cycle, for then we feel we must further tighten up our defenses. Thus, neurosis is self-perpetuating. A life of defenses is a serious addiction that uses all of our energies and resources. Conversely, when we choose a life that is open, full of feeling, and reasonably undefended, a lot of our natural energy is liberated.

It may seem foolish to attempt to persuade a person who has had a great deal of pain in his personal life to give up the negative outlook that he acquired for perfectly valid reasons. Nevertheless, maintaining cynical attitudes is more damaging in the long run than taking chances and even actually being hurt again.

The choice of a life-style which cuts off feelings and is largely self-protective can be termed "self-nourishing." It rests on the illusion that one can feed and take care of oneself without the help of others. It is a life of pseudoindependence as contrasted with a life of real independence. Self-nourishing gives one the illusion of self-sufficiency, while it actually sacrifices more and more real existence and satisfaction with other people. The more an individual has been emotionally deprived and frustrated in his early life, the more he will rely on addictive defenses that give the illusion of self-sufficiency and that further incapacitate him.

There are five aspects of this neurotic choice to live an inward existence: (1) addiction to physical substances, (2) addiction to routines and habitual responses, (3) masturbation as self-gratification and pain reliever, (4) addiction to compulsive sex and work, (5) fantasy, the great painkiller, discussed in the next chapter.

Addiction to Physical Substances

Addiction is here defined not as a chemical reaction but as a psychological dependency. Food is used for survival by all of us, but for some it takes on a separate, special meaning. It can be used as a substitute for love, affection, and acceptance. For others it may be used in an attempt to relieve the boredom of an emotionally dead existence. Food may be used to cut off feelings of emotional hunger that many small children feel when their parents withhold love from them. Many mothers offer food as a substitute for the affection they may be unable to give.

Chronic dieters may sometimes have pleasant memories of mealtimes when their mothers offered them huge quantities of good food. Sharon recalls dinnertime as the only "happy" time at her house when she was growing up.

We didn't talk much, we just ate. Actually, we wolfed down our food, because Mom was always in a rush to get the table cleared and everything cleaned up. She loved to cook for us, but she didn't like to waste time socializing at the table. I always looked forward to dinner anyway. I was always hungry as a kid and by the time I was eighteen, I weighed 155. I used to go on lots of different crash diets. I could lose about twenty pounds in two months, but at a certain point I would start to feel awful. Not hungry, but depressed, like I had nothing to look forward to if I couldn't have what I wanted to eat. I felt empty and lonely. It was so strange. Just as I would get to a size where I began to look good and people started noticing me, I would break my diet. I went on an eating binge when a boy finally asked me for my first date. I don't know why; I guess I was just scared to go out and I wanted to spoil it somehow.

Sharon's homelife was devoid of much human contact. Both parents worked while she was growing up and Sharon had only dinnertime to look forward to as a chance for some kind of contact. Since there was none forthcoming, even when the three of them were together around the table, Sharon turned to food in an attempt to fill her hunger for emotional contact.

The same type of dependence may be present in relation to alcohol, cigarettes, and drugs of various kinds. Once a person becomes addicted to any of these substances, he must go "cold turkey," in a sense, to break the dependency. This is because the anxiety that has been lessened and eased by the "drug" comes to the foreground once the addictive substance is removed. Hard drugs are used by people whose need to cut off feeling is the most desperate. In the same way alcohol may be used in increasing amounts when other defenses have failed to suppress pain and anxiety. An alcoholic who comes for therapy will do almost anything to change himself except break his dependency on alcohol.

Alex worked for a large hotel in the catering department. There was free liquor available at all times and many of Alex's fellow employees drank on the job. For over eight years Alex had been drunk every day at work. On his days off he drank even more. Eventually, he was threatened with the loss of his job and came for therapy in an attempt to, as he put it, "go on the wagon." During our talks he spoke of his father, who was also an alcoholic.

My father would drink down in the basement. When he got good and drunk, he yelled and banged on the walls. I'll never forget that terrible sound. It frightened my mother, who was a church-going lady and hated drink more than anyone else I've ever known. Why she married him I'll never know. My father called me brat as a regular nickname. He never called me by my real name. I hated his guts. When I was sixteen I ran away, lied about my age, and joined the navy. That's where I first started getting high myself. I swore that I would never be like my old man, but here I am in the same fix he was in.

Alex stayed away from drink for three months, and intense reactions soon followed this abstinence. In his therapy sessions he began to approach some of the rage he had felt toward his father for the way he had been treated. At this point he became frightened of facing his anger without the soothing effects of alcohol. In addition, he couldn't tolerate the new identity of being different from his father, who was still an alcoholic.

The anxiety of his change seemed unbearable to him without drink. He left therapy and started drinking again. Once more he was identifying with his father through alcohol. Many years later he returned to therapy and this time successfully broke with his father and with his addiction to alcohol. Giving up this dependency on alcohol was one of the most difficult things that Alex had ever done in his life. Much of his anger and anxiety during treatment had been reactions to his source of gratification being denied him and his having to face reality without a painkiller.

Most human beings carry around a tremendous reservoir of pain that they have for the most part successfully suppressed with painkillers of one type or another. Mind-expanding drugs like LSD may have the opposite effect from painkillers in that they allow the unfelt pains of childhood to flood the conscious mind. The pains are usually not experienced directly, however, because the truth and reality behind these pains from the past might be overwhelming. They appear symbolically as hallucinations with abstract meanings.

Addiction to Routines and Habitual Responses

There are an endless number of ritualistic or repetitive habits covering all aspects of human behavior that can be used to kill off feelings and pain. Almost any behavior that serves to reduce tension and anxiety, for whatever reason, can become addictive. A person suffering a high degree of tension and pain in his emotional life will often fall prey to habits that are tension reducers. Almost anything is preferable to the anxiety.

Compulsions illustrate this phenomenon. We can all remember repeating words and phrases over and over as children: "Step on a crack, break your mother's back." Children will count up to a certain number over and over again. Many adults make elaborate lists before going shopping. With disturbed children these rituals can take on immense proportions. In psychiatric institutions for children, it is considered almost a crime to make any change in the patient's schedule because of the intense panic and anxiety that is aroused. People who can be compulsive in their occupations, such as bookkeepers, accountants, and engineers, have the opportunity to cut off their painful feelings and to reduce their anxiety.

Many children sit glued to their television sets day after day. This routine effectively removes them from their daily lives. Many women spend hours in the beauty salon and in front of the mirror experimenting with hairstyles and makeup. Some men spend hours in a gym building their bodies and exercising to keep fit. These routines can become extremely self-involved and serve to soothe any anxiety about physical inadequacies. One young man whom I saw in therapy used exercising routines to hide from his deep feelings of inferiority.

Gary was concerned with the appearance of his body. When he was a young boy he was sickly and the men in his family ridiculed him unmercifully about being skinny. When he was sixteen he met an Olympic track star who took an interest in him and begin training him in track. Gary developed so much in the next two years that no one could ridicule his physique. But running and calisthenics slowly became an obsession with Gary, often to the exclusion of any social life. He was unsuccessful in keeping a relationship with any woman longer than a few months.

Gary never really faced the way he felt about himself or his body. Instead, he built a defense against feeling weak and inadequate by developing his body. His underlying feeling of being weak and unworthy kept him from letting a woman really care for him. His compulsive routines of exercise and running kept him removed from any awareness of feeling inadequate.

Routines like these are partially gratifying when, as in the case of Gary, the fantasy of having a strong body comes true. Yet the underlying pain and poor self-image still remain.

Masturbation as Self-Gratification and Pain Reliever

Sexuality begins when the child discovers that it is pleasant to suck not only to get milk but also for the simple sensation of the sucking response. Whenever he is in pain or hungry or fearful, he turns to his thumb or pacifier or the edge of his favorite blanket. Later, he discovers that touching his genitals also gives him pleasant sensations and relief from tension. He learns that he can make himself feel good with this form of self-gratification.

This process becomes more inward as the older child attaches fantasies to the physical and emotional gratification he is giving himself. Often, the parent discovers the child playing with himself and takes his hands off his genitals or delivers a lecture or simply frowns. The child now feels guilty and goes into hiding when he wishes to engage in this form of self-gratification. His inwardness is increased as he becomes secretive about this activity.

Gary felt tremendous guilt about masturbation. He imagined that the girls in school could tell just by looking at his face that he masturbated. He started masturbating after his uncle teased him about his small penis when he was about five years old. He reassured himself when he saw that he could get an erection from touching himself. This ability made him feel less weak and frail. Later, he fantasized that he would one day shock his relatives by showing off the size of his erect penis in front of them all.

When he began to be sexual with women in college, he had a lot of anxiety about being able to perform adequately. With each woman he dated, he experienced more anxiety when he started to really care for her. He found that he needed to resort to the same kind of fantasy he had entertained as a child to remain aroused and have an orgasm. His method of self-gratification had become preferable to taking a chance on real gratification from someone he could love.

Addiction to Compulsive Sex and Work

Society does not view the "workaholic" as it does the alcoholic, nor does it usually look on sex as an addiction. However, millions of people use work and sex as pain relievers and tension reducers. There also exist elements of fantasy and inwardness in the compulsive behavior of people who use these otherwise "good" activities to soothe themselves.

Mike was such a person, using both work and compulsive sex as crutches to help him through each difficult day. He was a successful salesman for a large computer company. Each morning he woke with a sense of impending disaster. "This is going to be the day when I'm not going to be able to meet my quota," he would think. As he left the house, his stomach was knotted with fear. By the time he reached the office, he was a bundle of driving energy. His fellow workers didn't know where his drive came from and they envied his sales record. But Mike was not an enviable person. Here was a man who was compulsively driven to work in order to cut off his feelings of fear and inadequacy.

I feel as if I'm on a speeding treadmill. I don't know why I have to go so fast. All I know is that if I slow my pace even a little, I become worried and anxious. When I get home at night, it takes one or two drinks before I can relax and enjoy my dinner. When my wife and I retire for the evening, I can't seem to get to sleep right away. If we're sexual I can usually fall asleep after a short time. Once I went on an extended business trip without my wife. I couldn't sleep at all. I really had a case of insomnia. I realized that I use sex as a sort of sleeping pill. Even though I know that I enjoy making love, I feel like I'm using my wife in some way that doesn't feel very real.

Sex and overwork were both painkillers for Mike. But they did not completely obscure his awareness of what was happening to him. Some people are more cut off than Mike. They are not aware that they have deadened themselves with habitual overwork and compulsive, routine sex.

Almost any routine that we can consistently depend on is capable of becoming an addiction in the sense that it may help ease those transition times, such as leaving one situation and entering a new one, when we would tend to feel anxious. Some people allow themselves a respite from habitual routines when they embark on a trip or vacation. They feel happier and more alive than at any other time in their lives. They have the energy that is released by breaking with fantasies and deadening routines. They don't feel very much anxiety because they are allowing themselves this freedom from routine for only a limited time. If these same people tried to imagine living their daily lives without routines and schedules for everything, they would undoubtedly be filled with anxiety.

The Damage in Cutting Off Feelings

Why is it so harmful to cut off feelings if this seems to reduce anxiety and pain? The answer is that anyone who is well defended becomes insensitive to himself and others in the area of his repression, and sometimes this insensitivity is extended to other areas. One may become capable of very self-destructive acts, much like an individual who is insensitive to pain on a neurological level and unknowingly leaves his hand in a fire, getting severely burned. In other words, feeling the pain is what makes us remove our hands from the fire.

Another inherent danger in cutting off feelings arises from the fact that they come back again after the drug has worn off. The relief is only temporary and you are thrown back into the conflict situation once again. Habitually cutting off feelings leaves you more maladapted generally in your ability to cope with your life.

In your urgency to avoid pain, you become unaware of yourself and, worse, can be destructive to others as well. In this manner you can certainly damage your children. If nothing else, they will unconsciously imitate your style of defense no matter what you teach on a verbal level. This process will lead them to distort and limit their life experiences in much the same style that you have. The illusions you maintain about yourself, the punishments you dole out when events don't go the way you want, the manipulations you use childishly to try to get what you want, the white lies you tell in the name of protection, the blame you place on others, these are all damaging to other people, especially your family. Thus, you can be destructive to others and also not feel the pain within yourself.

For many years I have known a man who seemed like a happy, well-adjusted person. As I got to know him better, I realized that Howard was a man whose best defense was "feeling good." He didn't suffer much emotionally. He wasn't miserable or unhappy. On the contrary, Howard enjoyed the "good life." He ran a large manufacturing business; his appearance was attractive to women; he loved adventure; he was charming and seemed full of life.

One day Howard told me about his adventure of skydiving. Jumping from the plane for the first time, he had noticed with curiosity that he felt absolutely no sense of fear. He had felt happy and somewhat excited, but he wondered about his lack of fear. This was Howard's first awareness that he felt very few feelings. Fear was only one emotion that he had dulled into a bland, contented state. Real love and affectionate feelings were not emotions he was familiar with either. He had divorced two wives and barely noticed their absence from his life. His children didn't know him because Howard related to them from the parental role only, never person to person. If he could keep his distance and his defenses, he would never have to feel the fear, the grief, and the desperation which had overwhelmed him when his father had died before he was two years old. Howard had very little access to these fears of abandonment, possibly because the traumatic event had occurred so early in his life.

Howard had learned to make himself feel good when he was very young, yet now this man's life was full of gaping holes. His experiences were extremely limited because his feelings were cut off from even the most unusual events in his life, like the experience of skydiving. Howard is in fact a sad human being. Even his business, which appeared so successful, was seriously threatened by his adventuristic style and his refusal to manage and cope in an adult manner.

There would be a tremendous sense of loss if one were to wake up someday and realize that one had missed his own life. But that is what we are doing when we choose to remain within our defensive structure and refuse to feel much for ourselves or others.

The Alternative: Feeling

The way out is to choose to feel all aspects of your life, the sadness and the joy. But it is important to make a distinction between real feelings and the sentimental emotionality that is an avoidance of feeling. Dramatic overreacting to the events in your everyday life is not really feeling.

For example, a woman entered my office one day crying and complaining that her husband had come home drunk, her children were ill and she needed help taking care of them, and her mother-in-law was visiting and taking over her home. This woman was distraught when she came in, but after a few minutes of nondramatic response to her complaints, she dried her eyes, sat up straight, looked at me, and smiled. She talked about other important things for the rest of the session and she was happy when she left. If her sadness and pain had been real, the feelings would have lasted through most of the session and would have formed the content of our talk. As it was, this woman's feelings were not real even though the events were. Her tears and upset had been overreactions, dramatic emotions having more to do with the past than the here and now.

It is sometimes difficult to distinguish between real emotions in the present and feelings from the past. However, it helps to ask yourself if you are feeling sorry for yourself or looking for a sympathetic response or for approval whenever you think that you are overreacting to someone or some event. This is what the woman who came into my office was searching for. When she didn't get the response she wanted, she dropped the miserable state she was in and began to relate to me as an adult. Prior to that she had been playing the victim.

Exposing Destructive Habits

Becoming aware that there are certain elements in your life that you have become dependent on is the first part of breaking those dependencies. You may already be aware that you depend on certain substances to make life more pleasant for yourself. Determining if these habits are addictive can help you take an objective view of them. You can then decide to stop using that substance for a predetermined length of time and observe the effects of abstinence on you. If you experience a great deal of anxiety or if you feel erratic mood swings, the chances are that you are dependent on this substance as a drug or painkiller.

If you think that you're using routines to soothe yourself and to relieve anxiety, you may want to try breaking one of them and see how you feel living without it. Dropping a routine or habitual pattern of behavior, for example, not performing a certain activity at a definite and regular time each day, could be anxiety producing. But it is exciting to lead a more spontaneous life and to experience a sense of not knowing what's happening next. You may feel as if you've been let out of prison; at the least your life will not be boring.

Breaking the Dependency

The more difficult step comes next. Deciding to put an end to your dependency requires a strong motivation on your part. It can be helpful to involve a close friend in your decision, whether to diet, stop smoking, or whatever habit you wish to break. The process will then be much easier. In fact, it could be important not to undertake this project alone. Talking with someone you can trust when you become anxious can help tremendously whenever you are tempted to return to your old habits. In addition, communicating your feelings to someone, whether they be ones of anger, depression, sadness, or anxiety, will relieve some of the discomfort.

The nature of painkillers is such that their ability to deaden our feelings is insidious and can catch us unaware. Becoming more sensitive to your feelings and to the feelings of others can help make you aware of the point at which you begin to cut off feelings. Bringing this awareness out into the open and voicing it to a friend may be all that is necessary to start you feeling again.

Rationalizing Habitual Behavior That Is Against Your Best Interests Is Always a Serious Matter.   I remember Christine, a cousin, who for years had been drinking alone while working at home on accounting problems for her husband's business firm. She still functioned fairly well, but because of her usual state of intoxication was cut off from any real contact with her husband and young son. One night she ran out of cigarettes and left the house after midnight to walk to the local liquor store to buy a pack. She never got there. The police called her husband and reported that she had evidently passed out in the street and been run over and killed.

Christine had always rationalized both her drinking and her smoking. Smoking made her "better able to concentrate on the figures." Drinking made her lose some of her inhibitions and let her "have a good time." It "relaxed" her. Yet her addictions were essentially the cause of her death.

Even though you may never get to the point where your particular self-destructive behaviors will literally make the difference between your living or dying, to not take the effects of them seriously is to value your life too lightly. It is never harmless to rationalize habits that you know are self-indulgent and self-destructive. Determination and even stubbornness can be used to fight deadening routines and habits. The realization that you are fighting your worst enemy, your defense system, is vital knowledge; it clarifies what the battle is about and whose side you are on.

In your struggle against these addictions, it is also necessary to use your knowledge of the inner voice to separate what you want from what the inner, negative voice may be telling you. Using the techniques previously described, answer it by behaving in your own best interests. Your reward for all your hard work will be that you will be gaining strength and freeing energy for more growth and development.

9

Fantasy—The Great Painkiller

Every human being is capable of creating an imaginary world within his own mind. The ability to fantasize can serve all of us well, for example, at those times when we choose to transform our daydreams into constructive actions. However, the inner world I want to describe here is one that can be used as an escape from a harsh reality, as a distraction from pain and worry, as a relief from anxiety, and as a substitute for satisfactions not present in the outside world. The child who is too young to physically leave his unpleasant surroundings can instead escape at will into his own fantasy.

If a child grew up in a totally nurturing environment, he would probably never use a fantasy world as an escape. However, all of us grew up in an emotional climate with some frustrations, and when frustration reached intolerable proportions, we retreated from the real world into fantasy and self-gratification.

Fantasy eases this pain much as a physical habit such as thumb sucking helps relieve a young child's frustration. Fantasy not only eases pain, it partially satisfies the original need as well. The world of fantasy is completely under the child's control. He can go into it whenever he needs it. It is obviously far more reliable than a mother, whose attention depends on so many variables. The child develops the illusion of self-sufficiency, feeling that he needs no one outside himself to give him satisfaction.

What could be wrong with fantasy and inner control? Why not relish the feeling of independence and freedom from needing other people? To begin with, we are not actually independent when we

[97]

are living in our heads. It's pseudoindependence, a defensive stance of imagined self-sufficiency. What's more, we become more and more maladapted to the real world if we pursue our goals in fantasy, only imagining that we are really pursuing them. Nowhere is this more obvious than in a mental hospital, where the dormitories are filled with people who have carried their inner world of fantasy to its logical conclusion. These individuals have been so emotionally damaged that they have nearly totally retreated from the real world.

This brings us to the second disadvantage of choosing a life of fantasy gratification over satisfying ourselves in the real world with real people. We always feel guilty when we reject people and seek satisfaction in illusions. The guilt comes from two major sources: without and within.

Guilt from Society

Even though there are strong unspoken pressures in society pushing us to satisfy our needs internally, there are also strong pressures against it. The child sucking his thumb is scolded and his thumb removed from his mouth. When he finds he likes touching his sex organs, his hands are slapped and he is told that that is not acceptable public behavior. Later on, when he seeks to masturbate for pleasure and self-fulfillment, this innocent activity also comes under strong social taboos. Indeed, in our culture all sexual activity is given a somewhat dirty connotation and is to be pursued only in private.

Other forms of self-nourishing are also given a dirty connotation, drinking and smoking, for example. In some religious groups these activities are even considered sinful.

In a similar way we must hide our fantasizing. Probably all of us at one time or another have suffered the rude awakening of being called on in class while we were daydreaming. We were, no doubt, awakened from our reverie by the sound of our classmates laughing at us.

I remember a similar incident that took place during a Little League ball game. A harmless fly ball was hit quite close to a little red-headed boy playing the outfield. It looked like an easy play, but the boy's mind was somewhere else and he made no effort to catch the ball. It was a disaster, with three runs scoring on the play. A few moments later he was scolded by his irate coach and broke into tears.

Internal Guilt

Because of this kind of external pressure, we get increasingly devious in our attempts to seek satisfaction in fantasy. We hide it from others and develop a sense of guilt and paranoia about it. If we rely heavily on this form of gratification, we can also develop an overwhelming feeling of self-hatred. We hate ourselves because we are secretive and rejecting of people who care for us. This self-hatred only furthers our sense of alienation.

In the course of seeking more and more gratification from within instead of from real people and real events in our lives, we deny ourselves mastery in the real world. To maintain this inner world, we must protect our illusions from other people's interference. So we *pretend* (to ourselves and others) that we want things from the external world—love, material success, good careers, etc.—while in fact maintaining our self-denial by sabotaging ourselves and complaining that we have been thwarted by other people or bad situations. We become phonies who do not want what we say we want from the real world.

The intrusion of the real world into our fantasy world would destroy our fantasies, so we must limit our sources of real gratification. We often choose to give up broad areas of success and achievement in the real world to protect our fantasy world: We fail at jobs, we undermine or destroy our personal relationships.

In pulling away from people, we develop a genuine sense of guilt because we have to make them look bad to justify isolating ourselves. So we say that the world is "no damned good," and to avoid becoming "dependent" on the people we are close to, we misperceive them and develop or hold on to a negative picture of them. Then we can still delude ourselves that we want "a nice relationship" with the opposite sex while we systematically ruin each new relationship.

In losing our compassion for others, we turn away from our feelings for ourselves as well. There is a kind of existential guilt in turning our backs on others and losing our sense of compassion, and all of this adds to our self-hatred and sense of isolation.

Protecting Our Fantasies

There are five circumstances that arouse aggression in us and that are important to know about because they reveal the ways in which we rely on fantasy and are defensive about its being interfered with: (1) a threat to our fantasies of omnipotence or greatness, possibly by real comparisons; (2) an intrusion on our self-feeding habits, such as smoking or drinking; (3) exposure of the fact that we don't want what we say we want; (4) being caught playing the victim or martyr; (5) having real success or achievement in our work or personal relationships.

1. THREATS TO SELF-AGGRANDIZING FANTASIES

When parents withhold love from their children, they often substitute praise and special treatment and exaggerate the importance of their children's accomplishments or unique traits. This buildup partially satisfies a child's need for recognition and he will crave more of this kind of flattery as he grows older. He will become overly sensitive to approval or criticism as he is pushed to build an idealized, fantasized image of himself that probably does not correspond to his real self. To the degree that a parent withholds real appreciation for the child as a person and instead gives him a false, inflated picture of himself, the child will be unable to tolerate any blow to his ego when he becomes an adult.

Marvin, for example, was reared by his aunt and grandmother following the death of his mother. Trying to make up to the three-year-old for his loss, these two women pampered him and doted on his every word and act. They treated him as though he were the smartest and cutest child they had ever known. As Marvin grew older he literally took over the household. He was not given chores to do and his room was always a shambles.

Many years later Marvin became involved with a woman who was very different from the two women who had raised him. Anne did not have a strong need to please or cater to a man. For Marvin to be attracted to this kind of woman was unusual; his ex-wife and other women friends had all fed his ego generously. Marvin thought that Anne, who was highly intelligent and successful in her own right, could help him in his business, which was growing rapidly, so he hired her as a business consultant, and they became closer friends.

Within a few months Anne knew enough about the business to realize that Marvin's style of management was having a destructive effect, yet he was enthusiastically talking about increased gross sales. Anne also sensed that Marvin didn't want to hear what she knew she must tell him.

Finally, she offered her criticisms and ideas about the way the company was being run. Marvin's first impulse was to angrily tell her, "You don't know what you're talking about," but he swallowed those words, knowing that she was too good a businessperson to have misjudged the situation. He was furious, nevertheless; he felt like the rug had been pulled out from under him. His whole image of himself as a shrewd businessperson was in danger of toppling.

His decision, made almost entirely unconsciously, was to get rid of Anne and keep his fantasy. He told her that he was interested in her ideas, but that he had to keep running the company with no changes for a few more months. Meanwhile, he slowly broke off their friendship and Anne stopped working for him. Months later Marvin instituted some of the changes she had suggested, passing them off as his own ideas. Marvin had preserved his image of himself as a great businessperson, but he had lost a valuable friend and ally.

We often compensate for self-hatred and feeling inadequate by feeling superior. This is a common form of defense because at the same time that our parents were building us up and fussing over us protectively, they were also rejecting our real attributes and qualities, our real selves. Deep down we sensed this rejection and learned to hate our real selves. As adults we may find that we alternately think we are either better or worse than other people. Both views are part of the unreal self-image we have. If we come into contact with someone or some situation where there is a possibility of direct comparison, then we have a chance to view ourselves realistically. Usually, we avoid such comparisons.

Real comparisons and legitimate competition tend to challenge our fantasies. For example, a direct comparison can occur when one person is promoted above others in an honest competition for the same position. If the decision is fair, it is clear to everyone involved that the best person has won. If one of the people who lost had an inflated image of himself, however, his fantasy will have been challenged.

Receiving Realistic Feedback

By selecting from among the people you know those who seem realistic, sensitive, and truthful, you can get honest feedback. This is what happened to Chuck when he gained some new friends after changing schools.

Chuck had an unrealistic picture of himself when he first came for therapy. He was fifteen at the time and was very involved in weight lifting and a body-building program at school. Chuck's parents had been extremely rejecting, so in a desperate attempt to give himself some sense of self-worth he had created a fantasy for himself. To compensate for being rejected, he tried to build his body into something to be admired. He imagined that he would be loved if he had a strong, handsome body.

Chuck joined a therapy group with his new friends and they soon gave him a more realistic view of himself than he had ever received from his family. First of all, most of the people in the group initially liked Chuck for his friendliness and his warmth. They couldn't understand why he was fascinated with weight lifting to the exclusion of other parts of his life. When they began to question him about it, he got defensive and angry. Soon, however, Chuck began to realize that the people in the group were not attacking or criticizing him. They liked him. His interactions with them helped him become aware that he had other qualities that were far more valuable and lovable than a built-up body. For the first time in his life, Chuck was recognized as a person with many traits, some positive and some negative. He dropped his defensiveness and his vanity about his body. He found that he preferred the friendship of the people in the group to the fantasy that had sustained him for many years. Unlike Marvin, who refused to give up his fantasy of being a great businessperson, Chuck began seeking and getting more satisfaction in the real world.

Even though Chuck had succeeded in his goal of building up his body, he had still been painfully self-conscious about it. He hadn't gained true self-assurance. He had been living the role of weight lifter instead of being himself.

If you are self-conscious about your movements, your speech, and your actions, it could be a sign that you have turned something that was once natural into a role. Once you are playing a role, reality fades and fantasy takes its place.

2. INTRUSIONS ON SELF-FEEDING HABIT PATTERNS

The more a person is hurt or scared when he is a child and small, the more he may tend to rely on self-feeding habits. Later, if he attempts to break these habits, he will experience a lot of pain and anxiety. He will also feel angry toward anyone who suggests that he give up a habit that has become precious to him.

A person who is very dependent on physical substances clutches his habit like someone who is drowning. In a lifesaving class you are told to approach a drowning person with extreme caution because he will grab and hold on to anyone with a death grip. He will even cling to a small piece of wood in a frantic desperation to save himself. The desperate need to hang on to his self-feeding habit that the addict experiences is very similar. He feels that his habit is sustaining him. Individuals who are heavily involved with drugs or alcohol often get intensely angry whenever their addiction is interfered with. They very often direct their hostility toward anyone who is involved in helping them withdraw from their addiction.

Breaking Self-Feeding Habits

Your self-feeding habits are substitutes for the love and affection that were withheld from you as a child, and it is important for you to face the fact that you will never be able to find the kind of love you didn't get then. But as an adult you no longer have the same kind of dependency needs.

The feelings of desperation that you will more than likely experience while trying to break these habits are mostly feelings from your past. You will be reexperiencing your original needs and your intense longing to have them satisfied. The feeling will slowly diminish in intensity as you start satisfying your present needs in the real world and give up your old forms of self-feeding.

3. YOU DON'T WANT WHAT YOU SAY YOU WANT

There is a huge discrepancy in our society between what people say they want and what they actually do. They do want things in fantasy, but they don't want them in reality and for a logical reason: It cuts into the fantasy process and jeopardizes it. If you fantasize something the worst thing that could happen is for you to have it in reality. At that point it's no longer under your control. You can no longer conjure it up in fantasy when you like. Your dream is now a reality that you have and that you may lose, for in reality nothing is forever. In fantasyland everything is forever, including you, which is why some people don't like to live in the real world, where they have to endure human limitations.

If you don't know that you and other people are defending fantasies, some of your behavior and other people's behavior may not make sense to you. Why would an individual slow down his productivity after a success? Why would a person pull away from you when you are really nice to him? If he has financial success, why isn't he happy about it? Any one of these questions may expose the fact that many people wish for and grant themselves satisfaction in fantasy while rejecting the real things they get.

If you have been deluding yourself about wanting certain things and then suddenly are given what you want, you may find yourself becoming angry and not knowing why, especially at the person who gave it to you. If you have only been wanting in fantasy, then getting for real will in a sense "call your bluff." Arlene had fantasized about many things throughout her life. One day she had a favorite dream of hers come true.

For years Arlene had driven an old VW to and from work, trying to conserve gas and knowing it would be years before she would have the money to buy another car. Arlene worked as a bookkeeper in a large business office several miles from her home. She worked hard and her three bosses appreciated her competence. One day on the way to work Arlene's car caught fire and was damaged beyond repair. The next day her bosses held a conference and decided to include her in the sales force, which would entitle her to a company car that she would only have to pay half the monthly payment on. They also voted to pay her first six months' car payments to express their appreciation for the contribution she had made over the years to the company. The following Friday at the weekly office party they presented her with a new bright red convertible.

Arlene was stunned. She had always wanted a convertible and had even told one of the secretaries about the kind of car she dreamed of having. Her bosses admitted that they had found out about her dream car from that very secretary. Everyone was happy at that Friday party—her bosses for giving her the car and Arlene for getting it.

Everyone's happiness was short-lived, however. In a few weeks Arlene was called into the head office, where she was told that there were some serious mistakes in her records. She promised to correct them. The next day she called in sick and was away from work for three days. This was erratic behavior for Arlene. Her fellow employees and her bosses were puzzled. She had always been lively and quick, but now she seemed dull and slow. Within a month she was again reprimanded for incorrect figures and the same men who had bought the car for her were considering firing her. She was told she had one more chance to redeem herself. Luckily, it was at this point that Arlene realized why she had been acting so strangely and got back to normal.

Arlene's reaction is one that occurs very often in everyday life. Most people are unaware of it when it happens, however, and the underlying anger usually passes unrecognized. The truth is that most people cannot tolerate actually getting what they want.

Establishing Real Goals

Establishing goals for yourself and working toward them, not endlessly entertaining fantasies about them, is important. Fantasy is not only a great painkiller, it is also a great time waster and energy drainer.

It's human nature to want things: love, sex, money, acknowledgment, etc. What you want and try to get for yourself need not interfere with other people and their desires. Wanting as much as you can get out of life harms no one. On the other hand, turning your back on wanting real gratification in your life does hurt other people. Self-denial creates an atmosphere of inhibition for yourself and others.

A pattern of self-denial inhibits your growth and is damaging to your sense of identity. A large part of a personal identity is related to what you want in life, the realistic goals you pursue, and what these goals mean to you. If you deny yourself small goals, you may go on to retreat from larger, more significant ones. If you deny yourself what you naturally want or if you don't attempt to get what you want, then you are going against your natural inclinations. This is usually self-destructive.

Jerry entered high school with a definite set of goals. He wanted to become the editor of the school paper by the time he was a senior, he wanted to be on the first-string football team by the time he was a junior, and he wanted a girl friend. He set out energetically to get what he wanted. Jerry was not a dreamer. He really went after each goal in a systematic, spirited manner. By the time he was a junior, he was on the first team and he was a star reporter on the school newspaper. He had begun to date one or two girls, and he was popular because he was so enthusiastic about life.

Halfway through his junior year, Jerry noticed Helen at a school dance. The next day and every day of the following week he stopped by her classroom and walked her home from school. As he got to know her better, he liked her more and more. He began to think she might be the girl he had always wanted. He knew that the next step would be to ask Helen for a real date. Before the next dance he made up his mind that he would ask Helen to dance with him and then would offer to drive her home. However, as he stood looking across the dance floor at Helen talking with some of her friends, he felt extremely awkward and paralyzed. He just couldn't walk across the floor and ask her to dance. He was terrified that she would say no. The evening passed without Jerry asking Helen to dance or offering to drive her home.

This was the first time in a year and a half that Jerry had not taken one of the steps that would bring him closer to one of his major goals. He had denied himself what he wanted out of a fear of rejection, and he rationalized by telling himself, "Helen isn't the only attractive girl I know; there are plenty of other girls who will go out with me." Gradually, over the next few months, Jerry became less energetic, less spirited, and more sullen. He was less popular even though he kept on with some of the activities he had begun during his sophomore year.

Jerry never became the editor of the school paper. He dated sporadically, but with little enthusiasm. He kept playing football; however, he was far less valuable to the team and his coach often had to replace him because his performance was poor. Jerry's retreat from pursuing one goal had far-reaching consequences: An attitude of retreat spread through his whole life. Jerry remained largely unaware that he had slowed down and blamed his failure to attain some of his goals on external circumstances.

Your activity reveals what you really want: consistent trying and active striving versus passive hoping, wishing, and daydreaming. Real accomplishment may not be what you dreamed it would be. There is a solid, good feeling of knowing that you have tried hard and that it worked. There may not be glory, admiration, or basking in other people's praise, though sometimes you get this too.

One famous author made his name and fame with his first novel. Thereafter, he was essentially paralyzed and wrote nothing that even came close to his first success. He spent his life living in the reflected glory of his first accomplishment. After his initial success he had stopped his daily activity of grinding out his ideas on paper. Instead, he spent the next few years touring the country, talking and lecturing about his first book. It wasn't that he had nothing more to say; he did, and he intended to develop his ideas further. He made the mistake of getting into the habit of thinking that he had all the time in the world to write. But in reality it is the active, present moment that has significance, not what might be accomplished tomorrow.

4. THREATS TO PLAYING THE VICTIM GAME

It is paradoxical that the reality of being close is often avoided by couples in preference to the fantasy of being mistreated by each other. Yet in light of what we know about the nature of fantasy, it doesn't seem so strange. To avoid the anxiety of being close, people often choose to revert to fantasy gratification. Whenever two people are deeply involved in the mutual victim game, they don't want to learn what they are really doing to each other, especially from a third person. They want pseudosolutions dealing with compromises or agreements that do not threaten their fantasies. An honest appraisal of their situation is a threat and is often met with anger.

In counseling couples, if I am able to make one of the people aware of the damage that his playing the victim is doing to himself and to his partner, he usually wants to stop. He wants to give up his stake in being right. As soon as he does, there is immediate improvement in the relationship. The other person is often deeply affected by realizing that his partner cares more about him than about being right, and he, too, is usually willing to give up his part of this victim game.

5. THREATS TO FANTASY WHEN WE HAVE
REAL SUCCESS OR ACHIEVEMENT

Nowhere are the dynamics of fantasy so apparent as in the outcomes of the numerous success stories of people who couldn't tolerate the realization of their efforts or enjoy the fruits of their successes. All too often failure followed success as the person retreated into himself and discontinued the efforts that had brought him success.

At the time of an important success, each person has to make a crucial choice: whether to hold on to inward image building or give up these fantasies and live his real success and continue to make further achievements. The wrong choice may have disastrous results for the individual and for the people who depend on him to continue being active and moving forward.

With the merger of his company and three other companies, Dan had within his reach the realization of everything he had been working toward for years. He had been the top salesman and then had taken over the position of president following the former president's retirement. Dan's sales ability was still vital to the success of his company and to the conglomerate that had just been formed. Dan had agreed to concentrate on increasing sales as part of his new responsibilities as head of the company, but within three months of the merger, the new company was in trouble. Dan's sales efforts had almost ceased, despite the support he had in this area. In effect he was sabotaging the very company he had been instrumental in forming.

For many years Dan had had a fantasy of being the president of a large company. He had pictured himself seated behind a huge desk, issuing orders and delegating responsibility. His associates, however, valued and had selected him for his outstanding sales ability, a facet of his personality on which Dan placed little importance. Once he became president he simply began acting the role he had pictured in fantasy.

At first it was hard for Dan to realize that he was the one who was responsible for the downward turn in profits, but there was no escaping the fact that he had indeed reacted to his success with anger toward his associates. His lack of sales effort was a direct, though not too obvious, punishment of his associates for making him the president of the new company. After he became aware of what he was doing, Dan set about remedying the damage he had done.

In pursuing goals it is better to have tried and failed than to have assured failure inwardly by pulling back. If you honestly strive to the best of your ability, you can still feel good about yourself even if you lose in competition. Knowing that you were active and not passive in the contest allows you to forgive yourself for "failure." Passively avoiding a real contest is more debilitating to you than a real failure. Imagining defeat or rejection in fantasy may not seem to be gratifying, but it does serve to prevent you from taking a chance on acting in the real world. Your retreat precludes failure, but it also precludes success. Each retreat further weakens your drive to seek gratification in the outside world. Thus, it is important for you not to turn your back on any opportunity to compete for something or someone you really want.

Fantasy is indeed the great painkiller. Its pervasive influence can be detected in almost every facet of our personalities. Just as a person can learn to live without other painkillers and self-protective defenses, so he can live without fantasies. Living without debilitating fantasy helps allow you to fully experience life. You will live your real life in the real world.

10

Bonds—Destructive Ties

Love one another, but make not a bond
of love:

. . . . .

And stand together yet not too near
together:
For the pillars of the temple stand apart,
And the oak tree and the cypress grow
not in each other's shadow.
KAHLIL GIBRAN, *The Prophet*

GERALD SAT IN MY OFFICE one day and told me the story about what had happened during a most important time in his life. It was the year he met Karen and married her. Now, three years later, he felt that he was once more approaching a turning point.

Nineteen seventy-five was my lucky year. Everything just seemed to come together. It was the year my poster was accepted as the official recruiting poster for the air force. It was the year I met Karen. When I went to Washington to accept the award for the poster, I was more excited than I had been since I made the first-string basketball team in high school. I'm not kidding you, I wasn't the cool, suave artist. I was really happy, and I guess it showed because when I was introduced to Karen, I could tell right away that she was attracted to me. Our eyes met as we shook hands, and it was like a shock of electricity had passed between us. It may sound corny now, but then I knew it was the start of something that was going to shake me, and it did.

We started dating immediately. I was scared to ask her for that first date, and I knew that if I didn't go ahead right then, my shyness might get the better of me. She accepted with no hesitation, and we went to dinner and to a rerun, interestingly enough, of the movie *Love Story*. The ending was very sad, when the girl dies, and Karen and I sat in the car afterward holding each other. She was crying a little, and I have to admit that I had tears in my eyes too. I swear I had never before felt so close to anyone as I felt to Karen during those few minutes before she went back into her rooming house.

I had to return to California within four days of meeting Karen. We made love the night before I left. She was so nice to me. I didn't feel nervous the way I usually feel when I'm with a woman for the first time. I remember she said, "Just do anything that you like. Anything you do feels good to me." I couldn't believe it; she was so open and relaxed and excited all at the same time. I knew I loved her.

No one had ever been like this with me sexually. She was so beautiful. I loved to look at her body, and she was so honest about everything. She asked me what I was feeling at different times while we were being sexual, and she told me what she was feeling, too. When I left the next morning, I knew I wanted her to be with me more than anything else I had ever wanted in my life.

Our phone calls were really something—a huge long-distance bill from Washington to Los Angeles. They were worth every penny and more. Once we talked for over an hour. We got to know each other by phone for those two weeks preceding her visit to California. Karen lost no time in arranging a week's vacation from her work. She loved seeing my studio and my paintings. She was an artist, too, and a pretty good one. She had never been able to support herself by painting and so had been working as an assistant interior designer. This was when I started talking to her about trying her talents in commercial art. She was really interested, and through some contacts of mine I was able to get her two jobs here in California.

On the basis of those two offers and a part-time position as a decorator in a furniture store, Karen moved to California and into my life completely. We were both so happy. Everything seemed to work out so smoothly with our efforts to be together. My life in those days felt like a walk in the clouds, yet solid, with my feet on the ground. We lived together three months before we talked about marriage. I couldn't wait to get home from the studio each night. The smile on her face when she saw me walking up the sidewalk was a study of glowing, happy anticipation. I wish I could have caught that expression on canvas.

Well, I hate to get to this part. It was slow and not too obvious, but something changed after we talked about marriage. I don't know exactly what it was, and we did recover some of what I call the Washington feeling on the day of our wedding. We were excited about getting married, but I had been vaguely dissatisfied during the weeks before the wedding. It was our sex life. Something was different. I felt tense myself and Karen had a hard time having an orgasm. She had always been so free before. That's one of the things that was so exciting about her; she had really loved making love.

Anyway, it got better for a little while during the honeymoon and then not so good again. I couldn't say anything to her about it because I was starting to get worried about myself, and I thought it would go away if I didn't focus on it. But I was less interested in making love after we were married. I sometimes had a hard time getting an erection. We stopped making love every night, I guess because I was worried, and Karen didn't seem to be too interested either.

Well, you know what has happened since then. When Karen and I first started talking to you, things had gotten pretty bad. I even started hating her for little things, like she looks terrible in the morning, she won't keep the apartment clean, she always asks me when I'm going to be home, she won't make friends with my artist friends; instead, she criticizes them and incidentally puts me down, too. I guess I wanted to tell you about the good time we had before you met us. We were really in love and we had so much in common. The art, the way we felt about people—it's like we were made for each other. Then all this other stuff came in to turn it all to garbage. It's horrible. I wish I knew a way out of it, but it seems almost too late.

Gerald and Karen's story wasn't over, however. These two people are still together, working through the crisis in their marriage. By the time they had consulted me, they had one child and another was on the way. Karen had developed a tremendous amount of resentment about getting pregnant again so soon after their daughter, Kristie, was born. Karen had wanted to open a studio of her own to get her foot in the door of commercial art. Conflicts had developed between them concerning the subject of Karen's career versus her being a homemaker and a mother.

In my talks with Karen, I was struck first by her description of the qualities that had originally attracted her to Gerald. I was also impressed by the degree of similarity between Karen's father and Gerald. Both men, according to Karen, were critical of her ability as an artist, her homemaking skills, and her physical appearance. When I suggested to her that she had essentially married her father, she vehemently protested that Gerald had never criticized her until after they had decided to be married.

So how could I know that he was going to be like this. He didn't pick me apart before we talked about marriage. Either he's changed drastically or else he was hiding his true colors until he "had" me. My father, on the other hand, was always lecturing me or telling me what was wrong with me. "Your dress is too short. Go change it." "Can't you at least make all B's at school? You're no dummy. Just show some sense." I felt rotten around him and tried to avoid any conversation with him.

You may be wondering why Gerald and Karen didn't separate if they were so miserable together. The truth is that neither of them wanted to split up, for good reasons and bad ones. They didn't want to have a broken family because of Kristie and the baby that was on the way. And they vaguely remembered what Gerald had called the good days, that they had once loved each other deeply. A bad reason was that they were also extremely dependent on each other in a malevolent way that was destructive for both of them. Essentially, their relationship had most of the symptoms of a bond.

Symptoms of a Bond

A bond is an imaginary connection with another person and is used to allay pain and anxiety. When a bond is broken, the under-lying pain surfaces. People form tremendous resistance to the truth to ward off the pain of breaking a bond. They will literally destroy themselves to hold on to the bonds, imagining that they are holding on to people.

The marriage in which Gerald and Karen were entangled was a bond. Their original love and friendship had almost vanished. Despite Karen's protests, she had been attracted to someone who had many of the characteristics of her father. She was now using Gerald to repeat the kind of unhappiness she had experienced in her original family. This destructive repetition on Karen's part was effectively destroying her real feelings for Gerald. A pattern of repetition is one of the signs that a good relationship has turned into a defended one.

When two people are first getting to know each other, there is usually a real friendship and an attraction between them. But as it matures signs of a destructive bond may appear. A man and a woman who once spent hours talking to each other about everything begin to be disinterested. They no longer look at each other or notice what the other person is feeling. They begin substituting role-deter-mined behaviors for real feelings.

In other words, they don't act the way they feel, but instead they act the way they think they are supposed to. They behave more like a "husband" or a "wife," a "mother" or a "father," than the real people. Their sexual attraction for each other begins to diminish; their sex life may become routine and dull. With Gerald and Karen, their sex life degenerated primarily because of Karen's initial sexual withholding. A progressive withholding of the sexual response and of affection on the part of one or both persons is often another symptom that a destructive bond has been formed between two people.

The form of love, for example, remembering anniversaries and birthdays, becomes more important than the real relationship. The pretense of love has taken the place of real love, yet both parties haven't even noticed that the original feelings are gone and that there is only a fantasy left. They may think the love is still there, yet much of the real contact is missing. They both suffer as a result of this lack of contact.

Gerald and Karen got into trouble almost immediately after making the commitment to be married. Their commitment had accurately reflected their feelings and desires. It had been a strong statement about their love for each other. However, as is so often the case, this commitment became a fantasy in their minds, a guarantee of future love and security. A bond exists only in the mind. It's a state of being that is not free and spontaneous but one in which the person imagines a permanent, unchangeable tie to the other. Imaginary ties create an illusion of security.

Both Karen and Gerald lived in dread of rejection. They fully expected that the other would confirm their underlying feelings of being bad, unwanted, and unlovable, feelings that each of them had experienced in their original families. On the other hand, they both desperately wanted the security and assurance of being loved. Gerald wanted Karen to remain in the home as a mother and wife so that he would have a tangible reminder that he was worthy of love. And one day I listened with sadness as they admitted their mutual reluctance to excel as artists for fear of losing the other's love.

Origins of a Bond

In many families where the parents are unable to express love for the child, the child may form a compensatory self-nourishing fantasy, a kind of self-bond. Karen had been raised in an environment that for the most part was barren of emotional contact and physical affection. Therefore, a gap existed in her emotional makeup. She was quieter and more reserved than Gerald. She was a good listener, fairly easygoing in her dealings with people, and usually agreeable with almost anything other people wanted to do.

She was attracted to Gerald because his affectionate nature seemed to fill a deep need within her. Initially, she had taken a chance and broken down some of her usual reserve and allowed herself to be loving and sexual with Gerald. As soon as he committed himself to her, Gerald became essential in her eyes as the only person who could make her feel good. She had turned a spontaneous, exciting, and risky experience into an expectation of having that gap within herself closed, that past need fulfilled. It was an unreal expectation because no one could have satisfied her needs from the past.

During periods of emotional deprivation, the child forms a fantasy in his mind of being at one with the parent, of being the same as the parent. This fantasy, like most fantasies, becomes a self-nourishing substitute for real gratification. The child becomes as dependent on this fantasy as he does on his other means of self-gratification: thumb sucking, nail biting, excessive television watching, and other activities that reduce his pain.

By taking in the rejecting attitudes of the parents and identifying with them through imitation and preserving them through the inner voice, the child forms a fantasy of being self-sufficient, of having everything he needs within himself. He is both the weak, bad child and the strong, good parent. This is his first bond, so to speak, a kind of close tie with his parents within himself—in effect, a self-bond.

As the child grows older, he re-creates the elements of this inner tie in his relationships with the significant new people in his life. This is what Karen did as soon as she believed that she had a guarantee of love from Gerald. The bond then became a style of relating between Karen and Gerald.

A bond may become like an agreement to destroy the real feelings in the relationship so that the partners don't have to experience the pain and sadness that real love would bring. Gerald and Karen felt this pain for the first time after they saw *Love Story* on their first date. The feelings of sadness made them feel close to each other, yet as soon as they tried to nail down these feelings and promise that their love would endure forever, their way of being together had changed. Karen began withholding one of the qualities that Gerald loved the most, her natural way of feeling sexually free with him.

Very soon the stage was set for each person to relive his past, listening to his inner voice and acting out his old responses. Gerald began to have thoughts about Karen that were similar to the ones his father had about his mother and about women in general. For example, regarding Karen's desire to open a studio: "If you let her take this step away from home, then you're through. You know that women are fickle. She'll soon find someone else to replace you."

Karen's inner thoughts seemed self-protective, but believing them put more distance between herself and Gerald. Some of the things her voice told her were "He may love you now, but don't count on its lasting forever," "He'll eventually get tired of you," "Find a career for yourself; you may need it someday."

These were the kinds of thoughts, partially unconscious, that caused this couple to both withhold their love and yet cling desperately to each other in fear of rejection. Their dependency on each other obscured the earlier truths that they had not been adequately loved or cared for as children, that in fact they had been injured by their parents' dishonest rejection of them. This form of dependency also acts as a painkiller against the fear of separation, the dread of being alone, the terror of being without an identity as defined by their parents. Gerald's intense fear of a loss of identity came out one day as he remembered a scene from his childhood. He was playing alone in a sandbox behind his family home:

I think I was in a sandbox or something small. Looking back, I know how destructive my parents had been to me and how much I had counted on things that they would do for me and never did, and how much my mother's praise drained me of my incentive. In spite of all that, it was so important that they be there, that whole image of them and me together. It's part of me, them and me there. All of the rest of it didn't matter as long as I could have them and everything that goes with them, all the images of the things that made up my life as a child.

It seems too drastic a step to take, when I think about walking away from that and how it would be. It feels like I could never go back and that something terrible would happen if I were to walk away. It's like walking away from myself. Even today there are people who may be destructive to me or whom I don't need. But somehow or other it's just the idea that they're there. I don't want to walk away from them. It's like I transfer that old situation to them. I almost can't separate myself from the person or the situation or something terrible will happen.

If I really would ever walk away from them, there's nobody there. There's nothing. I just don't have anybody at all. It's that past, and those people, and that world that somehow define me. I can't imagine what I would be like if I wasn't like I am. It's really stepping off into nothingness.

Gerald experienced this memory at a time when he was considering separating from Karen. In his attempt to break the unhealthy ties of dependency, much anxiety surfaced and he became aware of his powerful need to "just have someone there."

The major cause of the deterioration of a relationship is the formation of a bond, that imaginary tie securely binding two individuals together as one. Understanding the concepts of a bond answers the questions that all of us have asked at one time or another: "Why did this love affair die?" or "Why did this marriage fail?"

Separation from bonds does not necessarily mean separation of the people involved. Once the bonds have been dissolved, a new basis for being together is possible, based on real feelings. At that point they will stay close if they really like each other and separate if they don't. In a good relationship there are no bonds.

Breaking Bonds: How to Get Loose

It is important to have some significant areas of your everyday life that don't involve your loved one. This does not mean maintaining a self-sufficient stance of imagining that you don't need the other person; that would be a self-bond. It does mean maintaining a separate existence.

A temporary separation may help you to recapture your independence and rekindle some of the excitement of the early days of your friendship. Going on separate vacations has helped many couples who were deeply involved in bonds. The individuals involved in temporary separations have returned with a renewed sense of their own aliveness and individuality.

There are many aspects to getting out of a bond, but the most basic one is being aware of the symptoms of a bond and acknowledging that you may be experiencing some of those symptoms. Knowing this is freeing in itself. You now know why your relationship has gone sour. You know what to watch out for. And you now can learn to live without these unhealthy ties of dependence.

Try not to make or ask for unrealistic commitments about feelings. Given the nature of love—a feeling that comes and goes, is weak or strong, and is affected by many variables—commitments that guarantee continuing love are unreal. However, a commitment that expresses a desire to be associated with another person for a long time, perhaps for a lifetime, can be an expression of deep feeling without becoming an attempt to find "ultimate" security.

Giving promises or trying to extract promises from a loved one may be a substitute for the hope that your parents might someday really love you. If you have found someone who appreciates you and likes you for who you are, you have what you want and need as an adult, but not what you needed as a child. This is a critical point!

Living and loving in reality is not what your fantasy pictured love to be. Love is daily contact, friendliness, caring, companionship, hard work, honesty, pain, sadness, happiness, anxiety, and tenderness and occurs in a non-dramatic way. It is living a simple, uncomplicated life with someone you like and get along well with. That may not be your fantasy of unconditional love, but it's a real opportunity to fulfill your adult needs for love and sex.

Avoid the impulse to merge with someone else for security. If you notice that you are less attracted to your husband or wife or lover, it may be that the two of you have so merged your personalities that you feel like "we" (an entity). There have to be two separate personalities for the attraction to occur *between*. As the quote at the beginning of this chapter indicates, two pillars leaning on each other for support would have a hard time supporting a temple, a marriage, or each other for that matter.

Many times opposites do attract, and two people in a relationship may complement each other in their traits. For example, in some marriages the husband may be more outgoing and talkative than his wife, who may be quiet and more reserved. These different traits, which originally attracted two people to each other, may eventually become the source of irritation between them. As the years go by, the husband may become even more extroverted and become known as the spokesman for the couple, while the wife becomes even quieter. The couple may come to exist as a unit composed, in a sense, of these two complementary halves. The husband may find himself nagging his wife about the trait he once was attracted by: "Why don't you ever say anything when we go out with other couples? You're so quiet and shy, it's embarrassing." She might retort: "You never let me get a word in. You always interrupt me if I do start to talk."

If one or both of you have sold out your individuality to each other, for whatever purpose, then your basic attraction to each other is jeopardized. You cannot be attracted to your own arm. This is very often how people in a bond feel, like an appendage of the other person.

Security is not found in merging two personalities. A person has only himself ultimately. It's unreasonable to reduce yourself to being half a couple. If you do you will lose your full self, and you are the only real security you can ever have.

Each individual has separate and clear-cut boundaries. We all exist in separate skins. I cannot experience your pain, and you cannot feel my sadness. We can all empathize and identify with each other, but each person is born on his own and will die on his own, too. A mother who says to her child, "Now it's time for our nap. We must lie down and try to get some rest," is talking as though she and the child are one. The only connection that exists between a mother and her child is the physical connection that is present before the doctor cuts the umbilical cord. After that we are all separate. To pretend that there is any other connection through belonging is false and destructive.

You are essentially alone no matter how close you may be to someone you love. In fact, being very close in a genuine way to your loved one can make you feel very vulnerable and separate if you stay out of fantasy. Facing your separateness may cause anxiety, but it is far better to sweat through some real anxiety than to conjure up a fantasy of being together in an infinite sense. If you had met Gerald and Karen when they returned to the mainland after a vacation in Hawaii, you would have noticed that they looked far older than their real age, that they seemed dull and uninteresting, and that they were wearing matching shirt and muu-muu. There was very little separateness between them, and very little life and energy.

Try not to get involved in protecting others' defenses or in seeking protection for yours. A bond is a mutual protection society designed to protect defenses, fantasies, and vanity. Gerald and Karen were both extremely protective of each other and of their way of life. One of their favorite pastimes had been to come home after spending the evening with another couple and gossip about the other couple's problems. They often said to each other, "I'm glad we are not like the Smiths." They were very much like the other couple, but they got no honest feedback from their friends, nor did they ever tell their friends what they thought. Couples protect each other's bonds, but they protect their own even more.

Just what is protected in a bond? The freedom to act out anger and blame on each other, the freedom to be inward and not really relate, and the freedom to delude oneself about one's favorite vanities are a very few of the things protected. Couples in bonds rarely challenge each other in their defensive areas because for one to challenge would leave him open to "attack" from the other.

Keeping an honest communication going between you and your partner can do much to break a protection pact. Asking for honest feedback and not retaliating for any unpleasant information you hear will help your relationship. If you are just getting to know one another, try to be honest about your feelings, but not to the point of criticizing needlessly in the name of honesty. An exchange of feelings said with sensitivity is one of the most valuable gifts two people have to offer each other.

In fantasy you control the gratification you give yourself. In a bond you may control the gratification that your mate gives you. To break a bond it is essential to give up your forms of control. Whether you control by withholding your sexual response or love, by being the victim, or by provoking the other person's anger, it is necessary to give up using these methods of control. It is important for you to not allow anyone to control you either. Being free from control by your mate and not being controlling yourself can give you both back the kind of exciting feelings you originally had.

If you really love someone, you let them be and love them for what they are. That is how it was in the beginning with Karen and Gerald, but they stopped being free as soon as they began to talk of marriage. This didn't have to happen.

A loving friendship is not intrusive; it allows each person the amount of freedom he chooses to have. It allows each to be faithful or not, according to his choice. Some people may choose to be with one person exclusively, others may want more than one partner. Faithfulness has to be a personal matter of free choice, not a matter of rules or standards. People have no proprietary rights with respect to each other.

By remaining two separate individuals who have an ongoing close association with each other, you will keep the quality of excitement and romance alive between you. Your sexual contact will continue to be close and spontaneous, the way it was at the beginning of your relationship, if you remain friends who treat each other as equals and if you grant each other the amount of freedom each desires.

A Final Word About Breaking Bonds

There is no magic to breaking a bond. A person must fight to stay in a relationship of real feelings and not retreat to the manipulative and self-nourishing methods of comforting himself. To whatever degree an individual can do this, he will have become stronger and more fulfilled.

Breaking a bond is a painful process, but the alternative is to continue to live life defensively and on the run from one's feelings, that is, having one parent after another, one painkiller after another. In living without bonds, change, personal growth, and fulfillment become real possibilities.

Destructive Maneuvers

11

Man vs. Woman and the Myth of Jealousy

"LISTEN HERE, you bitch, don't you ever come to me again asking if we have enough money for you to buy a stupid party dress. You know just as well as I do how much money we have. You're the one who is supposed to balance the books."

"Jason, I just don't understand you. How can I keep the money straight when you never tell me what you spend? You don't give me one penny to spend on myself, yet you spend hundreds of dollars on that sports car of yours."

In the next room Kathy and Debbie sat up in bed listening to the shouts from their parents' bedroom. They could hear their mother, Sheila, sobbing and Jason's loud voice. It was hard to recognize that voice as their father's because he spoke so softly during the day. But these nighttime fights were getting to be a regular part of Kathy's and Debbie's life.

Jason and Sheila were obviously no longer friends. If men and women were able to see each other as equals and treat each other as equals rather than in terms of stereotypes, then they could be friends.

As it stands now, hostility, distrust, and jealousy between men and woman in our society have reached such vast proportions that they have enormous social significance. There is not only a high rate of divorce but many young adults are cynical about the idea of lasting relationships and the whole subject of marriage. Most men and women are so destructive to each other in their personal and sexual relationships that it is inevitable that children born into the climate of their mutual hate will be seriously affected by it.

There are many reasons for the tension and pain in male-female relationships. Four important sources are sexism, male vanity, female manipulation and control, withholding and jealousy.

Sexist Attitudes

Jason and Sheila did not relate to each other honestly or as equals, yet these two adversaries in the argument above were both responsible, competent adults. Jason had graduated from Harvard Medical School several years before this particular argument, and Sheila was an RN in pediatrics and a certified teacher of a natural-childbirth method. She had also helped Jason when he was starting his practice in internal medicine. However, these two "normal," capable adults had been indoctrinated during childhood with biases that were now destroying their marriage and their happiness. They had been taught, by the words and actions of their parents, lessons we have all learned well.

Long before we entered kindergarten, most of us learned attitudes about the opposite sex that are similar to attitudes of racial bigotry. We learned the prevailing misconceptions that exist about men and women in our society. Now that we are adults, these biases can interfere with our chances of attaining happiness in our relationships with the opposite sex.

For example, Sheila had learned, especially from her mother, that men are mean and brutal. Threats of "Just wait till your father gets home, he'll take care of you" had always frightened Sheila. She also learned that men are more sexual than women, they want sex more often than women. She learned many other clichés about sex and about men, statements that were not necessarily true, but Sheila believed them.

The attitudes about men that Sheila learned from her mother are not isolated idiosyncratic examples. They are widespread in our culture. In spite of many advances in recent years in the direction of equality between the sexes, there still exist deeply held prejudices passed down from previous generations. It is impossible to change these ingrained attitudes within the short span of one generation.

From her mother's behavior Sheila had learned that men are after only one thing with a woman, sex, and women have to put up with it. Her mother conveyed this message to her in many ways: by stay-ing up late sewing when her father wanted her mother to come to bed, by warning her that she had better not get too friendly with boys because they might become aroused and then it would be "too late."

Many of us have learned that men are generally unfeeling and tough, that they don't want the kind of love and devotion women want. The stereotype is, men don't want marriage or kids and some-how have to be talked into it. Once they are married they will prob-ably be unfaithful. We may have been taught that men are more logical and intelligent than women, that they are more powerful physically and don't fall apart under stress the way women do.

We have been taught to categorize people and stereotype them ac-cording to their sex. Even though some of the stereotyped qualities are true for some men—for example, many men are physically stronger than most women—the uncritical acceptance of stereotyping has a destructive effect on our lives.

Like many other men, Jason had many of these same beliefs about men and felt pressured to fulfill the "male" image. Jason adopted a tough exterior as a defense against his short height and slight build and his feelings of tenderness, which he felt were weaknesses. The truth was that Jason was neither tough nor soft, but simply a human being who had compassion for others.

Most men have learned numerous misconceptions about women by imitating their fathers' behavior and from observing how both parents related to each other. For example, women are second-class citizens, but they're more emotional and intuitive than men; they know more about children and interpersonal relationships. Women, in contrast to men, aren't logical or mechanical. They are often scatterbrained and childlike and must be protected.

As an adult, Jason found it natural to relate to Sheila as her su-perior because he had learned that "women are less important than men and are vocationally inferior." He had been affronted by the presence of the few women he knew in medical school and was never interested in dating them. He felt comfortable with nurses who seemed to "know their place" in relation to the male doctors.

These attitudes, these false assumptions about men and women, have been impressed upon most of us by our parents. Learned prejudicial attitudes are firmly entrenched before we reach school age. As we progress through school, these attitudes are reinforced and supported by the unspoken biases of our teachers and by the arrangement of educational programs.

The school represents the combined defenses and attitudes of all of us and as such, places a strong social pressure on children and young people to conform to these attitudes. Again, the behavior of the teachers and the policies of the school system have a larger effect than words or lectures. For example, boys and girls are separated at every opportunity: separate lines to the lunchroom and to recess, separate physical education courses, separate sports, separate clubs— Boy Scouts, Girl Scouts, Little League—separate sex education courses.

In addition to the physical separation of the sexes, hostility between the sexes is either ignored or accepted as normal by teachers and students. Real friendship between a boy and a girl is often labeled puppy love and the two young people are ridiculed by their friends and teased by adults. The separation, differential treatment, and acceptance of hostility have destructive effects on male-female relationships.

Without minimizing the impact the school system has on the growing person, the war between men and women begins long before the school system adds its negative biases to the child's mind. As soon as definite distinctions are made between girls and boys about the "proper" behaviors each one should exhibit and the "proper" ways to treat each sex, sexism has started. First, there are toys. Most little boys are still given playthings of a mechanical nature, while girls are given dolls. Yet, very young boys in a free play situation often choose a doll when presented with a doll and a mechanical toy. This occurs at a time before the boy has been made to feel ashamed of his choice.

When Sheila was a child, she envied her younger brother who had been given an elaborate train set the previous Christmas that she was not allowed to play with. The next Christmas she asked for a train but received an expensive dollhouse with miniature furniture. When she complained, she was told by her mother that she should be very grateful to get such a costly gift.

Sheila grew up to be disdainful of women and angry and envious toward men. While talking with me one day, she painfully remembered asking her mother over and over, "Why can't I go out to play? Why can't I wrestle, play ball, and build forts like my brothers?" Her mother said, "Can't you ever understand? They're boys and you're a girl." Sheila cried for many minutes, saying, "I don't really want to be a boy, I just want to play." To please her mother, who, incidentally, disliked boys, she tried from that point on to be more like a girl.

Sheila began to retreat from many of the active and independent qualities with which she could have identified, qualities that her brothers possessed. From this time on she was different: cleaner, nicer, and quieter than her brothers. Gradually, she gave up much of her independence and learned to control in a passive manner. Most little girls assimilate this kind of passive orientation within the context of learning the proper sex-role behaviors.

In our society most men and women lack trust in one another and have cynical attitudes that destroy their attempts at friendship and at being sexual. This lack of trust is supported by social pressure from other men and women. Men and women who rarely talk to each other, who are subtly abusive and disrespectful to one another, significantly contribute to a social pressure. It is one of the major misfortunes of the era that men and women are so alienated from each other.

Despite the public acknowledgment in recent years that women are interested in sex and have a right to seek sexual satisfaction, there still exists a relatively common view that a man is more sexual than a woman. He is thought to have more sexual experiences and more sexual fantasies, to be more sexually aggressive and, overall, to be more sexually oriented than women. Men are considered to be more random in their sexuality and to want variety in their sex life, which women supposedly don't want. Men are thought to be more impersonal in their sexual encounters, relating to a woman not as a person but as a sex object. It is widely believed, on the other hand, that women are more loving, emotional, and faithful. All of these views are stereotypes and put people into artificial categories. The views are often incorrect and in some cases their reverse may be true.

SEXIST FEELINGS ARE LIKE ANY OTHER
FORM OF PREJUDICE

Many of the above distinctions are prejudicial toward one sex or the other. Both men and women want essentially the same things in life and the same things with each other. They want sex, love, affection, success, dignity, and self-fulfillment. They want to be recognized first as persons, then as men and women.

Assigning all the emotional, people-oriented functions to women cuts men off from a significant portion of their lives. How many fathers have missed their own children's growing up simply because they believed that they knew nothing about infants or young children? How much of the presupposed fear and awkwardness of the father in relation to his baby is a direct result of these sexist attitudes? How many times have you read magazine articles or books that advise the mother to guide her husband into having an interest in his own baby?

The whole tone of this advice is condescending to the father even in view of the fact that he might be somewhat anxious. The fact that many fathers might be better than the mothers at child rearing is largely neglected. This is only one area in which the division of labor reflects prejudices and is thus destructive to everyone involved. The mother, the father, and especially the young child suffer from this stifling of contact.

Even if you feel that you have gone far beyond the attitudes your parents held about men and women, from time to time you probably still slip into old attitudes about special abilities or handicaps that each sex is supposed to possess. You may discover that some of your time-honored, favorite attitudes will be shattered if you begin to explore this subject further.

Refusing to support sexist attitudes and hostility between the sexes whenever you come across it—in school, at work, or in your personal life—will do much to improve your relationships. You can effectively remove your support of these general attitudes only by personally giving up your own sexist views.

Male Vanity

Men are taught that they should be the king of the house—the one and only choice of their mates, the great lover and sex partner, superior to other males.

Jason and Sheila had been friends for years with the Petersons, another doctor and his wife. Dr. Peterson, a gynecologist, had told his wife that something was wrong with her sexually because she had never experienced an orgasm in all their years of marriage. He had led her to believe that he was an experienced lover because he had been involved with many women. Recently, he divorced his wife and married a woman he had been having an affair with for some time. His wife was extremely depressed for months and blamed her frigidity for the failure of their marriage. However, as time passed she cautiously began to go out with men and eventually became brave enough to begin a sexual relationship with one man who had become a good friend over the months. She was astounded at what she found out from this first experience with a man other than her husband. She discovered that she was fully responsive sexually with her new lover. She had believed that her husband was normal, when the truth was he had always experienced premature ejaculation, which allowed her no time to become aroused. She had had nothing to compare her experience with while she was married. Her husband's buildup of himself as a good lover had gone unchallenged.

Needless to say, this experience was an eye-opener for her. But it is only slightly more dramatic than some of the other realities that are protected by male vanity. In many marriages there is a strong commitment to flattering the man and shielding him from comparison with other men. This special treatment of the head of the household is not only destructive to the man but it exhausts the woman and twists her psyche out of shape. She caters to him in his presence and hates him behind his back. The man, on the other hand, knows at some level that the buildup is a lie, but he craves it. Since he cannot tolerate real comparisons with other men, his male friendships are limited.

Jason experienced a lot of tension about his performance sexually and anxiety about his abilities as a doctor. These were both areas in which he was praised and flattered by Sheila. In their arguments at night, however, her real hatred for him emerged. One day in my office, Jason haltingly explored some of the issues concerning Sheila's treatment of him and how it made him feel.

Sheila has always admired the fact that I'm a doctor. She worked for years to help me get through med school. She was very proud when I opened my office. She was prouder than my mother, if that is possible. She fussed a lot about decoration of the waiting room and the examining rooms. She spent some of her own money on extra touches, plants and expensive accessories. I liked that, but I was also a little embarrassed that I was getting more attention than my associate.

Even though she had had a boyfriend before we were married, Sheila always told me that she was not very attracted to him and that sex with him wasn't like it was with me. After we make love she always says how great it is, but I can't tell if she's really excited or not. Sometimes she seems to feel really good, but other times she just lies there. Sometimes I feel bad after we make love, really unsure of myself, but those are the times she reassures me that everything was great.

At that point in his life, Jason was becoming aware that his relationship with Sheila was based to a large extent on her false buildup of his qualities as a strong man. This buildup had undermined his self-confidence and contributed to his attempts to project a macho image of himself to his fellow associates. In recent years he joined hunting expeditions with a group of internists, not because he enjoyed the activity (he hated killing animals) but for the purpose of gaining prestige among his "friends." In reality Jason was very much alienated from a friendship with any of these men other than on a superficial basis.

The buildup of the so-called male ego is widely supported in our society. Flattering male vanity is one form of female control and manipulation, and some women's magazine articles are full of advice on how to accomplish this. Many men contribute to this destructive process by insisting on special treatment and flattery from their mates. The more insecure the man, the more he demands a buildup.

Faithfulness to one man is an essential ingredient for safeguarding male vanity. The woman must be faithful or the man's vanity is totally shattered. Any possibility of a comparison sexually or any trace of an attraction on the part of "his woman" to any other man stirs up deep feelings of insecurity in the man. Many men have experienced these feelings as intense feelings of dying or being killed. What is being killed is the man's fantasy that he is the only one, the best in his small kingdom, his family. His vanity is shattered, but not his total being, although it may feel like that to him.

Female Control and Withholding

Men control activities like war, scientific ideas, mechanical matters, politics, and abstract ideas. Women, however, control everything of importance in the area of feeling and interpersonal relationships, that is, the social world. They control activities in the home, its furnishings and decoration, mealtime routines, child raising, and social life with friends of the couple. Since they were little girls, they have been practicing the management of family affairs by observing their mothers and playing with their dolls. It's the little girl rather than the son who can usually get her daddy to do anything she wants. It's the little girl who observes her mother manipulating her father to get what she wants, while perhaps withholding affection, sex, or small everyday courtesies from him.

There is no more powerful manipulation than a woman holding back her sexual response after having been initially loving and sexual toward a man. Normally, the man's sexual response, his ability to become aroused and complete the sex act, depends on the woman's wanting him and not withholding her sexual response from him. If she is not really there with him as a sexual partner and is withholding, there are only two ways open to him that will allow him to be able to continue being sexual. He can fantasize to remain aroused or he may work hard to have enough physical contact and simple friction to accomplish sexual satisfaction. Neither of these methods leaves the man feeling very good because he has lost contact with his partner and has had a largely fantasized experience and a more masturbatory kind of sexuality. He has essentially lost his manhood by retreating to a form of self-gratification which he may have practiced while still a boy.

The content of his fantasies may also cause him considerable guilt. The cumulative effect of a number of encounters where the woman is sexually withholding may be an emotional castration of the man. There is a tremendous unconscious rage within each man to whom this happens. This anger rarely comes into awareness because he usually blames himself as the one with the sexual problem.

Male vanity and female control together contribute vastly to the destruction of good relations between men and women. Germaine Greer has summarized how men and women become enemies using the security of false buildup and special attention to each other's vanity:

> As soon as we find ourselves working at being indispensable, rigging up a pattern of vulnerability in our loved ones, we ought to know that our love has taken the socially sanctioned form of egotism. Every wife who slaves to keep herself pretty, to cook her husband's favorite meals, to build up his pride and confidence in himself at the expense of his reality, to be his closest and effectively his only friend, to encourage him to reject the concensus of opinion and find reassurance only in her arms is binding her mate to her with hoops of steel that will strangle them both. Every time a woman makes herself laugh at her husband's often-told jokes, she betrays him. The man who looks to his woman and says, "What would I do without you?" is already destroyed.

Jealousy and Withholding

A person usually experiences jealousy most intensely when he denies his own competitive feelings. It is a reaction to his own withholding. If an individual holds back his feelings of sexuality for any reason, he often becomes emotionally hungry as a result. He will then tend to focus on what his rival is getting and will feel cheated. Essentially his jealous feelings are covering over the fact that his own self-denial is preventing him from pursuing his goals.

Competition and jealousy are both terms that are used in relation to rivalry, yet they are very different behaviorally. Competition is a healthy, active striving for goals in relation to a rival, whereas jealousy is a passive, hating, and self-hating brooding over a potential loss to the rival. Being jealous is similar to the orientation of playing the victim: It is a passive state, one's focus is on the rival of the loved one and away from one's own desires, and one tends to blame others for any loss.

Healthy competitors can be friends, whereas those with childish, passive jealous tendencies find it difficult to relate to others successfully. It is very difficult for men to be friends in our society precisely because this issue arises so often. Rivals or even potential rivals rarely get past the point of being superficially friendly. They are unable to appreciate the fact that they may have a certain kinship with each other because they are both attracted to the same goal.

Jealousy may or may not be a biologically determined emotion, but we may never be able to discover this as long as we all support with sympathy the "victims" of a rivalrous situation. In a few countries, killing a rival while in a jealous rage is lightly sentenced by the court. It would be interesting to observe the opposite, a society in which jealousy did not arouse the sympathy and protection of others and was not implicitly supported by social sanctions.

We would probably not be so sympathetic to the "injured" person of an extramarital affair if we didn't have a belief that people can own one another or that wives and husbands belong to each other. Each person has his own sexuality, which cannot be owned by another. Your body is your own and belongs to no one else. You and your mate may choose to remain monogamous or to have other relationships. Both of you need to be operating out of free choice. When you choose to be sexually free, jealous feelings are bound to arise, but these feelings can often be traced to withholding, self-denial, and to retreating from closeness within the relationship. Sometimes jealous feelings can be traced back to feelings you experienced as a small child watching your parents going into their bedroom and shutting the door. This left-out feeling can be devastating to a child and may be triggered in rivalrous situations when you are grown.

If you have occasion to feel jealous, it may be that you are holding back your own wants and expressions of affection from the ones you are closest to. To see your rival pursuing what he wants while you are denying yourself is what makes you feel envious and jealous.

Limiting the freedom of someone else—and limiting your own freedom—can never bring you real happiness, but deciding from free choice that one or both of you wants an exclusive sexual relationship could be a source of deep satisfaction. Making choices about the kind of relationship you want to have can only take place between the two of you if you have a real friendship.

Becoming a real friend with your lover based on the kinship you feel with him as a fellow human being can create the most solid foundation you can have for a relationship. Feelings of understanding and empathy can replace old fears and prejudices between the two of you. This is what happened with Jason and Sheila during one of their sessions with me. Sheila had been talking about how she felt about men while she was growing up. She realized that her mother felt the same way. Knowing how her mother had treated her own father made her want to have a better relationship than her mother had had with her father. She looked across the room and saw Jason looking at her, not with anger as she had expected, but with tenderness. She had a feeling of certainty that her mother had been wrong about men, that her whole upbringing had been warped, that most of what she had been hearing as an adult from her women friends was just plain incorrect. She felt that Jason was a person just like her. She saw that they both had been damaged in their ability to receive and express tenderness, affection, and loving feelings. She went over and sat down beside him. They were once more friends and companions.

We hold the key to what our children will become. Whether they will feel that members of the opposite sex are strange creatures to be hated, feared, and looked down upon, or whether they will develop a real kinship and love with people of the other sex rests largely with us. Their attitudes will depend on your attitudes. It is vitally important to stop this kind of damage to our young people before they, too, perpetuate the hostility through another generation.

12

Clean Sex, Dirty Sex

S EX IS ONE FORM OF COMMUNICATION between men and women. The sexual act may be fun, playful, sensuous, emotional, affectionate, serious, carefree, or a combination of these, depending on the mood of the participants. Sex adds more to our general feelings of well-being than perhaps any other activity, yet if we look at ourselves through the eyes of society, we feel guilty for our healthy sexuality. If we look at sex through our parents' eyes, we may feel ashamed of what we do in our own bedrooms. Most of us have been brain-washed to one degree or another and many times are unaware that even as adults our views of sex are distorted.

Have you ever wondered why in this enlightened age direct talk about sexual matters is considered to be improper in polite society? Why it is that people giggle nervously when sexual subjects are raised? Or why so-called dirty jokes are considered dirty? Why is sex such a private matter that we would be arrested for exhibiting our sexual organs in public? Why are our sexuality and our sexual functions such a matter for secrecy?

There is no question that virtually all of us have developed a negative point of view about our bodies; those parts that are sexual have especially been imbued with a dirty connotation. On an intellectual level we all agree that our sexual functions are a simple and natural part of our makeup and that a dirty point of view must have been a learned response. No one questions that feeling dirty about our sexuality has made it an area that is fraught with anxiety and pain, yet most people still have negative attitudes toward sexuality in

spite of recent movements toward sexual freedom. There has been
some improvement, but considerable damage remains. Attitudes
about sex affect all aspects of our functioning and feeling bad about
our sexuality hurts us in all ways.

One of the basic indications of how we feel about sex is how we
feel about our bodies, and since many of us have been damaged by
our parents' attitudes about nudity, our attitudes toward sex were
similarly affected.

One evening while visiting friends, I watched their small eighteen-
month-old daughter running joyfully through the living room. She
had no clothes on and was not embarrassed in the least in front of
her parents or their friends. I knew that by the time this little girl
was five or six she would be mortified if someone saw her naked.
By that age she would have lost the delight she had taken in being
nude and instead would be very self-conscious. A basic attitude would
have been imparted to her in those intervening years that would
cause her to feel shame about her unclothed body.

Children may have their first contact with these "dirty" attitudes
toward their bodies when they are being diapered. They pick up the
verbal and nonverbal clues that communicate the disgust and, at the
least, the displeasure the parents often feel. Later, the child may
associate the functions of the genital area with the functions of the
anal area, which by now to him is dirty. In grammar school, "bath-
room" jokes are often the predecessors of the "dirty," or sexual, joke.

Many people are offended when they are confronted with nudity,
and many feel deep shame about their own bodies:

Cynthia, a divorced schoolteacher in her forties, had been close
friends with her next door neighbor for twenty years. Cynthia was
a very active woman, especially in outdoor activities. One summer
Cynthia and several friends spent two weeks on a long canoe trip in
an isolated area. The group enjoyed swimming and naked sunbathing in that wilderness area. Cynthia, while at first very embarrassed,
came to feel natural about this and felt good about her body for the
first time in her life.

A few days after returning home, Cynthia enjoyed an afternoon of
nude sunbathing alone on her patio. Her backyard was surrounded
by a high wall and was private except for one corner of her neigh-

bor's window that overlooked the yard. Cynthia felt slightly hesitant as she gazed up at the window, but she noticed the curtains were drawn shut. She thought nothing more about it.

During the next week Cynthia's neighbor barely spoke to her and acted strangely when Cynthia tried to strike up a conversation with her. Finally, Cynthia asked her friend what was wrong. Cynthia's friend said that she didn't know how she could still be friends with her since she had observed her sunbathing naked. She said other things, such as: "But Cynthia, you're just not that kind of person," and "Well, Cynthia, what about my husband? You know men when they get to be that age . . . well!" Cynthia immediately felt guilty for making her friend so upset.

As a result Cynthia not only retreated from her good natural feelings about her body and her sexuality but her entire mood changed and her sense of spontaneity was dampened. She felt more resigned and defeated in general.

Many people like Cynthia have adopted their parents' views of nudity and their parents' destructive attitudes about their own bodies. This in turn has the powerful effect of drastically lowering their self-esteem, for many of a person's good feelings about himself originate from good feelings about his own body and sexuality.

We have learned to feel that there is a danger in exposing our nude bodies, a danger of retaliation or of a sexual assault. Yet, in nudist colonies and nude beaches, this exposure doesn't lead to rampant sexuality and anarchy. The human body is natural and nice-looking if it's not disfigured or extremely obese. There are many people who have found that they enjoy swimming nude, and they haven't suffered a decline in their morality, despite the predictions to the contrary of some religious groups.

Two Distinct Kinds of Sex

Clean sex is a natural extension of affectionate feelings. It is not an activity separate from other aspects of a relationship. Clean sex includes affection and closeness. A dirty view of sex sees it as an activity that should be kept hidden, remain a secret, be thought of as entirely separate from the rest of normal daily activities. A dirty view of sex sees it as a subject unfit for social conversation, a subject not to be discussed with children, or a subject to be spoken of only in professional circles using clinical terms.

If sex is seen as dirty, then there is embarrassment when the subject comes up with our children. Marjorie came from a background where the parents had tried to overcome their embarrassment about sex. Their basic attitudes existed unchanged since their own childhood, however, hidden under their more liberal, modern views. Marjorie was shocked when she first learned where babies came from when she was about eight years old.

When some kids told me that my parents had intercourse, I felt angry at them and told them, "My parents wouldn't do anything like that." Obviously, to have that reaction I must have already learned that very negative attitude from my parents through their secretiveness. I'd already accepted the idea that sex was dirty, particularly my father's part. I think some of my feelings were because the genitals are located in the same area as the place for excretory functions.

Later, my sister and I heard about sex from other kids, and my sister asked my mother about it. My mother then explained the whole thing to the two of us. I thought it was horrible. I felt angry at men and at my father. I said: "Oh, how awful! I'm only going to do that when I want to have a baby!" My mother laughed and said: "You'll change your mind when you get older." There seemed to be something tough about her laugh when she said that. I couldn't believe her because I had already learned her real feelings about sex and about my father from the way she was with my father. I knew she joked about having sex with my father but in a very disrespectful way.

Marjorie's mother tried to convey the feeling that sex was enjoyable. Her comment didn't relieve Marjorie's fear, but rather increased it. Marjorie was receiving a mixed message about sex and was more confused about her feelings than before.

In spite of some of the advances achieved by the sexual revolution, the double messages in relation to sex are some of the most contradictory messages we receive and cause an incredible amount of suffering.

For example, it would seem natural that men and women want sex equally, yet most women who were recently polled about their favorite activity chose reading over sex, with sewing running one point behind sex. Most men chose sex. Many women are dishonest about their desire for sex. Everybody says that children should learn healthy attitudes about sex, yet very few parents discuss this important matter personally and openly with their own children. Everybody says that sex is just another function of the human body, like eating or sleeping, yet no one makes off-color jokes about these other functions.

Rather than learning new sexual techniques, which can be helpful to some individuals, a much more far-reaching remedy would be an honest reevaluation of our sexual attitudes and sexist biases.

Sexism creeps into many of the "lessons" that both men and women learn while growing up. Often the language describing these activities is indicative of this dirty view of sex as being bad:

A man has to talk a woman into sex, and a woman "gives in" to a man if sex does occur.

A man has "scored," or "made it," or "triumphs" over the woman if they have sex together, whereas a woman has "fallen for his line."

Sex outside marriage may seem more romantic and more exciting, yet it is sneered at as illicit or "cheating."

Married love and sex are seen as dull but "clean" because they are legally sanctioned by society.

Engaging in oral, anal, or other forms of sex besides man-on-top intercourse is looked on as having dirty sex. The "missionary" position is seen as a part of married life and thus is acceptable, while other forms of sex may be seen as abnormal or shameful. In particular, anal sex is considered dirty by many couples because to them that area of the body is considered unacceptable and untouchable.

Many women feel that having intercourse while pregnant is somehow inappropriate with the approaching maternal state. They may find themselves thinking: "Now that I'm pregnant, why have sex?" They may compulsively worry about infecting the baby by having sexual contact, thus confirming their view of sex as dirty.

Some people even look upon childbirth as dirty, especially when the couple permit friends and family to remain in the room during the actual birth. For example, recently, in a popular syndicated newspaper column, this touchy subject was the stimulus for an overflow of letters. The columnist's original comment had been in reply to a letter from a reader who wrote that she "was upset because her married daughter planned to let her 3-year-old son and 19-year-old unmarried sister witness the birth of her second child."

The columnist's reply, read by millions, was, "There is no better way to learn about the miracle of life than to witness childbirth. I see nothing shocking or immodest about it. A 3-year-old should find it a fascinating and educational experience." After noting the phenomenal increase in mail, the columnist commented that "letters are running 100 to 1 against my answer."

This is indeed a sad commentary on the large part of our adult population who would take the time to write these letters. In spite of the fact that this might not be a totally unbiased sampling of our population, the angry interest expressed on this subject was shocking in its intensity and vitriolic feeling.

In another letter in the same column, a woman revealed that her four-year-old son attended childbirth classes with her and her husband and also witnessed the birth of his little brother. She concluded: "Childbirth has nothing to do with modesty. It is God's greatest miracle. Since we all came into the world in the same way, why should anyone find it disgusting or loathsome? No name, please. My husband is a state senator.—Anonymous." This woman felt too intimidated by social pressure to reveal her identity for fear of injuring her husband's political career.

As children grow older there are opportunities for them to learn some of the facts about sex without as much of the attendant embarrassment that is usually felt by their parents when dealing with this subject. There is an opportunity to learn objective facts and correct attitudes in sex education classes at school. However, these classes are still opposed by some parents, who refuse to let their children attend. Many have gone so far as to prevent these classes from even being taught.

There are a myriad of other attitudes that together make up society's view of sex as a dirty, separate activity that men and women share. Many men and women have stated that they really enjoy working with members of the opposite sex, that they like going dancing, to the movies, out to dinner, talking, being affectionate with each other, but that as soon as they think about being sexual, especially for the first time with a particular partner, they become awkward, shy, and fearful. They tend to think of sex as something strange, out of the mainstream of their lives, and their partner as someone belonging to a different species.

Some young people experience extreme reactions when they reach their teenage years because they have learned that sex is an activity that is completely taboo and that discussing it is out of the question. They have been given such a twisted, distorted feeling about their own sexuality that they find it very difficult to express their emerging sexual desires. Michelle was such a young person who grew up in an atmosphere that was very destructive to her sexuality.

Michelle's mother was an intrusive, controlling, sexless woman who had always longed for a little girl "to keep me company when my husband is out of town." Michelle did become her mother's companion and, as the years passed, also became more and more quiet and withdrawn. Her teachers praised her, however, saying she was the ideal student and perfectly behaved. The only concern they had was that she never played with other children at recess and seemed to have no close friends. Michelle was required to report home immediately after school and discouraged from bringing anyone home with her.

The longing of Michelle's mother to have a pal wasn't the only factor that was operating to kill any of Michelle's spontaneous desires. Her father possessed a warped, sneering attitude about sex. He watched Michelle carefully as she developed for any signs of her budding sexuality. One of Michelle's most embarrassing memories was of a time when she was fourteen. One morning, as Michelle was about to leave for school, her father stared at her breasts and said, "Better put on a sweater before some boy catches a glimpse of those two little mountain peaks." Most of the time, however, he said nothing, he just stared at her.

Michelle knew that her mother and father slept in separate beds, that her mother never mentioned sex, and that her father was interested in her body. Being unable to put all these conflicting attitudes toward sex together forced her to do the only things she could do: *not* think of sex, *not want* any attention from boys, *not want* to be active at school and draw attention to herself, *not want* nice clothes (they might show off her figure too well) , etc. In other words, Michelle grew up wanting very little for herself. Her self-denial and quiet acceptance of the drab homelife continued until she turned seventeen.

Then there was a sudden change. Michelle seemed to blossom and come alive; she was more sparkling than she had been since she was an infant. She was accepted into a circle of friends and began going to dances and movies with them. She kept one secret, however, and it was the key to her happiness. Michelle had a boyfriend, Tim. She loved going out with him and looked forward to their dates. She wanted to have a sexual relationship with him and finally got up enough nerve to tell him so. Tim was surprised because he had always thought that girls didn't like sex very much. As their sexual relationship developed, Michelle became even more radiant and energetic. Wanting sex with Tim had caused Michelle to become alive to other parts of her life. Coming home from dates with Tim, however, she made sure that she arranged her face into the familiar slightly frowning, nonexpressive face that her parents were used to.

Nevertheless, her parents couldn't help noticing the change in Michelle after a number of weeks had gone by, and they began questioning her about her life and restricting her activities. They both accused her of being on drugs and spent many long hours interrogating her about drugs and boys. A curfew of ten o'clock was set, and on one occasion, when Michelle arrived home twenty minutes late from a date, her father restricted her to the house for a period of two weeks. Michelle was desperate; she wasn't allowed to go to school, and yet she had to make her grades. For a girl who was as serious and conscientious a student as Michelle, this was the last straw.

One evening while her parents visited friends, Michelle ran away and several weeks later was picked up by police in another state. The conflict between her parents' dirty view of sex, their total avoidance of wanting anything sexual for themselves, and Michelle's newly awakened feelings of wanting sex and love had put too much stress on Michelle. Michelle's life outside her home, which had been innocent and drug free and fun loving, had given her a sense of aliveness, but the life inside her home of emotional deadness and suppression and dirty views about sex had already done her almost irreparable damage. The central contradiction between clean sex and dirty sex together with her guilt and incestuous fears triggered her running away.

Sexual experiences will probably not be emotionally fulfilling if there aren't genuine feelings between the two people. Many people feel worse after relating to a sexual partner on a mechanical, unfeeling level because they feel more alienated, inward, and cut off from their feelings than before. Sex is often used as a narcotic or painkiller, but it not only kills off anxiety and sad feelings, it cuts you off from feelings for yourself in general, and that doesn't feel good. It is as if you and your sexual partner "soothe each other to sleep." This sleepy, deadened state, where we may temporarily be free of pain, is not really what we want.

Sex also picks up a dirty connotation when it involves fantasy and has a masturbatory quality. When we were young we often gratified our needs through thumb sucking, masturbation, and fantasies. We received partial satisfaction through these experiences; however, we also developed a sense of shame and guilt because we were often punished for these activities. Today, we feel especially bad if we fantasize about a person other than our sex partner during the actual sex act. We often feel like we are being disloyal.

Using fantasy pulls us away from our lover just when we would naturally want to feel closest. It is virtually impossible to remain in contact when we are fantasizing about another situation or another person. Men and women often resort to fantasy when they are withholding their real feelings, and on some level they know they are holding back, so this, too, adds guilt. It is in all these ways that fantasy interferes with a completely satisfying sexual experience, one that combines real relating with physical contact.

If either one of the partners withholds his affection or his sexual response, the sex act turns into a totally different activity. It then becomes a struggle between the self-critical inner voices of the man and woman and is no longer a natural, spontaneous act. It becomes a war between a dirty view of sex and our own healthy appetite for sex. The inner voice's effect may be detected in nervousness, awkwardness, a cutting off of feelings, distraction, or a tendency to fantasize during the sex act. You may be able to discern the specific subject matter of these inner thoughts that often interrupt the flow of sexual feelings. Women may have thoughts such as: "Don't let him touch you there, how can he like to do that? Don't let him kiss your vagina. You may not be clean. Don't move around so much, he'll think you're a whore." A man's voice might say: "You're not going to be able to satisfy her. You're probably not doing it right. Don't have an orgasm too quickly—you're supposed to please *her*. Don't be so selfish. She must think your body is ugly. Your penis is too small, how can she like it."

Our learned sexist attitudes and our dirty view of sex come back to haunt us as adults just at those times when we want so much to be open in our sexual feelings. When desire is self-denied, when we turn our backs on our natural desire for sex, we tend to distort what's happening and feel that we are being denied and exploited by the other person.

Withholding one's spontaneous expression of a sexual response can be a deeply ingrained, unconscious behavior. It is often combined with other withholding behaviors that are not very obvious. The way a person walks, sits, talks, or works may express a holding back of spontaneous actions just as much as how a person behaves sexually. For example, Kathy always managed to lag about two steps behind her husband, Milt. She was rarely ready to leave for a date or dinner when he was. One day they took a long drive into the country. They had made love that morning and were feeling romantic and close to each other. Milt stopped the car when he spotted a beautiful knoll covered with long grass, flowers, and towering oak trees.

"Let's climb to the top of that hill and look at the view," he suggested to Kathy in a burst of enthusiasm. Kathy's response was, "I'm not about to go climbing around in the long grass; besides it's too far to walk. I don't feel like it." This statement of Kathy's and others just like it were just as deadening as if she had held back her sexual feelings from Milt earlier in the day. Milt's enthusiasm was killed for that moment and for the afternoon. He suppressed his anger at her general obstinacy and meanness and lost his friendly feelings toward her. For Milt to engage in clean sex with Kathy in the future, he will first have to resolve the hostility that had been aroused by her withholding in other ways.

Establishing Clean, Healthy Attitudes About Sex

Men and women are not very different in their sexuality. Men are not beasts driven by their sexual needs. Women are no less sexual than men even though there is a tendency in our society for women to deny their sexuality.

Your sexuality is one of the most tender, fragile parts of you. Try to be sensitive to and understanding of both your own sexuality and that of your lover. A relationship of deep trust can develop between two people who have been damaged in their sexuality if they are willing to give up the tough, cynical, dirty views of sex they learned as children.

LEARNING TO COMBINE SEX AND FRIENDSHIP

Develop compassion for the person who is closest to you. If he has trouble in the area of his sexuality, don't condemn him. One way to remain friends during the sex act is to remain in communication throughout the act whether by talking, looking, or touching each other affectionately. Let your loved one know when you become cut off from your sexual feelings or if you are distracted by inner thoughts. An honest response is the most valuable gift one friend can give to another.

Gradually replacing sexual fantasies and masturbatory practices with real relating is ultimately more fulfilling. Reveal your fantasies to someone you can trust, either your lover or a close friend. Exposing hidden fantasies to the light of day is similar to giving away secrets. The individual can feel freer and more open. The guilt that you may have felt about these fantasies will be relieved, and you will feel easier about relating in a more spontaneous way.

At first it may be difficult to feel comfortable being sexual without relying on fantasies. If, however, you stay in contact with your partner during the sex act, you'll find that the awkwardness will slowly dissipate. When you're making love, try keeping the lights on and looking at each other. Talk to each other about what you are feeling. Go slowly and be tender and affectionate with each other.

Your love making is not a performance at which you must succeed or fail. Along with dirty connotations, sex has taken on the air of a performance in our culture. This causes a great deal of misery to those people who continually measure their love making against some standard. Remember that sex is just another dimension of your life. It is not a contest to be judged by you or by others. Combining real friendship with sexual feelings takes out the pressure to perform.

If You Can't Have Mature Sexual Relationships, It Doesn't Mean That Sex Is Bad or That You Shouldn't Be Sexual At All.   There is another social pressure that insists that "casual" sex is bad, harmful, or at least undesirable. Often, a woman will use this to justify her denial of her real desire for sex. She pretends that she can develop her sexual attraction only *after* she knows the man better. The truth is that most women, as well as men, enjoy making love and that it is not necessary to wait to enjoy sex until you are more sexually developed or until the relationship has matured to a certain point that meets a certain standard.

To deny yourself a sexual experience because the relationship isn't deep enough or you're not in love can be an abnormal form of self-denial. Any two people meeting for the first time may be attracted to one another and want to make love. Their choice of whether to be sexual or not should be based on their free choice and not on some arbitrary standard. As long as the individuals are friendly and respectful and nonexploitive, their love making cannot be bad or dirty. If, however, their meeting and having sex is part of a compulsive pattern of using sex to kill pain or ease tensions, then the act could be destructive.

Be easy on yourself concerning your sexuality and what you expect of yourself in relationships. You will be able to tell if a particular experience is not a constructive one for you. If it isn't, you won't feel very good from it afterward even though it may have felt good for the moment. Learning to trust your own feelings about which experiences contribute to your sense of well-being and which do not will help your development in this area.

You Can Really Develop as a Sexual Person If You Are Open to Criticism and Experiences That Promote Growth.   You don't have to be inward and self-critical in this sensitive area. Learning how to be more sexually alive and mature is not a matter of techniques; it is more a matter of your state of mind, of whose point of view you are expressing. Your own point of view as an adult man or woman is that you want closeness with another human being, and the kind of closeness that you love the most is one where sex and friendship come together in making love. This is the closest contact and the most rewarding one you can ever hope to find. This is your opinion, and these are your real feelings; the dirty points of view about sex have been imposed on you from outside. If you can be aware of the times when you are not operating from your own point of view in relation to sex, you will be well on your way to fuller experiences.

In your move toward better sexual experiences, choose lovers who are sensitive and emotionally spontaneous in their sexuality. Ask your loved one to be honest with you and to tell you the ways in which he or she sees you sexually. Be open to suggestions about behaviors you can change to make the sexual relationship better between the two of you. Try to speak honestly about your feelings as well. You don't have to keep anything secret from your mate. Remember that your feelings about your sexuality are at the center of your sense of well-being. Hurt and insecurity in this area can be healed by becoming friends with the one you love.

13

Vanity—How It Hurts You

Peter, a man whom I have known for ten years, is constantly trying to convince people that he is an exceptionally talented architect. His close friends, however, are unimpressed by his bragging, by his long, involved explanations of the projects he has successfully planned and executed, by his name dropping, or by his insistence on always being the one to pick up the check at dinner and charge it to his company, of which he is the president. They like Peter when he isn't doing any of these things. His close friends, who have known him for years, like him when he is in an entirely different mood, when he isn't being vain. They love his sense of humor and his ability to put others at ease with his warmth and easygoing manner. However, when Peter is in his role, he is phony and unreal.

Vanity involves having a fantasized image of yourself that you feel you need to protect at all costs. You may feel as though your life depends on keeping up that image. As a child you exaggerated and desperately hung on to whatever role or trait your parents doted on to compensate for their real rejection of you. Today you maintain this fantasy image because you feel it is the most valuable part of your personality and because you want to avoid the underlying pain of your parents' rejection.

However, the people close to you love you for characteristics other than those which make up your vanity. They probably like you for traits that you may take for granted because they are a natural part of you. By ignoring or underrating these simple qualities, you are doing yourself a great disservice.

For example, Peter's view of himself didn't coincide at all with that of his friends. He placed no value on his sense of humor, his easy affability, or his capacity to make others enjoy themselves being around him. He failed to notice that as soon as he started talking about his latest project, his friends began to look bored, even annoyed. For many years Peter's friends helped protect his image and never told him that he had an inflated view of himself. They may have sensed his desperate need to hold on to his fantasy. Undoubtedly, they felt his unspoken pleas for protection of his vanity. In not confronting Peter with their perceptions about him, however, they were also doing him a great disservice. Until he entered therapy he had never challenged this image, which was also his strongest defense against feeling his real sense of worth.

Developmental Aspects of Vanity

"Vanity" is an image we build for ourselves to substitute for a lack of real interest and real recognition from our parents. When our parents were unable to express their love for us, they substituted a false buildup of us. They offered us praise and special treatment instead of real affection. They often focused on one or two traits, our physical appearance or a unique talent, instead of acknowledging us as people. As we grew older we incorporated the rejection along with a fantasy about our special traits and capabilities. We began to treat ourselves the same way our parents did.

This process becomes a form of self-gratification which we use as a substitute for the love we didn't receive. However, we only fantasize about a positive life and good image of ourselves. We seek from others the pretense of love, the kind of treatment we originally received from our parents. If our parents had been honest about the times when they held back their real affection and interest and had not tried to substitute praise, false approval, and flattery, we would not have grown up craving this false kind of recognition.

A family friend remembers Peter as a four-year-old. He remembers one special trait Peter developed precociously and that his mother, Cora, loved to talk about. Cora had been a high school English teacher before Peter was born. She took great pleasure in teaching Peter to read when he was four. At evening bridge parties she brought the small boy, dressed in his pajamas, into the living room and had him "read" nursery rhymes to her friends. As the friend recalled, "Peter seemed to enjoy these times" and "glowed" from the women's applause.

As Peter grew older, this family friend, a swimming instructor, had many occasions to observe Peter as he built more and more parts of his image.

I had a small group of boys each summer for swimming lessons. Peter was in this group for three consecutive summers. He was the loudest. He always shouted the minute he spotted me, "Hey, Mr. Jenkins, look at me. I'm going to do this back flip—haven't I gotten better since last summer? Don't you think I'm better than Danny or Jim now?" He was rarely quiet, but was always asking for praise or approval. When his mother arrived at the end of each lesson, he bragged to her, even lying or exaggerating the small amounts of encouragement I had given him during the lesson.

Peter was almost unbearable by the time the third summer rolled around. The other kids couldn't stand him and would get into arguments with him about who was the best swimmer or diver. I always ended up lecturing to the guys about losing sight of the real goals of swimming— enjoyment and team spirit and so forth.

It was a pain in the neck to have Peter in that class, especially after the boys began swimming competitively as a team. Looking back, I think Cora had a large part in getting Peter to have such a swelled head, but I know he was miserable, he never smiled. After I gave him a compliment, he seemed to gloat over the other boys, but he had more of a smirk on his face than a smile.

Peter couldn't take simple recognition for what it was—either he had to exaggerate it and use it to build more of his fantasized image or he had to reject it. Peter's fantasized view of himself, specifically in relation to swimming, was that he was the best swimmer and the best diver on the team. Any contrary information, such as losing a race, was excused and blamed on unusual circumstances. Any matter-of-fact real acknowledgment, such as Mr. Jenkins's evaluation that "Peter is probably the best anchorman of the relay team, but he does poorly as a lead-off swimmer" was angrily rejected by Peter, because he couldn't use it to build the image he had of himself as the greatest.

The more we build our vanity, the more unsure we become about ourselves and our capabilities. In fact, our vanity mocks our true abilities and belittles us constantly. Vanity can be pictured as a brittle, beautiful shell which covers an increasingly weakened real self. The self-hatred of a vain child (or adult) exists because he is trying to believe the lie that his parents love him, but deep down he realizes he is being rejected and deprived. He doesn't know why he feels bad and unloved because his parents seem to be acting as if they love him. They are fussing over him and telling him how well he performs. He begins to hate himself simply for being in pain and not knowing why he is hurting. The special treatment and praise he receives makes him feel better for a short time and soon he seeks it as a painkiller. The vain person becomes increasingly addicted to this kind of painkiller, especially if this is all that is offered in the midst of a noncaring environment.

As Peter grew older he clamored for more and more attention from parental figures. Peter's underlying hatred of himself was contributed to by his father's chronic disapproval. Sam, Peter's father, was a small businessman and had been a football star during his college years. He tried to counterbalance his wife's buildup of Peter by criticizing him. His negative attitude toward Peter was expressed as follows:

That boy was being ruined by his mother until I took him in hand. She was making a sissy out of him, even that swimming team was her idea. It's not my idea of a real manly sport. She always bragged about him to his face . . . well, I never did that. I never said one word of praise to his face. When he was thirteen I took over and taught him the clothing business from the ground up. I also insisted that he go out for football and basketball in high school, which he did. I taught him the value of hard work and real manliness. But he was completely ungrateful and turned his back on the business opportunities I offered him. He began studying art and architecture—a sissy subject as far as I'm concerned.

By withholding any natural good feelings for Peter and maintaining his critical attitude, his father further damaged Peter's shaky sense of reality about himself. For instance, to compensate for inferior feelings about his body, Peter prided himself on being a fastidious dresser and as he became well off, he spent much time and money on clothes. He enjoyed the admiring looks he got from women whenever he made his entrance into a fine restaurant. Indeed, most of Peter's efforts, aside from business, were directed toward eliciting admiration and praise from women. It was in Peter's relationships with women that the continuation of this defense of vanity was guaranteed. Peter demanded from any woman he became involved with all the false pride, flattery, fussing over, and special attention that he had received from his mother.

Peter's first wife, Natalie, adored him. Being from a relatively poor family and having worked as a bank teller after graduation, she felt insecure and unsophisticated in relation to Peter. Essentially, she was "taken under his wing" in a kind of Pygmalion affair. After a whirlwind courtship of six weeks, Peter and Natalie were married. Recalling those first months together, Natalie told me of the gradual tension that developed between them because of Peter's subtle insistence that he receive the kind of treatment from Natalie that would build up his vanity.

I didn't know very much about sex. Peter really helped me learn to enjoy making love. If I was scared or nervous, he was patient and gentle. I felt at that time that he was sort of like a guide, an expert, almost like a teacher. I started telling him each time we made love how much I liked sex with him and how I appreciated his being so patient with me. Only much later did I realize that Peter was disappointed at times when I didn't feel very good sexually with him. It was like a blow to his ego somehow if I didn't have an orgasm.

I became tense and nervous as the months passed. I felt like I owed him something because he had been so nice with me sexually when we were first together. Peter had also provided me with everything materially I could ever want. We had a beautiful home overlooking the whole city and bay.

We traveled a lot. I had my own car and an unlimited amount of money to spend, but I began to feel discontented. I wanted to return to school—to attend college—but Peter said that he would rather have me working in the architectural business. He seemed to want me around all the time. I thought that I was such a lucky girl to have Peter as a husband that it was a long time before I started to notice that he wanted me to be with him and pay attention to him only to flatter his ego and make him feel good. I guess I was afraid not to do any of these things because I might lose him.

Peter and Natalie had formed a bond based on the mutual protection of Peter's vanity and Natalie's dependence and insecurity. Peter is not a particularly unusual person. His insistence on maintaining his fantasized self-image and the demands he placed upon Natalie to protect this image at all costs are similar to the behavior of many men and women who demand this buildup from their mates, with destructive results. A person associated with a vain person has to pretend to feel more than he really does toward him, has to deceive him about reality, and has to lie to himself in the process.

How Female Control Works with Male Vanity

When a man is vain the woman in his life has much leverage in her manipulation and control. Since her responses to him are not spontaneous and genuine but rather manufactured, she can control just how "good" she is going to make him feel. She also is able to choose and control exactly what she can make him feel good about by focusing on certain traits and building him up in those areas.

At the onset of their relationship, Natalie had spontaneously responded to Peter and had developed as a woman sexually. As Peter demanded more and more protection of his vanity, however, Natalie began to withhold her sexual responses.

Sometimes she tried to pretend that she had experienced an orgasm, other times she was just "too tired" to make love. Natalie's sexual withholding was a kind of unconscious revenge against Peter's insistence on a buildup from her. When she pretended to respond sexually, it was out of a sense of guilt about the meanness of her withholding. As the months passed, Peter became more and more confused, desperate, and emotionally hungry for other forms of reassurance from her. Indeed, Natalie now had Peter under control, but again she felt tremendous guilt when she saw that Peter felt bad. She redoubled her efforts to make him feel better in other areas of his life. She agreed to work at his office, she praised his efforts at painting and sculpting, she shopped with him for an extensive wardrobe—and she became more and more drained of energy. She began to look older than her twenty-six years. One day, Natalie literally came to her senses and decided to take an independent stand.

Her deteriorating looks and general physical health caused her to take a serious look at herself and at her marriage. She told Peter that she was quitting her job at his office and was returning to college. Peter was so shaken by this development that he sought help through psychotherapy. His confusion was obvious when he talked to the therapist during his first session:

I feel like the rug has been pulled out from under me, like I've been betrayed. After all I've given her, all I've taught her. Look, doctor, for months she's been giving me the run-around sexually. I used to think that Natalie liked going to bed with me more than anything else in the world. It drives me crazy the way she acts now. I don't know what to think. I think I hate her, yet I don't see how I could live without her. And now this latest move—going out on her own, going back to school. What if she meets some other guy? I know she'll be unfaithful. If she is, then that's the end. No wife of mine is going to show me up by having an affair. I'll get rid of her so fast it'll make her head swim.

Peter's vanity couldn't withstand the blow dealt by Natalie's move toward independence, and the couple separated soon after. It is important to note that Peter had been weakened by Natalie's buildup and by her sexual withholding during the course of their marriage. It was not Natalie's desire for independence that caused the end of this relationship, it was the slow erosion of Peter's sense of self-worth by Natalie's false buildup and protection of his image, a position she had felt forced to adopt. This marriage may have been doomed from the start by the mutual protection pact made by Peter and Natalie—an implicit agreement to maintain Peter's fantasized image of himself at all costs.

Over the years, Peter suffered many setbacks in the other area of his life that was important to him, his career. Here, too, his vanity didn't protect him; instead, it damaged him greatly.

Vanity Compensates for Self-Hatred

In his work Peter continued to act out the false buildup he had incorporated from his parents as well as his self-hatred. This self-hatred was expressed in some extremely self-destructive traits which he attempted to disguise by bragging about his talents. For example, over the period of ten years during which I have known him, Peter's company twice approached a position of bankruptcy. In addition, several large projects were drafted by Peter without consulting his partners and large amounts of money were lost. This self-destructive style was, in a sense, the other side of the coin in relation to Peter's vanity. Peter often came to the brink of ruin only to be saved by his partners, but he maintained a fantasy that he had saved the company without help. This fantasy contributed to the image he had of himself as a self-made man who could take care of himself in any contingency. This fantasy also served the purpose of blurring Peter's awareness of his failure, thus preventing him from experiencing the depths of the self-hatred he would have felt without the fantasy.

Peter's self-destructiveness was the self-hating side of vanity, which all of us experience to a degree. If we have been built up to expect great things of ourselves and then find out that we are less than perfect, we begin to hate ourselves. We tear ourselves apart for the least mistake because we have exaggerated our talents. If our fantasized image is disturbed by the intrusion of reality, we are left to cope with the self-hatred that always underlies our vanity. Self-criticism and self-hatred are painful and debilitating to us, thus we attempt at all costs to maintain our vanity.

Vanity is useless as a protection against the negative feelings that we have about ourselves, and there is always a fear of the exposure of the "real person" underneath. Peter firmly believed that his friends didn't really know him as well as they thought. He once had the thought that if anyone ever became really close to him, that person would find out that Peter was worthless and unlovable. These feelings of self-doubt and deep insecurity were barely conscious. Peter rarely felt the sinking feelings of these doubts because he used his image of himself as a brilliant businessman and talented architect to hide these other, negative emotions from himself. Peter had been so confused in his early life by his mother's treatment of him that he now had very little reality left about himself. This man's perception of himself and his world had been truly distorted by his vanity.

Buildup of Vanity Creates Unconscious Pressure and Guilt

Many years ago when I was living on the East Coast, I treated a woman who was surrounded by people who adored her, "loved" her, admired her, but who never responded to her for herself. She was completely affected. She had no contact with her feelings, and she was extremely anxious, often physically ill, and frightened. She and her husband were quite wealthy, living on a private island with their own boat and dock. The day that she first came in to see me I was stunned. She was remarkably beautiful and she carried herself that way. She had beautiful long blond hair and an excellent figure. She was the female image in every man's fantasy, the kind of woman that most other women envy and resent on sight.

People come up to me on the street and ask for my autograph. They ask me what I do. They say, "Are you an actress or somebody?" "You must be famous or well known." "Who are you?" Who am I? I feel like nothing. I'm bothered by people. They don't even respect my privacy, gaping and gawking at me. Sure I like it sometimes, but it gets to be a bore.

The other day my mom and I were in a restaurant, really, with my own mom, and still a guy comes up and says, "It's been such a pleasure looking at you that I would appreciate it if you would allow me to pay for your lunch." People actually come up to me and touch me like I wasn't for real, like a curio. Men and women take my picture and come up to me and talk. Hell, even if a cop comes up to give me a ticket, he ends up asking me, "Is there anything I can do for you?"

Everybody does everything for me, especially my mom and my husband. It makes me feel like I'm retarded. I don't really feel that I'm good for anything or have any special value. Of course, my teacher who is really fantastic, thinks I have a good career ahead, but I'm plagued by doubts.

Guys are always saying they love me, even my boss, and he's over sixty. How do you think that makes me feel? The other day Marvin, who works in my husband's office, calls me over and tells me he's got to talk with me. He confesses that he can't work for loving me so much. He asks if there is any chance for him. These things make me feel very bad. I feel really guilty and sick to my stomach. Really physically sick. I haven't done anything to bring out these reactions.

My mother said, "You're a very special person because of the way that you're made physically. We just have to treat you differently. Everybody wants you—you're a very pretty girl." The other girls in my class just stopped speaking to me somewhere in junior high school, and I felt miserable and unpopular. I couldn't wait to get out of school. And my mother's attitude about sex was unbelievable. "We just don't mention those parts of the body, dear. Be sure you don't show anything. Don't forget your underwear. How can you dress like that? Don't you have any shame?"

This woman, Angela, had never been responded to as a real person. She existed as an empty, beautiful shell covering an inner world of fear and weakness. Until she entered therapy she had only received the kind of exaggerated attention that caused her to feel guilty and miserable. Her beauty was real and unusual, but her interactions with the people in her environment were exploitative and unreal. She knew she could control every situation with her beauty and seductiveness. Therapy confronted her with the first situation in her life that she couldn't control. It provided her with the first opportunity to be responded to for herself. In fact, my not "falling" for her beauty angered her greatly. It was a tremendous contrast to her past and current experience.

Angela's therapy was a long and stormy one. As her vanity was intruded on by my own honest reactions to her, she became mean and explosive, but in a very self-destructive way. She could be quite savage and vindictive. "You'll be sorry you ever began to work with me," or "I really feel sorry for you," she would say. Near the end of one session, she said she really liked me and was acting more seductive than usual. She wanted to stay on for an extra hour because she felt it could "really be productive," and she knew it was my last hour of the day. I told her that I would not mind continuing the session and that I liked being with her, but I didn't feel it would be a good idea. She quickly retorted, "If that's the way you feel," and stomped out angrily. I knew something was up. Later in the evening I received a call from Angela's husband, who said that Angela was "distraught" and threatening to take pills "to end it all." I asked him to have her come to the phone, which she did, and the crisis passed.

It required many months for Angela to get used to being treated like a real person without resorting to angry threats and depressed states, all of which were manipulations to stop this intrusion into her inner world.

Angela had come to believe that her beauty was the only valuable quality she possessed. Near the end of her therapy, she faced some of the underlying feelings her vanity had been protecting.

You know, maybe that's why when I read of a murder it's so scary to me, like I'm going to get punished by some nutty, insane God—like my mother or dad. I'm going to be punished for being pretty or winning or for being sexual. You know, I feel pretty close to you. It's painful to be away from you. It's great to be able to feel, but these feelings are pretty painful. Maybe that's why I shut them off. Maybe I'll be able to feel these things toward my husband. It's like starting out again, only maybe this time I'll get a better chance at it.

Developing an Honest Sense of Ourselves

Vanity hurts us by weakening us even though we feel as if we depend on it for strength. It's a shared deceit and a pretense between two people in a bond. It begins in childhood as a substitute for real love and interest and continues because we become strongly addicted to the short-lived "high" that flattery and exaggerated praise often produce.

What can we do to get rid of these inflated images of ourselves which weaken us internally? First, we can recognize the areas in which we have vanity, and we can become aware that we don't need to think of ourselves in these exaggerated terms, nor do we need to elicit this buildup from others.

What You Thought Builds You Up, Really Tears You Down. Everyday life provides all of us with opportunities to have our vanity built up by other people. It may be difficult to believe that something which sounds positive—an overblown compliment, some excess praise, perhaps well deserved but exaggerated, or a special favor—can be the thing that really weakens you. It is hard to realize this truth on first appraisal, but remember the empty beauty of Angela or the shattered ego of Peter when Natalie took an independent step away from the buildup. You undoubtedly know some people who are vain—both men and women. You can feel the pull from them to listen to their every word, to pay attention to their complaints and their interests, often at your own expense. You probably know fairly accurately those areas of their lives for which they ask protection. You know where to tread lightly.

Try to observe yourself as you would one of your friends who is vain. What words of approval make you feel especially proud of yourself? Are there some traits you have about which you feel doubtful and insecure? Do you compare yourself with others and feel superior, or do you feel inferior most of the time? Did one or both of your parents often proudly tell their friends about your unique qualities? If you are criticized, do you either think that the other person is absolutely wrong or sink into a black depression of self-hatred? Vanity leaves no room for you to see yourself in a realistic way or to have compassion for yourself. This is how vanity hurts you —and the hurt is deep. It does not come from the real acknowledgment, positive and negative, of your friends. The hurt comes from within, from old feelings of insecurity covered over by years of being shielded against real information about yourself, your human strengths and weaknesses.

Don't Ask for Protection

Asking to be misled or deceived puts pressure on others and aggravates your own fears. Innate personality traits such as intelligence or physical attributes such as tallness or shortness or beauty are very often the things we are most vain about. Any quality, good or bad, that we feel is unchangeable is more likely to be defended by our vanity. We all ask to be spared any comments on things we "can't help." We send out strong signals which say, "Don't tamper with this, I'm too sensitive about it." It is true that some few qualities can't be changed, but to exclude these from our communications is to ask for protection. It's like pretending that some things are just too unbearable, too embarrassing to hear, especially if they are negative. It may be painful to realize that one is a relatively unattractive person or not as smart as some people, but it is far better than deluding oneself and asking one's friends to take part in the delusion. One can never relax when deception is taking place because there is the ever-present danger that one's secret weaknesses are going to be revealed.

Deception has a destructive effect on a vain person. It creates fear and anxiety, a feeling that there is something terrible within him that has to be protected or hidden. To protect a vain person from reality is just as damaging as offering sympathy to one who feels like a victim. There can be little easygoing friendly communication with a very vain person. In the earlier example, Peter had very little awareness of the strain under which he placed his real friends. They couldn't relate to him during the times when he was asking for protection or insisting on the business tycoon image he had of himself. Neither could his wife, Natalie, communicate with him on a real level almost from the beginning of their marriage. As long as Peter subtly pleaded for protection of his fantasized image, he was cut off from most close human relationships.

Try to elicit realistic feedback from the people who have integrity in their personal responses to others. You are probably aware of whom you turn to when you feel the need for praise and false buildup and who is less likely to flatter you.

Don't Ask to Be Preferred

In a relationship it is never valid to expect to be preferred at all times or in all areas by someone you are close to. Even if you are married, it is still unrealistic to expect that you would be chosen as the one most desired at every moment. Even though there are strong messages in society that this indeed is the meaning of marriage, permanent all-encompassing preferences are unreal and do not have the same meaning as a simple commitment reflecting the real feelings of a couple.

A person who is neurotic in relation to vanity wants all or nothing and is eventually assured of getting nothing if he clings to his vanity. He is like the child who must have the whole bottle of milk, or he won't take any. For him the bottle is always half-empty, never half-full. He continually focuses on what he isn't getting, quite forgetting what he does get.

A man I know married a famous movie star and instead of being happy that she had chosen him from among several other eligible suitors began to complain about her early hours at the studio, her long trips on location, her time away from him for personal appearances. He started going on location with her, much to the neglect of his own profession. He was terrified that he would lose her, that she would meet a man on one of these trips who would sweep her off her feet. He watched her every move while she was filming, trying to determine if she still felt that he was the most important man in her life. At home he tried to restrict her activities and questioned her about appointments she made with agents or other men. He was even jealous of her hairdresser, an older man who had been in her life for years and for whom she had real affection.

He became more and more obsessed and possessive of "his" woman until nothing could allay his fears and hunger. By his actions he finally drove her away, even though she really had loved and cared deeply for him. She didn't want to break up her marriage; she wanted to have children with this man and eventually to retire from filmmaking into a more "normal" life, but he made it impossible for her to continue to be with him. In asking her to always choose his company over all others, he succeeded in destroying her loving feelings toward him.

Judgmental Attitudes Are Harmful

No one has the right to judge you. You must do that for yourself. Our parents taught us that we were either good or bad depending on how they judged our behavior, especially our performance. We all have such strong habit patterns that it may be difficult at first not to search for praise and a good evaluation from others. If you are looking for this kind of approval, you are still seeking a connection with a symbolic parent and are not acting independently.

The good-bad dichotomy has even been translated into whether one is "OK" or "not OK." This does not take the destructiveness out of external evaluations. No one else can judge whether you are "OK" or not in any given moment. No one is able to look into your mind and tell you whether what you're thinking or feeling is all right. A person can make an objective comment on your behavior, which may simply be an observation, or he may state how he feels about you, but he has no right to make evaluations about you in relation to some standard that he has set up in his mind. Only you can truly judge yourself. You can share what you think about yourself with others, without soliciting approval or agreement. To continue to seek a buildup from others is to maintain your vanity and, in fact, add strength to that outer shell of protectiveness that so weakens you internally.

It is far better to admit your doubts, fears, or weaknesses than to try to be reassured about them. Don't get others to reassure you with statements such as, "Oh, you'll do well," "I have every confidence in you," "You're really good at such and such," and "You have nothing to worry about." Being reassured may be temporarily satisfying, but you'll probably feel more dependent and fearful in the long run. If a vain and fearful person is told, "Don't worry," his fears and feelings of helplessness are increased.

In relation to seeking support, it is true that everyone would like to have someone with whom to share his feelings of anxiety or self-doubt. This kind of sharing, however, is not the same as seeking to borrow someone else's strength or to get someone on one's side or to obtain advice about what to do. All these behaviors implicitly place the supporting person in the parental role and the one seeking support in the child's role, still trying to get something from the parent. To attempt to get unconditional love and acceptance from another adult is also unreal. No one can offer another person that kind of unqualified warmth and support. Adults can share their lives with each other in realistic ways and offer each other love and honest communication, which very often may include revealing negative feelings and perceptions.

Vanity and the Inner Voice

In those areas of our lives in which we can become very ego-involved, we may feel a strong pressure to perform—in our sexual lives, in creative work such as art or writing, in our careers, in athletics, in speaking before people. In all these areas vanity can be our downfall. For example, in athletics the inner voice plays a tremendous part in maintaining vanity. It can work against you in opposing ways. First it builds you up as a fantastic player, say in baseball, telling you that your batting average is really terrific for the season, that you're a great fielder, etc. But when you step up to that plate, you are under a lot of pressure to continue that "great" batting average. You become tense and are more likely to miss and strike out. Then your inner voice really attacks you, telling you that you let down the team, that everyone hates you for striking out, that your batting record is ruined, essentially that you're no good.

Be aware of your tendency to try to perform up to a certain

standard in other important areas of your life. Life is not an exam which you have to pass.

Avoid Categorizing Yourself

Learn to accept an ongoing, ever-changing identity. In reality there are very few "negative" traits that are immutable. Even our innate characteristics can be improved if we face our vanity about these attributes. Instead, we may tend to cover over some of our "worse points" with vanity about our more desirable traits; the plain woman who stresses her intelligence and puts down other women's beauty as being unimportant is compensating with vanity.

It is also important to remember that vanity includes thinking that you are the worst. Vanity always includes self-hatred, conscious or unconscious. Once you have a realistic picture of yourself, you can be free to decide which of your characteristics you want to change.

One of the most important aspects of vanity is the fact that growth is limited in any area where vanity is strong or where an inflated fantasized image is desperately being held on to. You can't change something you are hiding from.

There is still another reason why many people choose to keep their fantasized images intact: They feel the need for a definition of themselves, for a strong sense of a static identity. When we were young, our parents defined us in every way imaginable. They told us who we looked like, whether we were good or bad, who we had inherited our personality traits from, and what we would probably be when we grew up. They guessed out loud at what we were thinking, what we were feeling, whether we were tired, happy, cross, shy, outgoing, etc.

They built our identity for us in thousands of words and actions. As adults we still feel like we need some steady definition of ourselves, some identity we can depend on. Vanity often supplies us with this kind of identity—a static identity resulting in emotional stagnation and lack of change.

In reality your identity may change from one situation to the next, from one year to the next. Real life doesn't dictate that you must be consistently and at all times "outgoing, brilliant, sensitive, nice, humorous," or however you think of yourself. Something so changeable as a person's identity cannot be categorized. It may be anxiety producing to think of yourself in free terms, but it is also a more exciting way to think of yourself. You can learn to be yourself in each new situation that comes up. You won't have to try to keep up that front that symbolizes your image. If you give away this fantasy picture of yourself, you will find that you are far more relaxed around other people than you have ever been. You won't have to struggle to get approval and praise from others, and your relationships will improve as a result of this tension being removed.

Vanity is a fantasy that has served for many years to keep you cut off from the small child within you, the little kid who felt real pain and joy. Your fantasized image stands between you and the feeling part of yourself. Vanity has diminished the feelings of compassion and tenderness you have toward yourself and consequently toward others. If you break away from fantasy, you can become reacquainted with yourself. You will know that the core of your personal experience is centered in you, not in what other people think of you or in the image you have presented to others. You will realize that your life is dynamic.

14

Power—How You Avoid It

Positive, natural power is what is exercised in the honest, direct pursuit of one's self-interests. Nothing could be healthier and more moral than a person seeking the full development of his potential and pursuing his own goals in a direct manner while at the same time being sensitive to others who are pursuing their goals. Perversely enough, there is an implicit tenet in the Judeo-Christian ethic and other similar philosophies that endorses self-effacing and self-denying behavior. The pride taken in this self-denying behavior is humanly immoral and injures large numbers of people who are going after what they want in life.

Most people are not pursuing their goals at the expense of others, but their positive strivings are tinged with guilt nonetheless. This guilt is powerful and damaging and limits our development. One of the most harmful double messages we receive from society has to do with the acquisition of things that would make us all happy: money, success, sexual attractiveness, open affection, and fame. Strangely enough, all are given an immoral, dirty meaning, while at the same time people in our society profess to believe in open competition.

On a deep unconscious level, most people feel or would feel ashamed of being powerful, influential, wealthy, attractive, talented, or successful. We often try to hide or cover up our successes. In our everyday lives we can observe symptoms of our recoiling from success, particularly after receiving public recognition. Yet all of us know at least one person who fits the description of a person who is happily fulfilling himself to the best of his abilities.

This type of person seems to have many facets to his personality. He is action oriented and has original ideas and practical suggestions about how to get things done. He is persuasive yet not dictatorial in getting his opinions accepted by others. He seems to be a natural leader who is spontaneous and exciting to be with, who seeks out adventure and unusual situations. He has charm and an open attitude toward sex, is affectionate and cares for other people, and most noticeable of all, seems unafraid and unapologetic about his successes.

These individuals are rare in our culture for two major reasons. First of all, because of the tremendous effect of social pressure, which labels a wealthy man "filthy rich," which judges successful people as "selfish, sinful, and bad," which distrusts all government officials and accuses them of being corrupt, and which puts down beauty and attractiveness as being "only skin deep." All of these evaluations cause many people with ability to give up their power or to tone down their outstanding capabilities. Many people feel guilt and shame in relation to others who are less successful, and so to relieve these unpleasant feelings they give up some of their wanting and their pursuit of goals.

Secondly, people give up their real power because they don't want to be adult. They want the kind of indirect and manipulative power they learned as children and which early in life they discovered could get them the things they wanted. Positive power is one of the most significant symbols of being an adult; negative power is a symbol of remaining a child. You cannot honestly pursue your goals in life as a responsible adult if you are still using negative power to control those around you.

The Development of Negative Power

Positive power can be defined as direct, goal-oriented behavior using all of one's resources. It is persuasive and logical rather than manipulative in relation to other people. It is strong rather than oppressive or hostile.

Negative power can be defined as any behavior that controls or elicits a response from another person through manipulation of his feelings, i.e., guilt, anger, pity, sympathy, remorse, or even sense of rejection.

Negative power is very often effective, but the cost to the individual using it is great. The adult who persists in using manipulative forms of control not only does damage to others but also limits his own development. He seldom achieves his goals in a legitimate manner. He often succeeds when his rivals capitulate because of his vicious techniques of arousing their sense of guilt. A person who uses negative power places himself in an arrested state of development from which he can never aspire to real power and strength.

We all learned about negative power and how to use it long before we became adults. As infants and as very young children, we really were powerless in terms of being dependent on our parents for our very survival. At that time we soon learned that we could get our parent's attention by crying, whining, nagging, sulking, throwing temper tantrums, refusing to eat, refusing to go to bed, being sick, or pretending to be more helpless than we really were.

Many parents often give a child what he is begging for just to get him to be quiet or to get rid of him. Thus, they further reinforce the child's use of this negative kind of power or control.

A sulking child is an artist at stimulating unpleasant emotions in his parents to get what he wants. Everyday life in many families consists of one episode after another of negative power being used by the child and the subsequent capitulations of the parents in the face of this manipulation.

A child as young as one or two may already know how to exploit his parents for as much as he can get out of them. Little children are not the pure, innocent beings we like to think they are. They learn the "game" quickly, and if they are allowed to keep succeeding at this game, they may be thoroughly corrupt by the time they reach kindergarten. These manipulations do not disappear when the child becomes an adult. The behavior will continue in more subtle forms unless strenuously interfered with by the parents. This disturbing behavior *can* be stopped by parents who refuse to allow these manipulations to succeed.

If you have any children or if any of your friends have children, you are probably well acquainted with the use of negative power on the part of these small "helpless" people. In public places you can observe the constant struggle between parents and children over the issue of control. The child usually wins, often by thoroughly embarrassing the parent to get what he wants. He knows his parents well and senses that they would be too mortified to really do in public what would be necessary to control his behavior.

One morning a mother brought her two-year-old girl into my office. She had been unable to hire a sitter for the time period of her session. The interaction between the two was a power struggle which the little girl won. Ellen clung to her mother and at first was only interested in trying to get some candy out of her mother's purse. The mother had promised Ellen that if she were good she could have the candy following the session. Ellen began her assault by whining "candy, candy" over and over. She dug into her mother's purse and spilled the contents all over the floor.

After about five minutes of trying to carry on a conversation with me over the din of Ellen's loud whimpers, the mother finally gave in and produced the candy for her daughter. However, the candy occupied Ellen's attention for the brief period it took her to consume it, and she was off once more, crying and whining for more.

I was amazed at the amount of attention Ellen demanded from her mother. At my suggestion the mother put Ellen off her lap onto the floor just to see what she would do. This woman was highly nervous as her daughter wandered around the office, which was fairly "child-proof." At one point Ellen tripped and fell. She proceeded to let out several ear-piercing screams. The mother rushed over and gathered up Ellen, and that was the end of our conversation.

I asked this mother if this was the way Ellen was at home, or if it was the unfamiliar office setting that was upsetting to her. She told me that this was normal behavior for Ellen, that she rarely had a a moment to herself because Ellen was after her from morning till night whining for something or other. "I guess she's just going through the 'terrible two's.' " She spoke with resignation.

Ellen was not going through a "phase" as her mother believed. I wondered when this mother thought that her little self-indulged daughter was going to change someday. Why didn't this mother use her real power (she was, after all, bigger and stronger than her daughter) to put a stop to the obnoxious behavior that constantly interrupted her everyday life? Essentially, she had failed to realize that the only way her daughter was going to learn how to be an adult was by fitting into her mother's world. Instead, this mother was more willing to fit herself into her daughter's world. Ellen was being allowed to act out her impulsive, indulgent behavior without any regard for the intrusion of this behavior on others.

How many of us know adults whose patterns are similar to Ellen's? Techniques of childish manipulation persist into our adult lives and cause all kinds of unnecessary damage to all concerned. Many children are never stopped from acting out these behaviors and are never made to change into decent adults by their parents. We may even physically punish them over and over again, but we do not really stop them. The "terrible two's" and the "troublesome teens" and other so-called phases are only the progressively more subtle acting out of the same negative behavior.

Negative Power in Adults

If you avoid pursuing what you want in life in direct ways, then you are self-denying and probably exert control by indirect, manipulative means. Adult negative power is just an older, more sophisticated version of methods that the child used to control his parents. An adult can manipulate others through a sense of guilt, through acting powerless, through being sick or weak, or possibly even through being mentally ill.

The tyranny of the sick is one of the most finely developed forms of blackmail known to man. A close friend of mine was successfully manipulated by the sickness of his mother just at a time in his life when he was striking out on his own.

Henry and I were both seventeen the summer we planned to drive across the country from New York to California in our old '36 Ford. We had carefully made all the necessary arrangements and gotten permission from all the parents concerned. I left my house early one June morning to pick Henry up at his home across town. When I arrived there, Henry stood in the front yard with no bags looking so dejected that I was alarmed. When I asked him what was going on, he replied that he couldn't go with me on the trip because his mother had developed severe chest pains during the night and had pleaded with him not to go on the trip as planned. She was terrified that she would have to go to the hospital and might never see him again. She was convinced that she was having a heart attack. Henry's father prevailed upon him not to leave at this time because it might make Henry's mother feel worse, and her condition might become critical as a result. He would be blamed if anything happened to his mother. I had to leave on the trip without Henry. His mother went to the hospital where they kept her three days for observation without finding anything wrong.

Twenty years later, Henry's mother died. Her feigned illness of that original summer had succeeded in preventing Henry from experiencing something he would have remembered all his life. Henry's mother had not wanted him to leave her, but knowing that she couldn't stop him by legitimate means, she had, probably largely unconsciously, resorted to this extreme form of negative power which brought her the results she wanted.

Conventional Power and the Illusion of Power

Both negative power and positive real power are effective, but the price of negative power is very great as we saw in the case of Henry and his mother. Henry's mother had gone to such lengths to get her way that she had actually made herself physically ill. This was, of course, detrimental to her as well as to Henry.

Most people claim that they want the positions of authority, independence, leadership, and status that power would give them. Yet they do not want the accompanying responsibility and sense of aloneness.

They may use the manipulations of negative power in their attempts to obtain and retain the implements and tools of power, that is, money, prestige, status, or a position of influence. The story of Leonard, a man who had many capabilities and strengths yet who shunned real power, could be a story about many of us and our illusion of power and our flight from assuming real authority.

By the time I met Leonard, he had already achieved an unusual amount of success. He was forty, married, had four children, and had had an interesting career. Graduating at the head of his class from the U.S. Naval Academy, he became interested in flying and transferred to the air force. He quickly rose to the position of lieutenant colonel, retired, and took over the job of executive vice-president in a large computer company. This man had an advanced degree in physics and mathematics and enjoyed outdoor activities such as sailing and skiing. It seemed that Leonard had all the qualifications of a leader, and furthermore, he expressed a strong desire to become the president of the computer company.

Leonard really believed what he stated, that he wanted to be a leader and that he wanted power and influence. But in the two years following our first meeting, situations changed radically in Leonard's life which served to challenge his desire for more power.

The first event had to do with Leonard's capabilities as a seaman and his longing to be the captain of a sailboat large enough to make ocean crossings. When half a dozen of his friends from the academy and from his office decided to purchase a vessel for cruising the Pacific Islands, Leonard thought his dream had come true. One of the other men had an extensive knowledge of the sea and aspired to the position of captain also. Leonard's knowledge of navigation and engine mechanics and his ability to handle small boats, which he had learned at the academy, all seemed to point in the direction of his being captain of this ship. But as it turned out, the other crew members soon discovered that Leonard lacked the ability to assume the final responsibility the captaincy demanded.

It was on one of the practice sails that Leonard's friends slowly came to the realization that he was not captain material despite his air of bravado and his extensive knowledge. On a short cruise an emergency arose when part of the rigging broke, tearing one of the large sails to shreds. Leonard froze, then called frantically to the other men to go forward and secure the loose lines and sail. His orders, however, were given in such a manner that only one man, Mike, who also had some sailing experience, knew what to do to avoid further damage to the ship. This single event shook the confidence of the crew in Leonard because of the dangerous situation and Leonard's garbled orders.

Most of the time on the rest of the other practice cruises, Leonard could be found sitting at the chart room table, studying a course or plotting figures for navigation. He rarely took the wheel and relied almost totally on the other men for most of the important decisions. He held conferences where he pretended to be the leader while actually depending almost completely on the opinions of the crew, especially Mike, for his final decisions.

The week before the ship was to take its first ocean cruise, crossing from California to Hawaii and then on to Tahiti, the group of men and their wives and children met to elect their captain. He would be the one to have the final say-so during any emergency and would have the final word on most of the course planning and general operation of the ship. Mike easily won the election.

Leonard was crushed even though his friends had honestly told him of their anxieties from previous sails. They were concerned with a safe crossing, especially with their wives and children aboard. Leonard went along to the islands as the navigator, but he was quiet and sulky for the duration of the sail. His dark looks made Mike highly uncomfortable and caused him to feel extremely guilty for being chosen captain. Everyone was relieved when the outline of Diamond Head appeared on the horizon because Leonard had succeeded in making everyone's crossing miserable. He had not really wanted the responsibility for the lives of the crew and their passengers, yet he acted insulted when he was turned down in the election for this position.

His retreat from personal power showed up in his personal relationships and in his professional life as well. A year later Leonard was offered the presidency of his company. Acceptance of this position would necessitate a move to the East Coast. But after agonizing over his conflicting feelings, Leonard did not accept the offer. His wife refused to move to the East Coast, insisting that the move would be too disruptive to the children. Leonard was afraid to press the point, and so he remained as one of the vice-presidents. Over the next few years, he was given less responsibility.

By not taking the position of president, he had weakened himself to a very great degree. By refusing to take control over his family situation, he could use his wife's reluctance to move as his eternal excuse for missing this once-in-a-lifetime opportunity. Leonard had not relished the responsibility of the presidency, just as he had withdrawn from final authority on the ship. The truth is that Leonard wanted the illusion of power without the hard work, dedication, and responsibility.

Avoiding Real Power May Lead to a More Authoritarian Power Structure.   An individual who prefers authoritarian rule has a negative viewpoint about human nature. He believes that man has a basically evil nature and uncontrollable impulses that must be curbed by laws and rules. He relies on external sources to judge and punish or reward him and others. He is extremely fearful of freedom and democracy in the true sense of the word. He is basically unconcerned with the issue of human rights as he strives to get to the top. He seems to want power simply for power's sake, not for what it might mean in his development as a human being.

Governments that are based on authoritarian rule, where the majority of people look to the government as the final word in every area of their lives, can come in forms as extreme as the Nazi government in World War II. Many people living under this regime carried out heinous crimes against other humans in part because they believed in the "values" of total obedience, submission, and loyalty to the leader, the one they trusted to guide them through an anxious age.

Negative Power vs. Positive Power

To fulfill one's potential is the real work of an individual's life, and it is that task that gives his life meaning. However, in many families this isn't what is taught, nor is it generally supported by society.

One of the principle functions of the family is the socialization of its children, that is, teaching them to become acceptable members of society. In a judgmental, authoritarian family atmosphere, where personal freedom is thoroughly suppressed, there is a high degree of hostility and destructiveness in all of the members. It follows that in a traditional "moralistic" society, where there are rigid controls and unnecessary rules, there will be a high degree of disrespect for others and their boundaries. The pursuit of power in this context becomes a ruthless battle based on fear and hatred of others.

A new salesman in a large real-estate office was told by his immediate superior: "Look, I'll be honest with you. Nobody here wants you to sell any piece of property. They're looking out for number one, and they'll do everything to steal your leads. But this shouldn't be news to you. That's life. You'll just have to hustle to make good here."

It's obvious that this boss was attempting to encourage the new man to work hard, make many sales, and so increase the income of both men, but the motivation was to be fear, suspicion, and hatred of his fellow real-estate agents. There was no suggestion of sharing or cooperation in this particular office force. The people here were pursuing conventional power in an atmosphere of hostility and intimidation. It would be very difficult for anyone to fulfill his true potential in such a destructive environment.

Steps Toward Personal Power Within the Context of Real Morality

DON'T CLING TO BEING A CHILD

Some people never grow up. Instead of actively seeking control of our lives and striving for happiness and success, some of us remain children. We think that we have all the time in the world to change. We forget that we are going to die; it could be tomorrow or twenty years from now. Carlos Castaneda, in his novel *Journey to Ixtlan*, suggested an allegorical cure for a child who stubbornly continued to use negative power. It was suggested that the child be taken to a place where he could see the corpse of a dead child and that he touch the body. The contact with this reality of death would cause the child to view the world in an entirely different way. He would see his childish whining for rewards and attention as petty, trivial, and totally irrelevant to his life. He would be startled and scared into stopping his destructive behavior. This unusual procedure for stopping a child's use of negative power might well be used as a reminder to everyone that there is no valid reason to waste time in clinging to the past.

You are no longer in the same position that you were in as a child. You can afford to take a chance on trying by legitimate means to get what you want in life. You may lose or you may win; the outcome is uncertain. However, you will learn a valuable lesson: Even if you lose, you won't die. You may be disappointed or angry, but you won't be totally overwhelmed.

DON'T SEEK ADVICE

No one can tell you how to attain your goals or what you want out of life. Only you can know yourself that well. Generally, when you seek advice from others, you are already biased and are really asking for confirmation. For example, if you want to have an extra-marital affair, you would know that the kind of advice you would get from your minister would tend to be moralistic and restrictive because it conflicts with his religious code of behavior and general morality. If you turned to a freewheeling friend of yours, you could expect the opposite sort of advice.

Overly dependent individuals often feel comfortable with advice from a very opinionated person, but their sense of security is short-lived and increases helplessness. Often it is better for our overall development to make a mistake on our own than to rely on others. There is generally an opportunity to rectify our mistakes. Most of our personal decisions are not as dramatic and world shaking as we think they are. The added drama comes from living in a childlike dependent way.

You may at times need help from someone who has more knowledge than you about the methods of achieving certain practical goals. In some cases, getting expert help from someone with superior and more specialized knowledge is a good idea. There may also be times when you are confused about your personal life. You may have been so cut off from knowing yourself that you could benefit from counseling. In that case, sessions with a competent psychologist or therapist could help you take the first steps toward learning to control your own destiny.

DON'T BE AFRAID TO MAKE MISTAKES

If you believe that you dare not fail, then you cannot act. Don't paralyze yourself by insisting on perfection, and don't berate yourself for mistakes. Simply correct them, and try again.

DON'T WHINE AND COMPLAIN OR MAKE EXCUSES

There are circumstances where you won't be able to get what you want, but this does not justify playing the victim and developing cynical attitudes.

James tried many different avenues in search of success and friendship during his lifetime, but he was very intolerant of anything less than immediate success. When he was older he realized that each time he tried something and it failed initially, he made a silent vow never to do it again, never to risk the humiliation of failure again. He even carried this principle into his everyday interactions with friends. Once, he wanted to have a serious talk with a friend and went to visit him during office hours. The friend was too preoccupied for the moment to pay close attention to James's conversation. James left the office vowing never to trouble his friend again with a serious matter. As a result James slowly became alienated from this friend, and after a few months the friendship no longer even existed. James complained for years afterward how his friend had given him the cold shoulder and that that was what had destroyed the friendship.

Direct Competition

Honest competition is healthy and moral, whereas retreating from competition is hurtful for all concerned. If two men are attempting to get the same job or date the same woman, there is necessarily a winner and a loser.

Backing away from your attempts to achieve your goals out of fear or guilt is damaging. If the other person loses, he may feel some pain involved in his loss, but you have still acted appropriately and morally. In expressing your honest opinions in an open and sensitive manner, you may sometimes hurt another individual, but unless you have deliberately set out to hurt him, the pain he feels only comes from inside him. You may have unknowingly threatened his defense system, and that is where his pain lies.

In competing, never inflict pain to get what you want. Running your opponent down or lying and cheating to get ahead are not honest competition. Expanding your energy on trying to undermine your competitor instead of making every effort to succeed for yourself is a distorted way of pursuing power.

In a good competition the contest is almost incidental—it's the attainment of the goal that is the essence. Focusing on the opponent rather than on the goal undermines the spirit of competing. In competing for the affections of someone of the opposite sex, some people get off the track and feel more anger and hatred toward the rival than they feel loving toward the object of their affections.

Many people lose sight of the goal because the contest alone becomes the primary focus of their attention. To be diverted in this way interferes with becoming more powerful.

It is valuable to seek objective criticism. Honestly stated perceptions of you are really gifts. You're lucky to find out the truth about yourself, even if it is a negative truth.

All of the above behaviors—clinging to being a child, seeking advice, seeking perfection in yourself, whining and complaining, withdrawing from competing—all of these behaviors make you feel powerless. They are all harmful actions and attitudes that are a burden to you. If you drop them, you will feel stronger immediately.

Positive Power Is Directly Linked to a Moral Social Order

There is a definite connection between positive power and a social order of implicit morality that would be conducive to personal growth and development for all of its members. In a society that supported the individual's straightforward pursuit of his goals, a person would also feel valued for himself. He would feel recognized and listened to and would have a strong sense of his own unique identity. Outward recognition would be personal, and it would include recognition of the person's sexuality. An acceptance of the whole person, a recognition of his body, of his feelings, and of his mind is needed by an individual to get a proper sense of his identity. Awareness of his basic nature comes first and is more important than recognition for performance.

In a positive atmosphere the individual would be responded to in nonjudgmental and nonparental terms. A healthy environment refrains from setting up unnecessary standards, roles, and rules and imposing these restrictions on our activities. This environment would be nonmanipulative, that is, not underhanded or tricky. People would not be used by others as tools for their own advancement. Instead, the relationship between people would be direct and honest. In a growth-enhancing atmosphere, people are seen in noncategorical, nonfixed ways. There is a feeling of fluidity, of mobility, of changeability, a feeling that people have the right to an opportunity to change.

People would be recognized as being capable of handling personal freedom and equality without total anarchy being the result. The fewer the restrictions on personal freedom, the more decent and less hostile people would be. Incidents of crime and disrespect of human rights would be minimal in a society uncluttered by unnecessary rules. Perversely, a heavily judgmental society produces the very crimes and destructiveness it strives to avoid.

A code of implicit morality would encourage real personal authority, not a power rule. The true authority in any situation is the natural authority, the person who knows the most about the situation or the activity, who is the most responsible, and the most concerned with other people.

Within a truly moral society, the ideal pursuit in life would be the accumulation of personal power, the pursuit of one's adult wishes, and the achievement of one's personal goals. This course of action is honestly selfish and direct and stands in contrast to the Judeo-Christian ethic and other philosophies that preach selflessness and self-sacrifice.

A truly moral person would favor honest selfishness over dishonest selflessness. Such a person is able to do what he wants to do and be what he wants to be without intruding on the rights of others. A person who is pursuing power in his personal life would necessarily have a blend of many different characteristics, but he would be more self-affirming than self-destructive in his actions. He would take care of himself, be independent, have a sense of responsibility for himself, be willing to take on responsibilities in the areas of his greatest capabilities, and have an optimistic outlook on life.

You are the one ultimately responsible for your life. Knowing your strengths and weaknesses leaves you free to go after power in a natural way. You will have a realistic self-concept. You won't desperately strive to fulfill unrealistic expectations from the past; nor will you need to hold back because you are afraid. You can know just where you stand and tolerate direct comparisons. You are free to approach life in a personal manner, harmonious with your true nature. Pursuing power is a truly moral endeavor, one that adds dimensions to your life and one that really makes life worth living.

15

You're Not Nice

ONE OF OUR STRONGEST, yet seemingly innocuous, defenses is an image we have of ourselves as "nice," "good," or "decent." This way of thinking of yourself as a good person would not be necessary if you hadn't grown up feeling unlovable and like a "bad" child. The need to maintain an image of being good or nice is a direct compensation for feeling worthless. If you had been raised in an emotionally nurturing environment, you would not think of yourself in evaluative terms, either good or bad.

The very process of thinking of yourself in terms of nice, good, or right is in itself "not nice." It places a burden on others to support your image. If your image of yourself is that you are good, generous, and giving, it may blind you to the injuries you commit each day. More important, you can't afford to admit into your consciousness all the so-called mean, petty, competitive thoughts that we all have about other people from time to time, because making those thoughts conscious would negate this nice image. With your mate, you may often be thinking, "He's wrong and I'm right," and trying to win points to prove that you're the innocent, well-meaning one. If someone criticizes you, you may feel devastated and hate yourself because this image has been damaged. Often, you will retaliate with anger at those who tell you an unflattering truth about yourself.

There is nothing wrong with thinking jealous, petty thoughts about your rival or wishing he would disappear or break a leg. These kinds of thoughts are just as natural and normal as any other thoughts you might have. Everyone has these supposedly "not nice" thoughts on occasion. Being aware of them will probably make your interactions with rivals more honest. On the other hand, keeping these thoughts partially unconscious increases your tendency to act them out.

Thoughts are not actions and cannot be labeled as bad or wrong. Giving up your nice image will allow you to get acquainted with that part of yourself that you previously thought of as bad and felt ashamed of. Then you won't have to keep pretending that these mean thoughts only occur in other people and keep imagining that *they* are hostile or wishing you ill.

Most people grew up in families that had an image of themselves as being better than other families, and they attempt to maintain this image in their current family. They feel that their way of doing things is the right way, and they desperately want their children to reflect this good image by being better behaved, friendlier, and smarter than the children of their friends and neighbors. These people are unintentionally acting out destructive behavior on members of their own families while defending their good image to the death.

One of the families I worked with illustrates a typically destructive interaction in a "nice" family. Julie and her parents came to see me for family counseling. It seemed that nine-year-old Julie wasn't fitting into the family image that her parents were determined to uphold. In fact, she disturbed this image to a large degree. During the past year Julie's behavior had taken a turn for the worst. She had developed a school phobia and often threw temper tantrums when her parents insisted she attend school. Julie's mother and father felt that they had been good parents and that all was well until Julie started acting up.

At the first session, without even introducing Julie to me, the mother launched into a recitation of her problems with Julie. Julie had seated herself unobstrusively in a chair near the door, completely out of the circle of conversation. I introduced myself to her and asked her to bring her chair in closer. Julie complied and returned my greeting: "Hello, Doctor . . ." Before she could even say my name, she was interrupted by her mother, who went on to describe the behavior we had all just witnessed.

"See how she slinks around, hoping not to draw attention to herself! This is just the way she acts at home, sneaky, like she's trying to hide something . . ."

Julie's father broke in to argue with the mother about Julie's misbehavior at home. Neither parent looked at Julie or even seemed to notice that she was in the same room. When I addressed a question to her, she leaned forward in her chair with definite interest on her face. I imagine she had rarely been asked by her parents what she thought about anything except in an intrusive way.

These parents spoke for Julie, talked about her as if she were not there, discussed her as if she were the source of their unhappiness, as if she were a thing, not a person. They did not give their daughter the consideration they would have given a stranger.

However, they were unaware of the harm they were inflicting on Julie until I pointed this out to them. For much of the session, Julie had been experiencing extreme discomfort, humiliation, and emotional pain, yet her parents had not even noticed.

Julie's parents had almost successfully blocked out Julie as a person. An extremely "close" couple before she was born, they could not tolerate her intrusion into their bond, so they had in effect shut her out. Her negativism was a pathetic attempt to get some attention from her parents.

This couple's image of themselves as good people was a defense against knowing about the destructiveness of their way of relating and its effect on Julie. Meanwhile, they had unintentionally created a toxic environment in their home. In fact, their good image protected them from knowing how they hurt Julie.

Maintaining a nice image of ourselves is a first-line defense against the awareness of our other defenses, our patterns of withholding, our playing the victim, etc. It is similar to a heavy layer of clothing we put on to protect ourselves against a cold, hostile environment when we were children, but it becomes inappropriate if we are living in a warmer, friendlier climate as adults. Our nice image is not only inappropriate and superfluous, it also keeps us from being honest about ourselves, and it causes us to punish the very people who offer us a warmer, more growth-enhancing environment. Hanging on to this image may keep us cut off from any genuinely positive impulses we might have toward others.

In defending an image of ourselves as nice and our families as good, decent people, we remain mostly unaware that we are acting out destructive behaviors. In ignorance, we are capable of committing atrocities in everyday life to the people closest to us. In the process of defending this image, we may unintentionally injure people who are innocent and who love us, acknowledge us, accept us, or give us value for being what we are. We often reject true friendship and prefer instead hostile and mutually disrespectful bonds and ties. There are several major damaging ways we react to others. We reject genuine compliments and personal appreciation, and we are distrustful and offensive when faced with unusually friendly or loving treatment. We attempt to suppress these responses in others.

Examples of Destructive Behavior

The ways in which we are destructive occur for the most part in the common, everyday interactions we have with other people. These actions are so much a part of our lives that they are often overlooked or their effects on us and on others shrugged off. But they all take their toll.

How many times have you tried to compliment someone, for example a woman who is wearing a new dress, and been met with a rejecting response like, "Oh, this dress, it's nothing."

A simple "thank you" would have made you feel much better. This woman was not being nice to you when she wouldn't accept your compliment.

Or, going to the other extreme, you may have congratulated a fellow employee on a job well done only to be treated to a full explanation of everything that went into that job. The recipient of your compliment may have praised and flattered himself in an effort to impress you still more.

An even more destructive way to reject compliments is to undo the very quality that earned the compliment in the first place. This is what Georgene did after she had been elected by the women in her professional club to represent them on a local television talk show. On the initial show she was a hit. Extremely articulate and attractive, she won compliments and applause from all her friends and from the other guest on the show. She was invited back to the next week's show.

During the week, Georgene unconsciously decided to hold back the qualities that had made her so popular on the show. She didn't get enough sleep the night before the show and so looked tired and haggard. She lost track of the subjects she wanted to cover during the interview and so was much less articulate. When her friends watched this second show, they were surprised and felt like fools for having praised her the previous week.

In a sense, Georgene was punishing the friends who had supported her in doing what she had wanted to do. Georgene had wanted, more than anything else, to appear on that particular television show. When she got what she wanted and received praise for it, she disowned her own wish and projected it onto her friends in the club. She became convinced that they were the ones who wanted her to be on the show and that they were pushing her to be on it a second time. Therefore, she wouldn't give them what "they wanted." She'd forgotten that originally she had wanted the success herself.

Most of us are suspicious of nice treatment. We think, "What's in it for him?" or "It's his job to be nice." You have probably noticed the kind of abusive treatment that perfectly polite waiters often receive at the hands of customers. Usually, however, it is the person who is closest to us who suffers the most from our suspicions about being liked or well treated. A friend of mine lightly dismissed the efforts of her nine-year-old daughter to make a birthday cake for her, saying, "Her father probably put her up to it; she would never have thought of it on her own." What this mother hadn't bothered to find out was that her daughter had indeed thought of making the cake herself and had spent hours mixing and frosting to get it just right. This mother's suspicion of her daughter's motives was a rejection of the girl's attempt to express love and appreciation.

When we distrust a friend's nice treatment of us, our cynicism makes him feel bad. One husband decided on the spur of the moment to bring some flowers home for his wife. As she placed them in a vase, she sarcastically* said to him, "Well, what have you been up to that would make you bring me flowers?" No doubt her husband will think twice before bringing her flowers again.

There are literally hundreds of ways in which individuals are not

---

* Sarcasm and so-called kidding often thinly disguise our attempts to push away people who are close to us and keep them at a distance.

nice to each other in their everyday interactions: the businessman who has had a hard day and so takes out his anger on the innocent salesperson; hostile, pointless arguments between a couple about their budget; loud outbursts of temper on the part of one family member that upsets the whole family; pushiness and aggressiveness on the part of individuals who insist upon having their own way. One can find countless examples of toxic personal interactions in one's own life.

The relationship of many doctors and nurses to their patients is often disrespectful. Their style of speaking condescendingly undermines patients as people: "Now we're going to have this little shot, it won't hurt very much. Now let's close our eyes." Such is the bedside manner of many physicians. The use of large words and jargon by people in specialized professions is often hostile. It's an attempt to establish proof of their superiority and their right to snobbery in relation to others.

On his first sailing trip, a friend of mine was with a captain who had had years of sailing experience. My friend had hoped to learn a lot on his first sail, but at the end of the day he came back feeling discouraged. He felt stupid and slow because he had had difficulty catching on to various sailing techniques. On reflection he realized that the captain had used many terms that he hadn't bothered to explain, and he had issued orders in a superior, condescending tone of voice. The captain, instead of being helpful, had been generally hostile.

There are people who instead of indulging in obviously aggressive, condescending, or hostile behavior act servile and overly submissive. For example, Pete had a secretary who exhibited such a hovering, eager-to-please attitude that she embarrassed Pete whenever clients were present. She served coffee to her boss and his clients with a quivering hand; she rarely said no to any request, even when it would have been reasonable to. This woman eventually made herself unemployable with her game of being an inferior. Pete fired her after many months when he could no longer tolerate her hostile attitude, which made him feel like a mean, critical slave driver.

A service person hates his imagined oppressor. An overly submissive person is not a "good" person. He makes others feel uncomfortable for being strong and capable. A servile person can cause a strong person to feel mean, tough, controlling, and harsh. Often a submissive person is quiet and reserved. A more vocal person can be made to feel loud and brash in comparison and as if he is controlling the conversation.

Trying to maintain a nice image of being generous while in fact being stingy and tight will push people away; your true stingy feelings will eventually be felt. One couple offered the use of the family car to guests who were visiting. The next morning they began to take back the offer by saying that the husband needed the car during the morning hours and that it had to go into the garage for repairs on the following day. They reassured their guests that any other time the car would be available for them.

This couple wanted to be seen as generous when in fact they were tight and withholding. This attitude pervaded every aspect of the visit. The guests became self-conscious about their presence in the home of this ungiving couple and eventually left for a motel, preferring to stay there than to feel that they were inconveniencing their hosts.

A major form of not being nice is lashing out at someone who intrudes on your defenses, who interrupts your fantasy world by offering you something real. The habitual response of anger and aggression to loving treatment is one of the most destructive patterns of behavior that can occur between two people.

An extremely vicious, destructive response is often set into motion once an individual's defenses are broken into by someone who loves that individual and who treats him with unusual respect, dignity, and genuine warmth. This is when some people are the least nice and the most punishing.

Several years ago in New York City, about half a dozen youths who had known each other since grammar school were persuaded by the most popular member, Steven, to accept a new boy into their group. The new member, Dirk, was a victim of polio and in fact often thought of himself as an "innocent" victim. He was small for his age and had a noticeable limp. At school he was the brunt of many jokes, being called "gimp" and "three legs" because of the cane he carried. Steven insisted that he not be teased by this group of friends, and his wish was respected. For many months Dirk enjoyed hanging out with Steven and his friends. He was not treated in any special, sympathetic way but was merely accepted as one of the fellows. Slowly Dirk relaxed and became more trusting about his friend's generosity. He began enjoying the company of some of the other boys.

One summer morning, however, when the gang was standing on a subway platform waiting for the uptown train, boredom set in and some of the youths started to tease Dirk sarcastically about his disability. Before Steven could utter a word, Dirk had grabbed him by the throat and tried to choke him. The others pulled Dirk away before Steven was seriously hurt. But Steven's wounds from this encounter were deep and not of a physical nature. He was unable to understand why the person he had befriended had turned on him in the midst of the painful teasing even though he had in no way participated in the abuse.

Dirk's hated image of himself as a cripple had been interfered with by Steven. He had begun to think of himself as a regular person instead of an innocent victim. He had let down some of his defenses and was thus more vulnerable at the moment when the young men had chosen to taunt him with verbal barbs. In his pain and distress, he had lashed out at the person who had been responsible for his lowering his defenses. He did not punish the youths who were causing him pain directly.

This extreme example of someone who lashed out physically against a friend provides a clue to the anger and hostility that is aroused in all of us by a significant person in our life who tempts us to lower our barriers and be vulnerable to pain once again. Anger and aggression in the face of love and friendship do not seem like perverse reactions when viewed in the light of the strong resistance that all of us have to any intrusion upon our defenses. When we are well defended, painful experiences do not feel so painful to us. When we are relatively undefended, we will necessarily feel more of everything that life offers us, including psychological pain. Thus, we hate the person who we feel is responsible for "luring" us into a less-defended position.

We may have been the ones who initially wanted to become less defended. We all want to be more open and to become more available to loving relationships. However, when we become resistant to going further in our development, if we become fearful and anxious, we often project our desire for love onto the other person. We begin to feel as if he is demanding love and trust from us, and we respond with anger and hostility. We deny our own desire to be free and spontaneous and punish the one whom we have allowed to make a dent in our armor. We feel as if the other person is causing us the pain instead of recognizing that it was we who wanted to change.

Many people choose to reject the real-life gratification and love and to return to the familiar world of fantasy. Whenever they choose fantasy, they will punish the one who made their fantasy become a reality.

It is obvious that the more deprived an individual was of warmth and love as a child, the more he will tend to punish those who respond to him with love and warmth as an adult. The only hope is to become conscious of this meanness by observing our own behaviors when faced with a possibility of having our fantasies come true. You may be completely unaware of the underlying anger against the person you love, but you *can* be aware of any specific punishing behavior in relation to him. It may often be enough just to admit to your loved one that you feel like pushing him away at the moment. Assure him that you won't act on that feeling. This punishing process can be avoided by your being honest about your reactions at these times.

You're Not Nice When You Are Being Self-Denying

In addition to the damaging impact we have on others when protecting a bond, we need to recognize the damaging effect of self-denying behavior on other people. If we are not honestly pursuing our own wants and instead are denying ourselves, we unintentionally hurt others. Unfortunately, self-denying, selfless behavior is seemingly sanctioned within many philosophic and religious persuasions. The effects of these insidious values and codes, which could even be considered immoral, are pervasive in our society.

It is also harmful to be dishonest about pursuing our goals and pretending to want success or love at the times when we are feeling cynical or negative and thus self-denying. Very often an outwardly good person is essentially self-righteous and noble about his goodness and is subtly punishing toward others who are not like him. He may see other people as selfish or bad, all the while insisting that he is right and good.

Remedying the Ways You Punish Others

LEARNING HOW YOU ARE NOT NICE IS THE FIRST STEP TOWARD CHANGING YOURSELF

It may be difficult at first to see yourself in some of these examples and easier to see your mate or your friend as the bad guy. This is a natural human reaction that is incidently strengthened by this defense of seeing yourself as okay and other as not so okay. In addition, our awareness of others is usually much sharper than our self-awareness and our self-knowledge. Man's resistance to looking into himself has a long history and is especially strong when that self-study threatens to turn up facts that man is loath to admit about himself.

It takes courage to face the truth that you may be punishing to someone who loves you and wishes you the best in life. You may feel that to be mean to one who is nice to you is a completely irrational way to act. This behavior only *seems* irrational. At some time or another we all lash out when the armor that has protected us throughout our lives is penetrated by love from someone who is significant to us.

We need to identify the specific ways we have of punishing others to change ourselves. You may be the kind of person who withdraws whenever you get too close to someone you could love. Perhaps you play the victim game and pretend that he is abusing you. It's possible that you feel indifferent and lose interest as things become nicer in your relationship. You may become more controlling and bossy, or you may go to the other extreme and become less communicative and quieter than you are ordinarily. It is helpful to realize that *any* radical change of behavior that is different from the behaviors you expressed at the beginning of your relationship is probably a form of punishment.

WHEN YOU DISCOVER THAT YOUR SEEMINGLY INNOCENT BEHAVIOR IS DESTRUCTIVE, YOU WILL WANT TO CHANGE

Very few people want to cause hurt, but nevertheless we do hurt others. Parents damage their children unintentionally, and the hurtful effects may persist for a lifetime. We don't mean to be destructive to others, especially to the people we care about deeply, but we often are. If we could visualize the results to our loved ones at those times we feel like being mean, sarcastic, or indifferent, we can learn to put their feelings ahead of any hostile urges we may be feeling. It is especially important to refrain from hurting others at those times when we are feeling pained or anxious ourselves. Don't confuse good intentions with actions. It's the action that counts. These insights you have gained can lead to changes in behavior.

Once you become aware of the ways you are not nice, you can begin working systematically to change them. Be open with people who are close to you about your destructive behavior. The other person may not want to hear about the negative way he has been treated; he may try to reassure you that he knows you have good intentions. Proceed with your plans to change in spite of reassurances. Some habits may be relatively easy to give up, and you will find yourself on the upgrade very soon. Other patterns that have been a part of your life-style since you were very young will require more time to change, but you can slowly gain control over these punishing qualities also.

Friends are the most valuable and precious things you will ever have in your life. Fortunate indeed is the person who has one or two real friends. It would be a terrible loss if you finally pushed those friends away from you. Remember that you are valuable to your loved ones just as they are valuable to you.

A final thought: Being hard on yourself or mean to yourself for your "faults" is not constructive. You are no different from most people. All of us have been destructive to other people without meaning to be. There is no reason to hate yourself or to use this information as criticism against yourself. It is just as harmful for you to punish yourself as it is to treat others badly. Treat yourself with the same kindness you want to extend to the people you love.

The Truth as Therapy
and Its Implications

16

Ten Steps Toward Cure
The Therapeutic Value of Friendship

THE IDEAS IN THIS BOOK point a way toward a richer, less-defended way of life. The source of the neurotic process is in the very defenses that protected us in our childhood, and a major portion of the solution to this human problem lies in knowing the truth about ourselves and our society. Once we know the truth, we have a chance at the alternatives to a defended way of life.

The alternative path presented here points in a direction that runs opposite to the road that most people travel in our society. Most people pathetically spend their lifetime protecting themselves with the barriers they erected as children. These barriers, these defenses, this inward style of living are unnecessary and indeed harmful to everyone. Instead, it is life affirming to struggle against the limitations that a defensive, self-protective life-style imposes upon us. In my opinion living with minimal defenses and maximum vulnerability is the only viable way to live. The following ten steps toward breaking down these defenses summarize the concepts and the practical methods that you can use in your fight to attain freedom.

1. Recognizing That You're Not Sick

Over the years I have noticed that most of the patients who came to me for therapy often seemed more "real" than other people I met in everyday life. Although they were in emotional pain, they expressed their thoughts and feelings more honestly. When they entered therapy they were closer to themselves than at other times in their lives and more compassionate to others as well. They were "healthier" than the average person because they were closer to their genuine feelings and less phony than many people who were not in therapy.

Your anxiety, pain, and sadness reflect an awakening; they are actually stirrings toward life. These "symptoms" signal a crack in your defense system. Even "abnormal" states of depression, anxiety, and phobias can be signs of progress because they are symptomatic of a break in your defenses. Properly understood and treated, these symptoms may lead you to a less-defended, more emotionally rich, and more productive life.

THERE IS NO PSYCHOLOGICAL SYMPTOM OR EMOTIONAL CONDITION THAT IS UNCHANGEABLE

You have the capacity to change. It is just a question of how much you want to, whether you are willing to go through the discomfort and anxiety involved in changing your self-concept. If you are willing, there is no limit to the progress you can make in your personal development. Working on understanding yourself is a first step in the direction of having a more active approach to life.

RECOGNIZING THAT YOU'RE NOT SICK HELPS YOUR MORALE

You don't have to feel like the passive victim of a sickness, nor do you have to get stuck blaming the past for your problems. Knowing that you're not strange or ill or different from other people is a large part of the battle.

Kate and Amelia were friends. Both had experienced similar problems while growing up. Their parents had been separated for most of their childhoods, and neither woman had adequately dealt with her painful feelings of rejection from her father. Both women married and began to reexperience anxiety and fears of being abandoned, this time by their husbands.

Kate felt extremely anxious, so nervous that she could hardly eat whenever her husband worked late. She fantasized about him being with another woman. She was so seriously concerned that she was developing an ulcer. Finally, she sought help from a therapist because she felt as if she were losing her mind. After her talk she felt tremendous relief just knowing that she wasn't crazy or sick. She felt very enthusiastic about continuing her discussions and was interested, too, in working on the relationship with her husband.

Amelia, on the other hand, slowly developed hypochondriacal symptoms over the years, laying the blame for her attacks of hysteria on a "nervous disposition I was born with." Amelia and her husband went their separate ways after several years of bitter arguments and recriminations. Kate developed as a person over the years and continued to improve the emotional quality of her marriage. Amelia deteriorated, while maintaining the belief that she was a "sick" person.

2. *Realizing That Your Pain Is Valid*

Your pain and anxiety are not abnormal. Recognizing that there is a reason for your pain can legitimize your condition for you. You really were damaged. The source of your pain lies in the fact that you suffered a certain amount of emotional deprivation and a certain degree of trauma when you were young and vulnerable. You are not the only person this has happened to. Most of us had similar experiences and sustained varying degrees of damage in our families. Just recognizing this can make you feel much better.

Most people cover up their feelings of pain and rejection, and many of us deny to ourselves that we were rejected. As a result we tend to think that we're abnormal. We start to get the feeling that our pain isn't valid, that we shouldn't be unhappy in the family where everybody else is "happy." However, the reality is that the people in our family, the people in society, and our friends are all attempting to cover up the fact that they are also in pain. Most of them are hiding their feeling of rejection and hurt.

Just understanding that your fears have a basis, that your pain is valid, that you're not innately peculiar or strange is a positive step. Realizing that different people have different fears and anxieties removes much of the shame you may have felt for feeling fearful.

Each person has different fears that are unique to his personality and his situation. You may be afraid of one thing while another person may be totally at ease in that situation. You may tremble with fear each time you have to take a plane trip, yet love the thrill of riding a motorcycle; your friend, on the other hand, may insist that he would never ride a motorcycle because he is afraid of an accident. You may be afraid of public speaking yet be at ease with individuals, while another person may enjoy speaking in front of a number of people and be unable to relate personally to anyone. These are the kinds of differences that exist in people's defense patterns. You should not be ruthlessly self-critical about your own defenses. Instead, feel confident and sensitive toward others in the areas where you feel strong and less defended, and gradually try to help yourself in a compassionate way in areas where you have been damaged.

3. Becoming Aware of Your Specific Defenses Against Feeling

Through knowledge of our defenses comes understanding. Through understanding comes change. It is important to become aware of your own specific defenses, whether they are habit patterns or dependencies on fantasy or painkillers. Identifying and understanding these defenses place them more under your conscious control. Gradually, with understanding and effort, you can reach a point where you have enough control to begin to let go of a particular defense. It is possible to challenge and change behavior patterns and lifelong rituals.

Your defenses are not you. A habitual defense seems and feels like a large part of your identity. However, a defense is still something you're doing or thinking that covers your real feelings. Do not mistake your defenses for your self. The specific habits or thought patterns that you make a virtue out of may be the very things that are killing you. It's very important to be aware of the specific defense and then to recapture the underlying feeling. Understanding a defense and knowing that it's legitimate to have built that defense, yet realizing that it is now limiting, is the first step toward getting out of it and back to true feelings.

GIVING UP SELF-FEEDING HABITS

Most of us at one time or another have been dependent upon certain habits that we used to partially relieve our emotional hunger and pain. Essentially, we became addicted to these habits. Overeating, drinking excessively, overwork, smoking, masturbating, using drugs, and compulsive and routine sex are all habits that relieve tension, anxiety, and pain.

It is important to realize that it will take time to break some of these self-feeding habits. It took you a number of years to become addicted in the first place. They cannot be stopped overnight nor without some pain and anxiety, but they can eventually be broken.

CHANGING RITUALS AND HABIT PATTERNS

Many people choose a seemingly innocuous painkiller that serves to soothe their hurts and fears. Examine the self-comforting habits that you have been using in your life. Try to see what it would be like without one of these painkillers or habits. This can be an interesting adventure in both knowing and helping yourself.

Routines are one of the greatest deadeners we can use to allay our anxieties, yet they seem so incidental, harmless, and so much a part of our lives. You probably know someone who says: "I can't do a thing until I have my morning cup of coffee." Or perhaps someone who holds to a rigid routine of arising at the same time each day and going through the same rituals down to the minutest detail of getting ready to go to work.

Many of our routines are carried on in private and are ways of taking care of ourselves. We can really isolate ourselves from others by insisting on rigid schedules and endless routines. We can watch television and read for hours; we can have ritualistic preparations for getting ready for bed; we can spend hours working tediously over a hobby or a project. Almost any activity can be used to kill off feeling.

If you are strenuously trying to break a long-standing habit, enlist the help of a friend and tell him any self-defeating thoughts. Doing this as a discipline breaks the secrecy of these thoughts. With its exposure lies the control of the behavior.

BEING AWARE OF THE "BAD" HABITS
OF WHICH YOU MAKE A VIRTUE

Don't be too proud of these defenses. They might have protected you in the past, but now they are killing you. Try not to end up like the old grandfather who proudly announced: "I'm a self-made man. I've always taken care of myself since my father deserted us when I was ten years old. I don't need anybody."

This old man never let anyone love him or "take care of him," and he succeeded in pushing all the members of his family away. He died alone one night in his luxurious home, sitting in front of his television set.

If you have the tendency to deny yourself and selflessly put other's desires before your own, don't be proud of it. "Selflessness" and "self-denial" are immoral because they inhibit and hurt others who are honestly striving toward self-fulfillment. If you think well of yourself, if you love yourself and don't deny yourself things in life, you will also naturally wish others well. It is moral to be selfish in the good sense of the word: pursuing your own goals while being sensitive and not intruding on others. Cultivate a healthy self-interest.

Defensiveness and stubbornness are also nothing to brag about. You may be rightfully proud that you "survived" your childhood, or that you grew up to be fairly successful "in spite of everything," but to be proud of the defenses that helped you protect yourself as a child is to hold on to a destructive behavior pattern.

Routines and self-feeding habits are some of the more straightforward defenses to break, simply because they are so obvious and your progress can be measured easily.

4. Understanding the Origins of Your Defenses Within Your Family

Most of us have been damaged innocently and inadvertently by people who were well meaning. Our parents did do the best they could. However, if their well-meaning efforts were limited by their own system of defenses, you necessarily experienced the resultant emotional distress. Your suffering and anxiety are nothing to be ashamed of. All of us have sustained some degree of damage in our developmental years and indeed are still vulnerable to an abrasive emotional climate.

FACING THE TRUTH ABOUT YOUR FAMILY

It frees you. Your parents could not possibly have given you everything you needed, simply because they had their own emotional inadequacies. Recall the times in your childhood that are particularly tinged with personal meaning. Pay special attention to the events that were painful, events that led to significant emotional or behavioral changes in you. One way to recall your feeling of yourself as a child is to be with children or observe them with their parents. Some parent-child interactions are painful to watch. See if you can get a sense of what the child is feeling and of what you felt in similar situations. These memories, these awarenesses, provide valuable information to help you attain independence and freedom.

REFRAINING FROM IDEALIZING YOUR PARENTS OR BEING OVERCRITICAL OF THEM

When you were very small, you were lovable, but if your parents could not express their love for you, you grew up feeling the opposite: that you were somehow unlovable. The child tends to see his parents as better than they really are and himself as bad, or unworthy of love. The child does this because he can't bear the truth that his parents are inadequate. That knowledge would leave him in a hopeless condition, so he chooses to assume that he is bad and that if he changes, they will love him. This keeps his hopes alive.

However, by idealizing your parents, by keeping an image of their being better and more loving than they really were, you necessarily have to keep your own negative self-image. You may carry this negative image and feeling of being unlovable with you all your life if you are not aware of this process. You will also never realize that there are people who can be more loving than your parents were.

It is also harmful to be overly critical of your parents and to blame them and feel revengeful for what they "did to you." Hatred of your parents bends you out of shape emotionally, just as much as idealizing them. Don't lead a life of blame and retribution. Rather, choose a life of understanding. Try to use your knowledge of the fact that you may be imitating the defense of one or both of your parents, or that certain events damaged you at critical points in your life, to get out of your habitual patterns of reliving the past.

5. *Breaking Destructive Bonds*

A bond is a fantasy of a permanent connection which you originally formed with your parents and now extend to significant people in your life. These illusions of connection serve to deaden you against pain and anxiety but virtually destroy you as a feeling person. Thus, it is vital to give up this destructive style of relating to those people who play a significant part in your life.

It is almost inevitable that couples who once felt mutual love and affection sooner or later form a bond with each other that cuts off the genuine feelings and substitutes a fantasy of love. Most of the couples whose stories are told in this book have been in a bond at one time or another. A popular song of the forties expresses the concept of a bond in poignant terms:

> Alone from night to night you'll find me,
> Too weak to break the chains that bind me.
> I need no shackles to remind me.
> I'm just a prisoner of love.
>
> What's the good of my caring, if someone is sharing
> Those arms with me?
> Although he has another, I can't have another,
> For I'm not free.

A bond is similar to an addiction. It is a dependency on another person for a sense of security that is actually false. There is a strong belief that your happiness depends totally on the other person. In addition, there is an implicit agreement between the two people to protect the defense system of the other, to never intrude (in the good sense of the word) on certain problem areas within the other's psyche.

Breaking a bond does not mean breaking up a relationship; on the contrary, it may lead to more closeness. It will help bring back the real feeling that was once between you.

Recognizing the symptoms of a bond that exist in your own current relationship provides very valuable information. If you identify the symptoms and understand the process of forming a bond, you have already made a major step in breaking these ties. You no longer need to feel futile about changing it for the better.

AVOIDING THE IMPULSE TO MERGE WITH
SOMEONE FOR SECURITY

If you feel like "a part" of the other person, the attraction you originally felt will be diminished to a considerable degree. If there is too much "togetherness" in your marriage or relationship, try doing more things independently. Many couples have felt a renewed and separate interest in each other after they returned from separate vacations. It is important to maintain a separate identity even while you are close. The idea of overlapping rather than merging or togetherness is important. You overlap with each other to the extent that you have real interests in common. You don't try to impose your interests on the other, and the other person respects your boundaries, too. Each individual has separate and clear-cut boundaries. We can empathize and identify with others, but each person is alone, was born on his own, and will die on his own.

MAKING UNREALISTIC COMMITMENTS ABOUT
FEELINGS IS DAMAGING

Don't try to promise that you will love someone forever. Love is a feeling that comes and goes, is weak or strong, depending on many variables. You can express a desire to be associated with another person for a lifetime without giving a false promise of love and guaranteed emotional security. You can stay out of fantasy about your feelings by being open in your communication, especially about negative feelings. Ask your mate to be honest about his feelings and perceptions about you, and don't punish him for what you hear. Explore sensitive areas in each other, areas in which you may have been damaged early in life.

Strive to "let the other person be," and love him for what he is. In the beginning of your relationship, you were both free and nonrestrictive of each other. Attempt to maintain or revive the spirit of those early times. Living up to the expectations and demands of the roles of a "husband" or "wife" is very detrimental; just be yourselves with each other. You can be compassionate about the other's faults, knowing that you have faults, too. All of us can struggle to overcome our resistance to real love and niceness and refrain from fault finding, blaming, disrespect, or building each other's vanity. Realize that your basic problem is in yourself and that the solution also lies within each of you. Breaking bonds can be a painful process, but it is well worth the struggle to reestablish an independent and mutually respectful love relationship.

6. Learning the Various Aspects of Your Vanity

Vanity represents a fantasized superior image of yourself which you imagine you cannot live without. You can live a more vital, realistic life without your vanity. Without a continual buildup of your vanity by yourself or by others, you will know what your real strengths and weaknesses are. If you realize that what you previously thought built you up and made you feel good is actually what has really torn you down, then you will have made a lot of progress toward giving up your vanity.

It is vital to your development to avoid flattery and exaggerated compliments. If your parents praised you for talent, special performances, looks, or athletic ability, you may still feel a need for this kind of treatment. You may have been built up to think much better of yourself in some areas than you really were. You can figure out if you are still subtly trying to get praise from others and refrain from attempting to elicit it. You will be far more relaxed around other people if you are not searching for flattery and approval.

Instead of praise, ask for real feedback from trusted friends. If you hear some constructive criticism, don't bother feeling terrible and hating yourself. You can use the information to change these undesirable behaviors or traits. It is impossible to begin to change things about yourself if they are covered by the buildup of vanity. Seeing yourself without the protection of vanity is a valuable process that can lead to positive changes in you.

In your relationships you don't need to be preferred at all times.

Permanent, all-encompassing preferences are unreal. Think about how much you already get from the one you love, not what he is not giving you. There are times when you will want the company of someone other than your mate and times that your mate will feel the same. Vanity is protected by the lie that husbands and wives always prefer each other. You can live more freely without that lie.

Giving up vanity will help you get rid of the unconscious pressure to perform. Your inner voice has a part in creating a pressure to perform in areas that are close to your ego, such as your career, sex, creativity, and athletic ability. First, the inner voice builds you up and tells you how great you are. You become tense because then you are expecting "great" things of yourself. You have a greater chance of failing because of this tenseness, and if you fail, the voice tears you apart with criticism. Relaxing and being yourself is more valuable, especially during sex, which is a loving activity, not a performance.

7. *Rejecting the Child-Victim Role*

Once you give up the idea that you are the passive victim of fate and that things always happen to you, you will be able to gain real control over your life in ways you had not thought possible. You will be giving up control of others through manipulating their guilt and other negative emotions. You will now be taking a chance on going after what you want without using old techniques of sulking, whining, pretending to be helpless or powerless, or other manifestations of negative power. You will respect yourself and know that what you get in the way of personal satisfaction is rightfully deserved.

If you have negative thoughts toward the people who are close to you, reveal them openly but not angrily or manipulatively and reaffirm your friendship by not acting out these thoughts or angry feelings against them. There is a crucial distinction between thoughts or feelings and actions. You may think the most angry, even murderous, thoughts and still be a loving person as long as you refrain from any action that expresses these thoughts. You can feel tremendous irrational anger toward someone you love, yet still not act in any way that would cause the other person hurt or pain.

It is important to be sensitive about the kinds of behavior and words that could possibly be abusive to the people close to you. Sarcasm, "humorous" ridicule, condescending remarks, jealous sulking, and a myriad of more subtle expressions of hostility can be eliminated from your behavior. Take full responsibility for your feelings.

8. Being Aware of Your Aversion to Nice Treatment and Learning to Increase Your Tolerance of It

One of the basic concepts presented in this book is that most people have a difficult time dealing with good experiences or with anyone caring deeply for them. Most people are also very resistant to the idea that they were disturbed in their families or that they suffered pain in their childhood. These two ideas are interrelated.

If most people reject a better life and nice treatment from others, and it seems from all my evidence that they do, then it necessarily follows that they were hurt and that they built up a defense against this hurt. If people hadn't suffered pain in their early lives, then they wouldn't need or have reason to reject a warm response or a better experience today.

If you have suffered from feelings of rejection, being loved will cause you pain and anxiety. Sometimes when you strongly feel your love for someone, you can feel yourself becoming sad. Feeling his love for you could also make you feel sad. For example, a happy ending in a movie can cause tears to come to your eyes. There is pain and sadness attached to tender feelings, but it is questionable whether we would feel this pain if we had been consistently treated with sensitivity and love. Why would that loving feeling cause pain if love and warmth had always been there?

All of our defenses are forged early in life to protect us against the pains of childhood and are maintained to keep us from having a different experience of life, one that would make us see what really happened to us as children. Better treatment today, if we would let it intrude into our defenses, would trigger the old pain from long ago, pain we worked so hard to cut off.

Perversely, we all tend to punish those who again cause us to feel pain through their loving treatment. Often, we strongly hate the one we love the most. These feelings of hatred and anger are mostly unconscious, but they cause us to lash out in punishing ways. We are afraid of taking another chance on someone and risk being rejected again, so we may push away the other person before he has a chance to reject us.

You really can learn to gradually increase your tolerance of the feelings of pain, anxiety, and sadness and have love in your life. The rewards of a loving relationship far outweigh the anxiety you may feel.

9. Developing Open Friendship and Communication Has Therapeutic Value

Real friendship is a dynamic, honest communication with feelings of respect and compassion between people. In a friendship you give your views and the other person is encouraged to present his. You're interested in the other person's perceptions of you, and you talk about these personal opinions and perceptions without being punishing to each other. You don't dump your frustrations on your friend: You don't mix him into your suffering or your struggle. You take responsibility for your own anxieties and problems without making your friend a part of them.

What makes friendship special and therapeutic is principally the quality of the communication. There is no subject that is taboo to friends in their talking with each other.

Feelings and ideas are shared with compassion for the sensitive areas in each other's life. Perhaps you have talked with a friend at times, received good feedback and even an interpretation that was correct about you, but you have come away from that conversation feeling bad. If so, your friend may have analyzed you without feeling empathy or understanding or caring about you as a whole person. Being analyzed is like being cut into different parts and only understood in fragments.

If you have become alienated from each other, you can get close again by revealing what you are thinking to your friend. It is important to say any negative thoughts and feelings in a way that won't cause your friend to feel defensive. In other words, take full responsibility for your hostile or cynical thoughts and feelings, even if some of your criticisms have some basis in reality.

A REAL FRIENDSHIP IS A MUTUAL INTERDEPENDENCY INSTEAD OF A FALSE DEPENDENCY

In that sense, it stands in contrast to a bond. There is no connection in it. There is free choice and equality. A friendship is based on a strong desire to share your life with another person because you simply like being with him.

Many people have acquaintances but few have the kind of friendship which expresses all of the qualities which have therapeutic value to both parties. Some people have one or two trusted friends to whom they feel they can tell anything. These people should feel very appreciative toward one another for this kind of friendship; it is a rare thing.

FRIENDSHIP BETWEEN A MAN AND A WOMAN ON A DEEP LEVEL IS ONE OF THE MOST DIFFICULT KINDS OF RELATIONSHIPS TO MAINTAIN

This is especially true in terms of communication. Talking to each other about the sensitive area of their sexuality, where most men and women have been damaged and where each feels vulnerable and defensive, often makes the difference between progressive alienation or continued closeness. Dave related to me a story about how he and his wife, Rosemary, had helped each other through a difficult period sexually and how they became better friends in the process.

We started having trouble making love when Rosemary and I were trying to have a baby. She began to get nervous and many nights she said that she didn't want to make love. When we did make love, she was often tense and that made me lose my erection. I started to feel like I just didn't want to bother with it anymore, so we got into the habit of just going to bed and going straight to sleep.

But we both wanted to have a baby so much that we finally started talking about this problem. Believe me, sex was the last thing I wanted to talk about to Rosemary, even though I usually talked everything over with her. She's really a good listener and has good ideas about me and about other people, too. I guess I trusted her enough to start to say something about how I felt sexually with her, but I was so anxious that night I almost decided to forget the whole thing. I almost didn't talk.

We got into bed and I just said to her, "I feel really nervous right now. I knew before I came to bed that I wanted to talk about why we don't make love very much anymore, but I don't know where to start. I feel like I don't want to go through the work of making love to you because it hasn't been very good lately, but I also know that I love you and want to share having a baby with you. I don't know what to do, though, to make things better between us sexually. But I really want to talk about it."

Rosemary started crying, but she said she didn't feel bad, just relieved that I had said what I did. She told me that she had felt tense for the last two months, since she stopped taking the Pill, because she didn't know if she would be able to get pregnant. She was worried that if she didn't have an orgasm, then she wouldn't get pregnant. . . . Intellectually, she knew that idea was foolish. But she still worried.

We both decided that when we came to bed we would just talk about whether we were anxious or not, and then see what we wanted to do. I also told her about being afraid of losing my erection. We talked about some of the strange ideas we had learned about sex when we were growing up. I really found out so much about Rosemary from those conversations at night. I felt so close to her and she to me. We made love that night and it was nicer than it had been in a long time. I felt as close to her that night as I did in the beginning of our relationship.

Dave and Rosemary continued to be close friends during these months. Their communication was close and it served to get them past their defensive fears of sex and pregnancy.

In talking with each other, good friends tend not to interrupt. Instead, they try to draw each other out. They are not approving or disapproving, not overly intrusive into each other's lives, not punishing for anything that is said.

In a real friendship you will experience a sense of your own separateness and individuality when you are exceptionally close to another person. It is paradoxical that in a friendship with deep love, compassion, and concern, we feel the most aware of our own aloneness and our own death. We feel that we have something to lose when we have a good friend. We fear the loss of that friend if we begin to care deeply for him.

Having the opportunity to be generous and giving to another person is very therapeutic. It leads to an anti-inward posture. If your friend means a lot to you, the natural impulse to share with him and to be giving of yourself and your possessions can be felt and expressed. It is a good practice to give of yourself any time that you feel caught up in self-hatred or self-criticism. It is one of the best antidotes for feeling inward and depressed. Learn to be generous with your time, your interest, and your material things. Sharing your innermost thoughts also breaks into your inward, secretive world.

IT IS IMPORTANT TO SHARE REAL-LIFE ACTIVITIES WITH A FRIEND

One cannot have a friendship in a vacuum. The activity doesn't necessarily have to be a project or a job; it can simply be standing together and sharing the appreciation of a sunset; it can be sharing ideas with each other; it can be an ongoing, deep interest in people; it can be almost anything as long as the two friends are equal. They may not be on the same level in skill or intelligence or knowledge of the activity, but they are equal in the sense of the absence of any parent-child roles in relation to each other.

If you ever have the occasion to need more professional help than your friend is qualified to offer, you may want to seek a therapist who has the same qualities as a real friend, plus professional expertise. This kind of psychotherapist would be nondefensive, have a nonjudgmental attitude, and be compassionate and honest in his communications with you. He should possess all of these qualities in addition to his specialized knowledge.

Developing a real friendship is a major step toward becoming a whole person.

10. Facing Your Own Death as a Reality in Your Life . . . Giving Each Day Importance and Meaning

Just as it is well worth it to risk becoming attached to someone you love, it is also worth it to become attached to your life, even though you are going to lose it in the end. Many people feel foolish on a deep level when they are excited and enthusiastic about life. They feel like suckers to value their lives so much, when their lives are going to be taken away from them at some time in the future, and they don't even know when it will happen. Their end is totally out of their control and they deeply resent this fact.

The Core of the Defense System, the One Basic Terror We All Defend Against, Is the Fear of Taking Another Chance on Life, on Loving Someone Again, and on Letting Someone Love Us. Because of the ways we were hurt in our childhood, some of us very deeply, we are fearful and extremely hesitant to be vulnerable again to rejection and hurt. Because we have anxiety about dying, about losing our own lives, we often pass our lives in indifference, cynicism, and detachment from real experiences. These two fears become confused in our minds, but they are related. In denying the basic terror of our own life ending someday, we often fear instead the loss of someone we love through being rejected. This fear of rejection stems from the emotional wounds we experienced in our upbringing by our parents.

Everything we do in life is determined by how we handle these basic fears. If we try to deny our death, we defend ourselves against living fully. If we face the fact of our death, we experience anxiety and life.

The thesis of this book is that it is far better to face this anxiety and this fear and to live a brave life. It is worthwhile to be totally involved participants in life rather than onlookers and observers.

There is no cure for the underlying fear and anger concerning the human condition, i.e., feeling attached to your life, to your own body, to your loved ones, all of which you are certain to lose in the long run. We simply need to face the nature of life realistically. However, you don't need to dwell morbidly on your inevitable death. It is far better to use this realization to make yourself cognizant of valuable time.

TAKE A CHANCE ON BEING A SUCKER,
LIVE YOUR LIFE FULLY

There's nothing better to do with your precious, fleeting moments. Wasting time in the half-alive state of protective measures erected against the realities of your life and death can doom you to a conventional, boring existence. Become more independent and live from your own point of view. Don't waste your time and your days in defensive maneuvers and trivial pursuits.

17

Critique of Traditional Psychotherapy

T HERE ARE A WIDE VARIETY OF SCHOOLS of thought affecting how psychological principles and theories are applied to the problems of human suffering. All have reported successes and failures. In addition to the efforts of dedicated professionals, there have been numerous offers of false hope and easy cures from other less than reliable sources. There is no simple and easy mechanical solution to human ills and psychological pain. However, people have developed and will continue to develop methods and theories to further enlighten us in the area of psychotherapy.

Personal Limitations of the Therapist

One of the major limitations to good psychotherapy is the therapist's own defense system. Often, this defense system is supported by the methods, theory, and systems he chooses to apply in his practice. Although expert in the field of human relations, the therapist is still a person with his own fears and limitations. Like other people, he may be cut off from his own personal feelings and may also be unwilling to make contact with that side of himself. The therapist who is cut off from his own feelings cannot fully feel with and experience his patient. Also, to the extent that the therapist has a stake in preserving his own personal defense system, he will have a stake in keeping the patient from achieving feelings and insight in those areas of his life. He will provide the same sort of interpersonal environment that the person experienced in his home where his defense system and subsequent neurosis originated.

Nicole originally entered therapy hoping to find help in forming some kind of lasting relationship with a man. A beautiful woman and highly intelligent, she found herself in her late twenties still single and dissatisfied with her life. Nicole was a warm, friendly person and very popular with men, but so far no man had expressed an interest in marrying her. At those times when Nicole was involved in two relationships, she felt guilty because of her religious background.

Nicole's therapist, although free thinking intellectually, was timid and shied away from this subject matter. When Nicole spoke of her religious upbringing and her resulting guilt about premarital sex and about her relationships, the therapist remained strangely silent in contrast to his usual style. At a deeper level, however, this therapist felt guilty about sex himself, yet he was removed from this guilt by his clinical attitudes toward sex and the human body. He could not discuss the delicate subject of sex in depth or in a nonclinical way with his attractive patient because of his own unconscious guilt.

Because of the therapist's nonresponse and noninterpretation of this area, both Nicole and he avoided confronting their guilt and fears about this subject. In fact, she picked up on his hidden shame and constricting attitudes, which further strengthened her feeling of guilt and wrongdoing.

Therapy can often become a case of the blind leading the blind. Therapists are no more likely than anyone else to be socially aware, perceptive, and sensitive to people. In fact, often people in other professions may be more immediately perceptive about human beings than some psychologists. Indeed, some therapists tend to misinterpret as an abnormality rather than a positive sign of change much of what their patients experience freely in the way of feeling.

The Traditional Therapist's View of the Defense System

When a patient first comes to therapy of his own volition, it is usually because there is a break in his defense system that is causing much discomfort and distress. At this point he is actually getting better, not worse. For some reason the person is feeling some of the pain and anxiety that he had previously managed to cut off by his defense system. Very often, the traditional therapist attempts to relieve the pain and avoid it instead of encouraging the patient to experience his feelings.

Henry's wife had been dead six months when his physician recommended that he enter psychotherapy because of his deepening depression. After the first few sessions, Henry began to approach some of the deep feelings that he had repressed following the shock of his wife's death. "You know, Doctor, I feel so guilty because I often wished that Margo would go away and leave me alone. About a year ago I had a nightmare in which she was killed in an airplane crash. In the dream I was free to marry anyone I wanted. I felt great and terrible at the same time. I've never thought about my own death before, but now I have so much anxiety that something will happen to me. It's an uncontrollable feeling."

As Henry was talking he became more and more intensely emotional. It was obvious that he was getting close to feeling some of the real pain and guilt associated with the death of his wife. At this point, however, Henry's therapist interrupted: "Henry, your feeling is really not uncontrollable. It feels so intense to you because of the grief you are still experiencing. Thoughts about death are common during this phase of working through your grief. You also seem to have a lot of guilt about hostile feelings toward your wife while she was alive. Do you recall any times when you experienced this hostility as a child toward one of your parents?"

The therapist's premature attempt to find structure and meaning in Henry's emotional condition interrupted a deep release of feeling that would have led Henry to his own personal insight into his life experiences and present-day trauma. He was able to avoid feelings of anxiety within himself by unconsciously cutting into his patient's flow of feelings. Henry's choice of a psychotherapist had been unfortunate. Despite his excellent reputation and financial success, Henry's therapist was well defended against feeling deeply about his own personal life. He had caused Henry to once again suppress his feelings and put up his defenses. In this way he unintentionally caused Henry to become more alienated from himself, which was this patient's basic problem to begin with. This therapist supported his patient's defense system, thus strengthening his neurosis.

The central issue is how the therapist views the patient's defense system. This will determine how respectful of the patient he is, how much he cares for people, and how much he will contribute to his patient's growth and sense of aliveness.

Therapists often make interpretations based on their own defense system. They have their own fears and their own resistances. They don't necessarily want to see the ways in which they're repeating patterns, the ways in which they are holding back or denying love, the ways in which they are destructive. They don't necessarily want to see what happened to them in their families or to recognize the damage that they are doing to their own children and even to their patients, especially in the stereotyped role-playing behavior that occurs in many therapies.

Dr. M. had been practicing psychotherapy for fifteen years with good success. Elderly patients with psychosomatic symptoms were often greatly improved after a few months in therapy with him. He received numerous referrals from local physicians because of his high rate of success with this particular type of patient. These older patients did not threaten Dr. M.'s defense in any major way, but another group of patients did—younger people.

Dr. M. was unintentionally destructive with his younger patients who exhibited more obvious emotional pain and distress than did his older, more insulated patients. This wasn't true in all his cases, but it was a fact that many of these younger patients were more alive, more rebellious, more volatile than the older ones. In one discussion group the teenagers began to talk very openly about their interactions with their parents. Dr. M. often chose these times to make long interpretations based on his theoretical orientation. These contributions served to slow down the tempo of the group and also took the edge off the emotion in these discussions.

Dr. M. had grown up in a restrictive environment and had never faced his own feelings of rebelliousness and dislike of the rigidity of his parents. In his present family he played the role of the father who could do no wrong, and he could tolerate very little disagreement from his children. Thus, Dr. M. had a blind spot which hindered his effectiveness with a wide range of people. He had become used to playing the role of father to his young patients. The aliveness, spontaneity, and emotion in the teenage discussion group threatened to cause him pain, so he unconsciously cut off their expression to protect himself.

Therapists generally recognize the destructive effects of trauma in a person's life history and subsequent personality development, but often they do not fully recognize that positive occurrences and favorable events are equally threatening to the defense system. There is not enough awareness of how deeply people have incorporated the defense systems of their parents and how desperately they refuse to live their lives without these defenses. There is an unwillingness to recognize the immensity of the underlying social pressure in our society and its impact on all of us. And there is a strong tendency not to see how terribly cut off people are from their feelings or how deeply cynical their hypotheses about life are when you get beneath the surface.

Professional Ethics and Allegience to Society

In the powerful play *Equus,* the psychiatrist, Dysert, is torn between his pledge to take away the pain and torment of his young patient, thus allowing him to return to society as a "safe," adjusted member, and his instinct to allow the boy to live with his pain, perhaps running the risk of turning a maladjusted, potentially dangerous person loose on society.* He chooses to blot out the pain and incidentally some of the most vital parts of the boy's personality rather than run a minor risk of harming society again.

This play depicted an extreme situation, but the psychiatrist's choice seemed typical: to cure the patient of his manifest symptoms and quickly readjust him to society, while leaving the core of the patient's neurosis intact. Dysert was tortured with guilt about the threats to the boy's spirit posed by the therapy. At one point Dysert cries out in anguish: "All right! I'll take it away! He'll be delivered from madness. What then? Do you think feelings like this can be simply reattached, like plasters? Stuck on to other objects we select?

* This type of threat is uncharacteristic of the typical therapy situation, but in other respects the analogy holds.

Look at him! . . . My desire might be to make this boy an ardent husband, a caring citizen, a worshipper of the abstract God. My achievement, however, is more likely to make a ghost . . ."

This play graphically illustrated the conflict that every therapist faces in his practice of psychotherapy. Professional ethics do protect the rights of the individual patient, but they are designed to protect him as a member of a group, of a larger entity—society. These ethics tend to protect the defense system of the individual and to facilitate his reentry and readjustment to society. However, society is representative of a pooling of all the defense systems of its individual members and as such supports and condones inward self-protective behaviors in all of us.

A therapist who places social conformity above the personal interests of his patient performs a great disservice. Just as the physician upholds the oath of Hippocrates, the therapist should be devoted to the cure of his patient above all other considerations, both personal and social.*

Dehumanizing Attitudes Toward the Patient

The slant and general tenor of the ethical codes of the profession, while rightfully protecting the patient from a therapist who might be manipulative or exploitative, is that a patient is weak, fragile, and in need of protection. This protective point of view about the patient subtly undermines his self-esteem. The tendency to regard a person as more helpless than he really is, more at the mercy of the therapist, gives a wrong feeling to the therapy. It implies that the person coming for therapy is inferior or childlike.

The medical model, which views the patient as ill or abnormal, is degrading to the person asking for help. Often the individual's "symptoms" are merely signs that his defenses are not working and that a stressful situation has provoked anxiety—which is often a sign of growth. To label these signs or symptoms as sick may be completely erroneous and may obscure the real problem. To approach

---

* There is one notable exception which applies to the condition where a patient could be considered to be physically harmful to himself or to other members of the community. Under no circumstances should he be allowed to act out violence on other persons or their property or upon himself.

a severely disturbed person as a "case" is extremely destructive to the patient and deeply interferes in the subsequent relationship between the doctor and the patient.

To assign a diagnostic label to an individual, even for the use or classification of the therapist or the insurance companies, is dehumanizing. It gives the person a distorted view of himself and encourages him to shrug off the responsibility for his pain and his life and to lay the blame on his "sickness."

It is in the area of marriage counseling that some of the most destructive work is done. Both persons in a couple are often seen as subordinate to the marital bond, yet it is exactly this type of bond that can be the most destructive element in the relationship. Many times marital counseling is directed toward strengthening bonds between individuals rather than helping them to be separate and independent persons. This is exactly the wrong kind of procedure because it further alienates both of them from themselves and eventually leads to more destruction in their relationship.

Instead of asking, "Can this marriage be saved?" one needs to ask, "Can these people be saved?" This does not mean that I am opposed to the institution of marriage. Quite the contrary, I feel that supporting individuals in breaking their bonds by exposing individual defenses is the only chance for people to experience close and genuine long-lasting relationships. However, many traditional therapies support togetherness instead of separateness and independence. The type of closeness they advocate is often more fantasy than real relating.

Of all the sources of mistruths about people and children, some of the worst offenders are the child-rearing books written by psychiatrists, physicians, and psychotherapists. They teach organized dishonesty and advocate role playing to an incredible degree. Parents are encouraged to hold out the promise of unconditional love by telling the child that his behavior is what is hated, never the child. These books teach parents what to say to their children when behavioral problems arise. However, they rarely stress the vital importance of actually stopping the child's misbehavior so that he will not grow into a manipulative, miserable adult.

The child-rearing model usually emphasizes the separation between adults and children. The child is viewed as a person to be manipulated. If he expresses views contrary to prevailing patterns in the family, many times he is not taken seriously or is even punished. Therapists can be guilty in this regard as well as parents.

Judith was sixteen when her parents sent her to a counselor. She had become progressively more unhappy during the previous year and was embarrassed that most of her girl friends were dating, yet she never had a date. After three sessions she began to relax and hesitantly talk about some of her thoughts about boys. The counselor encouraged her to say anything that she thought on any subject. Judith opened up even more and finally brought up one of the painful things that had been troubling her the most. She spoke of several times when she had rushed up to her father and hugged him when she was a small child, only to have him ridicule her affection.

As Judith related her embarrassment and humiliation from these events, she said, "I don't think my father wanted me to love him." When she began to cry, the counselor comforted her by saying, "I'm sure your father cares for you very much, but he might not know how to express it." Judith stopped cold, realizing that she was being sympathized with and that the counselor's words didn't ring true. She terminated therapy with him. Later, in psychotherapy, she repeated this story and explained that she couldn't tolerate the dishonest support.

This counselor's statement supported the myth that parents always love their children. Even though the counselor added the cliché that "he just didn't know how to express it," Judith knew that her sense of reality was being questioned. She closed up again and left treatment distrusting the whole process.

The whole emphasis on protecting the social process, which originally caused damage to the patient in the first place, is incorrect. The social conforming process is probably already one of the most destructive influences in a patient's life. In addition, religious teachings and philosophies in which the individual is taught that his innermost thoughts and feelings are dirty and bad are obviously detrimental to good mental health.

Yet technically, in relation to the ethical codes of our profession, these teachings can't be challenged. There is some leeway in practice regarding these matters; however, the ethical codes, procedures, and general approach to the patient that are taught in most clinical settings work against an honest one-to-one relationship which would permit maximum personal growth and help the person to feel for himself.

The procedure of introducing oneself as Dr. _____ and calling the person Mr. _____ rather than relating in a personal and equal manner is discriminating to the patient. These codes tend to limit the development of any real friendship between the patient and the therapist, yet the therapeutic value of friendship ranks high as a necessary factor for successful therapy, one that changes the patient's basic self-image.

Some Current Schools of Thought

Historically, psychoanalytical thought owes much to Freud's brilliant investigations into the unconscious mind, but Freud believed that defenses were necessary for an individual to live in society. Thus, according to psychoanalytical thought, some defenses are necessary for the person to function as a social being in a society. This supports the view that psychological defenses are essentially adaptive.

Recently, Arthur Janov made an important contribution to the subject of defenses. He discovered a more direct road to the unconscious. He described and implemented methods to facilitate the expression of a "primal," a deep emotional release that offered relief from tension and led to clear and penetrating personal insights. The information and interpretations coming from the patient himself during primals tend to support much of psychoanalytic theory.

Janov, in contrast to Freud, however, felt entirely different about defenses. He felt that defenses are unnecessary to the fully feeling person and in fact they are what cause the neurotic patient to feel tense and remain alienated from his feelings. He felt that defenses are a protection against feeling primal pain and that only through repeated expression and release could this reservoir of underlying pain be emptied and the patient cured of neurosis. It has been my experience, however, that the primal "pool of pain," as Janov termed the repressed emotional pains from childhood, cannot be drained and that repeated primal sessions will not necessarily alter an individual's basic style of defense.

The behaviorist school, with its theoretical basis in learning theory, has had an important function in education and psychological theory, but the learning model falls short of doing justice to the complex process of neurosis. Applying the learning models of conditioning to change a particular form of destructive behavior can be a valuable tool in the treatment of a person whose behavior is seriously damaging to himself and others. However, to apply this model to the whole spectrum of human suffering without taking into account the origins of the defensive behaviors and the underlying pain is not to perceive the patient as the full, complicated, feeling person he really is. To treat a symptom—fear, for example—as an entity instead of treating a person who is fearful is reductionistic and divides the person into fragments.

Because of their own defenses, bonds, etc., many proponents of other current therapies underestimate the damaging effects of the defense system to the individual's total existence. Instead, most of them tend to compartmentalize the person by emphasizing aspects of his personality or functions, his behavior, his philosophy, his search for meaning, his feelings. They underemphasize or completely neglect the fact that only through breaking neurotic bonds and defenses and establishing real friendship and equality can a person make contact with himself as a feeling person.

An individual can develop only by opening himself up to new experiences and through taking a chance again on getting close to others. A person cannot develop unless he really challenges the voice, that incorporated pattern of thought that runs his self-limiting, withholding life-style. He can improve if he is willing to move away from repetitive patterns, painkillers, and rituals and an inward style of life characterized by heavy dependence on self-nourishing fantasies. Most important, he will improve if he is willing to challenge his own resistance to change at crucial points in his therapy.

Neurotic Resistance

The essential problem of neurosis is in a person's life-style. It lies in his resistance to a better life, in his repetition of destructive patterns, in his basic withholding, in his listening to the voice, and in his incorporation of the parental ways of blocking out feelings. These defenses are not easily shattered even though most therapies attempt some penetration of the system. If the defense system is left intact, even though some symptoms are relieved and some changes made, the person will find other ways of cutting off and returning to a nonfeeling state.

If the methods and approaches to psychotherapy ultimately fail, it is because they don't successfully overcome the problems of resistance in therapy. The resistance to therapy is the same as the resistance to changing actual life patterns.

A therapist must fully appreciate the extent of a person's fear of a better life, his resistance to real friendship and equality, his need to maintain an inward system, and his basic style of self-protection. To a great extent traditional therapies fail to help a person to recover his feelings and to value himself as a person because they do not adequately challenge the life-style and behavior patterns that prevent pain and also maintain the neurosis.

The major problem in any therapy is that the individual is unwilling, because of his fear and guilt, to alter his defense system. He refuses to break symbolically with the people who played a part in the formation of this system: his family. The patient's resistance also centers around protecting himself from the terror of separation from his family and their incorporated voices and finally against facing his basic anxiety relating to separation and death.

The only way that neurosis can approach cure is by changing the defense system in the person's actual life, in his ongoing life outside the therapy office. Naturally, there is the greatest resistance to any therapy that directly challenges the defense system. Some people will leave therapy when they feel a threat to their deepest resistance. They sense what giving up certain defenses will mean in the light of how they live their everyday lives.

Dale was a wealthy young man who was beginning to get ahead in the motion picture industry. He came to therapy because of certain physical symptoms and a general feeling of boredom and emotional dullness. Dale was a name dropper and a phony person —charming, entertaining, and flashy. He felt that his personality was the reason for his success so far in show business. After several months of therapy, in one deeply emotional session he experienced the truth of what he was. "I'm a phony, I don't feel a thing, I just bullshit. I can't stand the way I am. I hate myself for being fake."

Following this important session and these insights about himself, Dale realized that he wanted to change the way that he was and feel like a real person instead of a fake. He wanted to feel his own feelings the way he had felt them in the session and not continue the kinds of acts which he put on for his friends and business acquaintances.

However, he also very quickly realized what this change would mean to him in terms of altering his life-style. Dale realized that he was always playing to an audience, even offscreen. He knew that he loved the praise, the parties, the Hollywood life. He was terrified that if he got rid of his phoniness he would have nothing, that he wouldn't be entertaining, that he would lose his popularity. Dale will never know if all these outcomes would have occurred. He left therapy long before he started changing. His resistance became activated long before he tampered very much with his defense structure.

Dale had been too frightened to live without a defense that to him seemed necessary to his survival. Everyone has the same kinds of fears that Dale had. We have found that people who challenge their destructive voice more and more directly become afraid. However, a person who has the courage to expose his innermost negative thoughts and discover how he hurts himself and others with his basic defensive process can achieve real independence and good feelings.

As a struggling person moves toward change, as he moves toward surpassing or developing beyond his family, he will undergo anxiety, and he will feel guilty about breaking the chain that binds him to generations of family history. The more a person values his life and has personal feelings about his life and the more he breaks away from his past and leads his own life, the more he will feel about himself as a person, both separate and alone.

I think the fundamental problem with psychotherapy is that both the therapist and the patient shy away from the challenge of breaking neurotic bonds and defenses; even if they don't, there is considerable difficult work to be done.

Successful Psychotherapy

As I said earlier, all therapies challenge the defense system to some degree and have some success and some value. However, there are certain characteristics of a therapeutic process that I value and would term "good" therapy. Successful therapy sensitively challenges the defense system and helps the person to feel. It helps people to break bonds and destructive dependencies. A good therapeutic process supports the truth and places it above any form of protecting false assumptions about the family, society, and people. It exposes the incorporated destructive voice and challenges it. A successful therapy comes from a respectful, equal interaction between the patient and the therapist and not from a superior-inferior role interaction.

Even in this good therapy, it is difficult to assess how far people will choose to go in their own development. And some patients improve even in "bad" therapy. They use the time and effort involved in talking about themselves to really change their patterns.

Personal Qualities of the Therapist That Are Conducive to Good Therapy

Even in very good therapy with a therapist who is understanding, sensitive, and highly capable, the patient may very well choose to protect his defense system rather than make changes in his life. Nevertheless, there are several dimensions and characteristics of a good therapist that can be stated.

To offer real assistance to his patients, the ideal therapist would be a person of unusual personal honesty and integrity. He would be sensitive and emotional toward himself and others. While strong in his optimism and belief in the possibility of personal growth and change, he would also be aware of the powerful resistance to change in his patients. He would not underestimate the strength of a person's defense system and would be sensitive to the fear underlying the resistance.

The therapist's personal life is very important because if a therapist is defensive in his personal life, he will necessarily be limited in the amount of help he is able to offer his patients. The good therapist would be just as aware and alive in his outside life as inside the office. With his patients and with his personal friends and family, he would be direct and nonmanipulative.

The good therapist would not only have completed the full training necessary for professional licensing and have proceeded through his own personal analysis or psychotherapy but he would be discerning in his choice of therapeutic techniques. He would comprehend the seriousness of the neurotic process and how widespread it is in our culture. He would not set himself apart from his patients as one who is completely "cured" of his own neurosis but would show his patients by his own behavior how to struggle against resistance and how to live less defensively. He would have compassion and respect for the person who is striving to live a better life and be able to predict at what points this person will meet the most resistance within himself.

In other words, he would have to know his patients' innermost feelings and fantasies and be sensitive to their unique methods and defenses. He would be open to new ideas and real experiences in each therapy session. He would be nondefensive about his mistakes and blind spots. Most important, he would be friendly and strive for an equal interaction with his patients.

If you find a therapist approaching these characteristics, you have an excellent opportunity to develop. He would be an unusual person, a strong and genuine human being. All of us in the profession of psychotherapy would do well to devote ourselves to the development of these personal qualities.

18

Denying Death—The Ultimate Defense

IN A FUNDAMENTAL SENSE the core of our defense centers around our anxiety about our lives ending. In fact, our own death, the total finality of this resolution, may fill us with terror if we look at it without our customary defenses. One wants to turn away from a life that is temporary and so obviously limited. The more that we value our lives, the more we have to lose. The choice then becomes one of either turning away from life because of its temporary quality or using the fact of our finite existence and certain death to enhance and give special meaning to our lives and the lives of others.

Solutions and pseudosolutions to the problem of death abound in our culture. Systems of belief have been built to deal with this reality. The fear of death is universal, but it is well hidden under elaborate belief systems and the individual defenses of all of us.

Much human activity is shaped by a desperate attempt to avoid the reality of death. Yet the fear of it haunts us as nothing else can.

Primitive peoples often celebrated death, but they usually held the belief that death was something akin to a promotion to a higher form of life, where one would enjoy eternity in an elevated position. Modern belief systems are usually more sophisticated versions of this belief. It is true that these beliefs could be valid. It may turn out that an afterlife does exist, but from our vantage point there is only uncertainty about the possibility of life after death. When these beliefs are used to deny our dread of death and to avoid the fact that these are tragic dimensions to our human condition, the belief transforms itself into a defense, which in turn is destructive to the individual.

Many atheists and other philosophers who affirm strong beliefs denying God often give a religious flavor to their philosophies and become defensive about their own personal beliefs. Some philosophers who have advocated radical social changes while attacking organized religion for offering false comfort have gone on to make similar claims for their own utopian views.

These beliefs do help allay some of the anxiety about dying, but the cost to the individual is tremendous. Whatever form of denial he uses, he cuts into his present-day experience to an enormous degree. In saving his soul he loses his body. He limits and restricts his life in a desperate trade-off—the hope to hold on to an everlasting life. The tragic figure of man becomes pathetic in the face of this denial.

Activities that may serve to give man dignity assume a quality of quiet desperation when used to avoid the idea of death. The belief that one's immortality may be assured through the perpetuation of creative works motivates many highly creative people. The desire to have sons to pass on the family name is another way to deny the despair that someday we will no longer be here. Acquisition of possessions, donations to charities in commemoration of our presence on this earth, beliefs that support the existence of something larger than ourselves—God, our country, any cause célèbre—all of these, while inherently good, may be used as parts of a monumental denial of this one terrible fact of human existence.

The presence of death is well hidden in our society. We are mostly removed from the routine contact with death that was available to our grandfathers. Animals whose flesh we consume aren't slaughtered in our presence, yet in the recent past our elders, many of whom lived on farms, were exposed to this reminder of death.

When we talked of the subject of death in one of our therapy groups, a young woman named Marjorie was obviously touched with sadness. She told us she had never thought about this subject before. Listening to others talk of death made her life seem ridiculous and trivial to her—the way she lived alone in a beautifully decorated apartment, the way she went from party to party searching for the right man, the empty contacts she made at the television studio where she worked, the endless treadmill of activities she used to fill up her hours and days, her longing for novel excitements to make her feel "high."

Her daily existence came into sharp focus during the short hour as we talked. This woman, who had been totally unaware that there was anything to think about in relation to her own death, was suddenly struck by the hard truths of her own life.

People who live in a way as to deny their own death often lead a trivial existence, as Marjorie did. When we attempt to deny the fact of death, we overreact to petty frustrations, we get caught up in efforts to hold on to a youthful appearance, we perform a multitude of unimportant acts to keep ourselves occupied so that we won't have time for quiet reflection on our lives. We become vain and set ourselves apart from other people so as not to feel our powerlessness against this inevitable end. We become cynical to avoid caring for our lives.

If our lives begin to go well, if we start to obtain long-worked-for goals, then the fear of death may erupt through our defense system. One sophisticated psychologist experienced a recurring nightmare of being trapped by death with no way out. He usually woke from this brief nightmare struggling physically and agonizingly to free himself of this inevitable trap. He felt imprisoned with the feeling of certainty of the end to his conscious existence. He felt terrified by the ending of his life and the agony of eternal nothingness, an ending he saw as inescapable. This dream only occurred when things were going extremely well in this man's life, when he was the most happy and excited about his life. During the dream, he experienced intense rage at his ultimate predicament. Paradoxically, he usually felt better and more in touch with his feelings in the days following his nightmares.

The human being is a superstitious creature in that he often believes that bad events follow good events, almost without exception. "The ax is bound to fall" if a sustained period of happiness has gone by. These superstitions may very well stem from a deep knowledge that we are indeed trapped by a "bad" ending, that no matter how fulfilling our life may be, we are going to lose it in the end. This superstition may be only the tip of the iceberg of fear, which we keep so well submerged.

It has been noted that nightmares appear in childhood with relative frequency after a certain age. It has been assumed that such nightmares are an expression of the child's unconscious fear of abandonment by his parents. This understanding may be partly true, but it may also be true that young children do become acutely aware of death at a certain age and repress it later. They first become afraid of their parents' death, then they may become increasingly conscious that they, too, have to die sometime. The fear of death is initially related to the fear of losing one's parents and remains closely associated symbolically with fear of loss of other important objects.

Years ago a young patient of mine, Leora, was on the road to health following a long struggle against intractable asthma, which had threatened her life. She told me, "Now that I'm feeling better, I'll probably get hit by a truck." Leora's story began in an atmosphere of despair.

They sent her home to die because there was nothing more that the hospital could do for her. Her death was imminent. She was eleven years old and had severe intractable asthma. She had been sent to a research center in Denver that accepted only the most serious cases and was often successful in helping children because of a unique and powerful medical and psychological approach.

A primary part of the treatment was to separate the children from their parents for a two-year period. During this time only two brief visits with loved ones were permitted. Somehow, the separation and the diminution of psychological stress were very valuable and some of the children improved immediately upon separation, despite the loneliness and hardship of the drastic "parentectomy." This unique method combined with good care and expert medical attention seemed to turn the trick—but not for Leora. The staff was still unable to control her symptoms after a year and a half. In fact, Leora was frail and dying and the situation seemed totally hopeless. Everyone felt that the best thing was to send her home to her family to spend what little time was left to her in normal surroundings.

Incidentally, she and I were leaving the institution at about the same time. I had just finished my training there and was about to start private practice in Los Angeles. Leora was from that city and they wanted me to continue her psychotherapy when she arrived home.

After consulting with her therapist in Denver, I prepared for Leora's first visit. My heart was pounding as I opened the door to the waiting room of my new office. I saw a very anxious little girl who looked very unhappy and who captured my imagination. I was ready to love her, I suppose, and to fight for her.

I became immediately involved that first session. I felt compassion for her terrible plight and could not accept the reality of her approaching death. I knew that I would do everything to avert that situation and felt that I was going to know her for a long time.

"Hello, Leora. I really want to meet you and to get to know you."

"Yeah, but— (wheezing) —what's the good of it—I've talked to—so many doctors, the hospital."

Her asthmatic symptoms scared me and I felt uncomfortable, like each breath might be her last. "Look, maybe it will be different here." "You'll follow me to the hospital and then to the grave," she declared.

I was chilled by the depths of her despair during those initial weeks. There was little hope or desire in her to live. She really wanted to die and wished to be released from her psychological as well as physical suffering.

As the months passed Leora began to talk of her secret world, her fantasies of being adopted, her suffering. And then the anger came and the wheezing stopped for the most part. Leora was angry at everything: her parents, me, her little sister. The internalized anger and self-hate began to flow in another direction—outward—and it splattered all over the place. She became a real bitch and her mother got very angry with her and insisted that she answer her with "Yes, mother dear" or choke. Very often Leora obliged. But as the anger came out, she began to feel better. However, this was not a smooth and continuous process. There were periods of regression and anxiety followed by remorse and depression and sometimes serious attacks requiring hospitalization and emergency treatment. But there was a general uphill trend in Leora's physical health.

More time passed and Leora and I had developed a good working relationship. During one stage she was enormously compulsive and ritualistic, planning her entire day and scheduling everything to the smallest detail. These routines reduced her anxiety about the sexual feelings she was beginning to experience as a young adolescent. She was much troubled at this time because she was jealous and competitive with her younger sister, who was more developed physically. Leora continued to be very small and underdeveloped for her age because of medications and this was very painful for her. As the years passed, Leora became relatively well and symptom free and her compulsive period passed. It was at this point that she made the remark about being hit by a truck.

There was an important and serious problem that we faced. The medication that had saved Leora's life many times when she had severe asthma attacks had perversely created many side effects. Repeated administration of large amounts of cortisone typically causes the adrenal cortex to atrophy, which can eventually lead to death.

We struggled with this problem for a long time and finally got Leora weaned from the drug. She was leading a somewhat normal life. It seemed as though a miracle was happening, and all of us involved felt optimistic. But our joy was short lived.

Suddenly, in the late afternoon one day, I got a call from the hospital. Leora had taken ill and her mother put her on the phone. Leora was screaming for help and was hysterically yelling, "Help me, I want to live, I don't want to die." She appeared in extreme agony and her voice pained me deeply.

I raced to the hospital and burst into her room, but all was quiet. She lay there silent and blue. She had just died. I sit here with tears streaming down my face as I remember that moment. I wanted to kiss her goodbye. When I had met her many years ago she had wanted to die, and now she had died an agonizing death screaming that she wanted to live.

My long experience with this young girl affected me greatly and made me more aware of the deep cynicism in all of us about the fate that waits for us. We feel extremely hesitant to become attached to a life that we are bound to lose sooner or later. We all face the same human condition. We are all of us tragic creatures because we are locked in a body which grows old and dies. Humans are the only animals that are aware of their own end and this is a genuinely sad aspect of the human condition. The only condition more pathetic than this is the attempt to deny the fact of existence and retreat from living in the face of our fear of dying.

In not dealing with our anxiety about death, we may abnormally focus on our fear of loss of others through rejection or even death. Just as we hesitate to value our own lives, which we will surely lose, we don't want to become too attached to others, because we will lose them also.

We may feel like suckers to invest so much of ourselves in a relationship that we will definitely lose in the long run. If we give in to this feeling, we may begin to withhold our real love. Thus, the fear of death can become the basic defense, the principal reason behind the destructive process of going inward and withholding our real feelings from others.

The fear of death is not simply a phobia or a neurotic fear of separation from the parent; it is a real fear. Death is a reality, and no one is to blame for it, certainly not those close to you. Don't punish the one who brings love to your life and causes you to value your life just because you are going to lose that life and the life of the one you love. It is important to value your fragile but precious existence and to develop a meaningful goal-directed life. Don't waste your days in activities that numb you to the realization that those days are numbered. As Castaneda wrote in *Tales of Power,* "That barking and the loneliness it creates, speaks of the feelings of men. Men for whom an entire life was like one Sunday afternoon, an afternoon which was not altogether miserable, but rather hot and dull and uncomfortable. They sweated and fussed a great deal. They didn't know where to go, or what to do. That afternoon left them with the memory of petty annoyances and tedium, and then suddenly it was over; it was already night."

When I was a boy, my grandfather shared my bedroom. I remember lying in bed at night listening to him struggling to catch his breath between paroxysms of coughing. He was old, and I sensed that he would die soon.

My grandfather had lived with us all my life and so I knew him very well. Having spent his life in a kind of half-miserable, yet somewhat comfortable daze, he was nearing the end. I was aware that he had no sense of his impending death. I dreaded the possibility that one morning he might suddenly wake up as from a sleep and realize that he was at the end, that only yesterday he had been a boy like me, and that he had spent the intervening years not really living. I was terrified that he would know that he had wasted his life in complaints, family feuds, and long hours at a job he couldn't stand. He would realize that it was too late—there was no time left to live.

In my mind, this would be the most horrible thing that could happen to my grandfather. I hoped so much that he would *not* "wake up," but just die peacefully without this unbearable realization. The years passed and he died, leaving me with a lasting impression of a man who had missed his own life.

From this experience came a strong motivation on my part to try to live my life differently from my grandfather. I never wanted to be faced with the kind of final realization that I had dreaded for him. I wanted to experience all the facets of my life, the good and the bad, the painful and joyful events.

There is no defense or protection against death, but there is a way to live that is life affirming and not life denying. Wake up to your life before it passes you by. It was Otto Rank who admitted that anxiety could not all be overcome therapeutically, and this is what he was talking about, that it is impossible to face the truth of human existence without anxiety. However, when this anxiety is experienced, the choice is clear: whether to restrict and numb our feelings in an attempt to escape the terror or to live fully, with humility, meaningful activity, and compassion for oneself and for others. We all share the same fate.